D1615576

First published in 2008 by
PALGRAVE MACMILLAN™
175 Fifth Avenue, New York, N.Y. 10010 and
Houndmills, Basingstoke, Hampshire, England RG21 6XS
Companies and representatives throughout the world.

PALGRAVE MACMILLAN is the global academic imprint of the Palgrave Macmillan division of St. Martin's Press, LLC and of Palgrave Macmillan Ltd. Macmillan® is a registered trademark in the United States, United Kingdom and other countries. Palgrave is a registered trademark in the European Union and other countries.

ISBN-13: 978–1–4039–7755–7
ISBN-10: 1–4039–7755–0

Library of Congress Cataloging-in-Publication Data

Haywood, Louise M.
    Sex, scandal, and sermon in fourteenth-century Spain : Juan Ruiz's
    Libro de Buen Amor / by Louise M. Haywood.
        p. cm.—(The new middle ages)
    Includes bibliographical references and index.
    ISBN 1–4039–7755–0
    1. Ruiz, Juan, fl. 1343. Libro de buen amor. 2. Ruiz, Juan, fl.
1343—Humor. 3. Body, Human, in literature. 4. Sex in literature.
I. Title. II. New Middle Ages (Palgrave Macmillan (Firm))

PQ6430.A1L534 2008
861'.1—dc22                                              2007031627

A catalogue record for this book is available from the British Library.

Design by Newgen Imaging Systems (P) Ltd., Chennai, India.

First edition: April 2008

10 9 8 7 6 5 4 3 2 1

Printed in the United States of America.

*To Jon and Jake*

E así como el niño faze cosa de que todos ríen, así el amador,
çiego del desordenado fuego del querer, así ha e pone en obra
cosa de que todos ríen e escarnesçen

[And thus like the child who does things that make everyone laugh,
so also the lover, blinded by the disordered fire of love, does things
and undertakes acts at which everyone laughs and mocks]

Juan de Mena, *Tratado de amor*, p. 379

# CONTENTS

# ACKNOWLEDGMENTS

The debts of gratitude that I have accumulated during the preparation of this book are many and manifold. I should like to thank the numerous colleagues and friends with whom I have discussed aspects of the project, and who have had the patience to hear the papers on which much of it is based. Particular thanks are due to members of the Medieval Hispanic Research Seminar at Queen Mary, University of London, especially, Alan Deyermond, Jane Whetnall, and Paco Bautista; the Association of Hispanists of Great Britain and Ireland; the Cambridge Hispanic Research Seminar; the Joint Research Seminar of the Universities of Durham and Newcastle; IMANA, particularly Nancy F. Marino, Joseph Snow, and Barbara Weissberger; and the International Courtly Literature Society (British Branch). Special thanks are due to Juan Carlos Bayo, Andrew M. Beresford, Rodrigo Cacho, Alicia C. de Ferraresi, Adriano Duque, Erik Ekman, Robert Folger, Esther Gómez Sierra, Carlos Heusch, Catherine Léglu, Bienvenido Morros, Francisco Rico, Rebeca Sanmartín Bastida, Alison Sinclair, Francisco Toro Ceballos, Isabel Torres and Mary-Anne Vetterling, all of whom facilitated access to documents, provided bibliographical references, or gave advice. I should also like to thank Dorothy Sherman Severin and Louise O. Vasvári, who have been an inspiration to me, and Robert Archer and Julian Weiss, who discussed the project with me in detail at a formative stage. My work has been enriched by the undergraduate students who have worked with me on the *Libro* over the years, and has acquired considerable depth through exchanges with my doctoral students, Geraldine Coates, Jan Gilbert, and Laura Vivanco. Emma Gatland heroically read a draft, and her comments have been invaluable. I should also like to thank the anonymous readers of my manuscript for their comments, which I found illuminating and very helpful.

I am indebted to the Master and Fellows of Trinity Hall, and to the University of Cambridge for two periods of sabbatical leave that saw the book through its formative stages, and for financial support to research and attend conferences in the United Kingdom, Spain, and the United States. I am grateful to the Arts and Humanities Research Council, whose

Research Leave Scheme, project number 11171, enabled me to complete my writing, and whose staff were enormously helpful. I also found the comments of their anonymous assessors invaluable and extend my thanks to them.

I should like to thank Jonathan Down for his unfailing generosity and support over the six or seven years that I have been engaged in the project that has produced this book; and Jake Haywood Down, our beautiful son, for his tolerance of all the time I spent working on this book. The generosity of our dear friends, Susan Bowie and Peter Beaver, is much appreciated. I am grateful for the love and support of my parents, Bill and Margaret Haywood. I also owe a debt of gratitude to Eddie Izzard, whose performances have been an inspiration and a source of great pleasure.

I should like to thank Vervuert Iberoamericana for permission to use reworked extracts from my "Imagen y palabra: algunos aspectos de la alegoría medieval," in *Las metamorfosis de la alegoría: discurso y sociedad en la Península Ibérica desde la Edada Media hasta la Edad contemporánea*, ed. Rebeca Sanmartín Bastida, Rosa Vidal Doval (Madrid: Vervuert Iberoamericana, 2005), pp. 105–25.

It remains to me to thank the series editor, Bonnie Wheeler, and the editorial team of Julia Cohen, Maran Elancheran, Farideh Koohi-Kamali and Kristy Lilas for their kind attention and support during the completion of this project.

Postscript: The present volume was already at press when I had the pleasure of organizing an international conference on the *Libro de Buen Amor*, and it would have been improved had I been able to cite articles by the following participants: María Luzdivina Cuesta Torre, José Palomares, Juan Paredes, Carmen Parrilla, Selena Simonatti, and Anthony N. Zahareas. The articles are published in *Juan Ruiz, Arcipreste de Hita, y el "Libro de Buen Amor": Homenaje a Alan Deyermond; II Congreso Internacional del Centro para la Edición de los Clásicos Españoles celebrado en Alcalá la Real mayo 2005*, ed. Francisco Toro Ceballos and Louise M. Haywood, with Francisco Bautista and Gerladine Coates (Alcalá la Real: Ayuntamiento & Centro para la Edición de los Clásicos Españoles, in press).

# INTRODUCTION

*For every preacher should give a good example in his deeds, and good doctrine in his words, since if he lives well and preaches not, he is as exemplary as his silence is harmful [. . .] For the preacher should be like a book and a mirror to his flock so that they may read in the deeds of their leader as if in a book, and see in the mirror what they should do.*

Thomas of Chobham, *Summa de arte praedicandi*[1]

*We need a mediator linked with us in our lowliness by reason of the mortal nature of his body, and yet able to render us truly divine assistance for our purification and liberation.*

St Augustine of Hippo, *De civitate Dei*[2]

The preacher lays claim to authority through his person and deeds, and through his words.[3] Robert of Basevorn in his *Forma praedicandi* of ca. 1300 makes this clear:

> Three things are necessary for the one exercising an act of preaching. The first is evidently purity of life [. . .] The second need for one actually preaching is competent knowledge [. . .] The third need is authority, with which the preacher is sent out by the Church.[4]

He is positioned in a lineage of authority that reaches back through the Church Fathers, and Peter the Apostle, to Christ, and even God himself.[5] Indeed the preacher is a mirror of Christ, mediating the Word, the authority of the Scriptures from a thoroughly embodied position; however, like Adam rather than Christ, he stands as a fallen being, susceptible, like his parishioners, to salvation and to sin.[6] The problems raised by the preacher's doubleness had long been recognized and discussed in preaching manuals by the fourteenth century, when Juan Ruiz composed his *Libro de Buen Amor*.[7] For example, in the early thirteenth century the Englishman, Thomas of Chobham, in the section of his *Summa de arte praedicandi* dedicated to this subject, deals equally with the way in which good example reinforces preaching, and poor example undermines its efficacy, particularly when publicly known.[8] Maurice of Scully and Humbert of Romans,

writing in the twelfth and thirteenth centuries, respectively, both insist that
the clergy enjoy a dignity that positions it above the congregation physically
and morally.[9]

Although little has yet been established about knowledge of preaching
manuals and theory in the peninsula, evidence of these concerns can be
found in other materials.[10] Whilst not dealing with preaching *per se*, *Partida*
I.vi of the Alfonsine legal code treats the secular clergy.[11] In common with
preaching manuals, it shows a anxiety about the bodily integrity of the
churchman: "Forma de omne complida es quando ha todos sus miembros
enteros e sanos e el que tal no fuere nol pueden llamar omne complido
quanto en facción e por ende no touo por bien Sancta Eglesia que a éstos
atales diessen orden sagrada" (I.vi.23; "The complete outward form of a
man is when all his members are whole and healthy, and whoever is not
thus cannot be called a complete man in his features and therefore Holy
Church decreed that men such as these should not receive holy orders").[12]
The law then moves on to define bodily integrity as consisting in the
individual's possession of all clearly visible members, such as arms, legs,
feet, hands, eyes, nose, ears and lips, and of concealed genital members:
"los miembros encubiertos que son uergonnosos de nombrar."[13] Minor
imperfections, such as loss of teeth or toes, having six fingers, or different-
sized eyes, are tolerated, as is slight damage to the fingers, provided the
individual is still able to take and administer the host. Martín Pérez's
*Libro de las confesiones* (1316) similarly expresses concern about the bodily
integrity, "yrregularidat que viene por mengua de mienbros," of the
clergy, and, also like Alfonso, he explains what degree of or reason for loss
is acceptable and what unacceptable, being more ready to tolerate that
which is less significant and hidden as being *sin escandalo* (II.11) than that
which is clearly visible. Martín dedicates some nine chapters to *escandalo*
(II.164–72), which he defines as, "dicho o fecho non derecho que da a
otro ocasion de caer en pecado" (wrongful words or deeds that lead others
into sin).[14]

Also debarred from clerical practice, according to the *Partidas*, are those
who are illegitimate, have had undue sexual experience or undergone
public penance, and those clergy who live in open association with women
who are not close relatives, keep concubines (*barraganas*), or frequent female
monasteries, particularly because their moral conduct is called into repute
through scrutiny.[15] Martín Pérez too is particularly clear that common
knowledge of clerical fornication is scandalous since it may lead others to
take up fornication by example or to practice it more, to lose their devotion
to the sacraments or their faith, and cause the steadfast to suffer greatly
because they see the devil's vassals in charge of the Lord's house.[16] Finally,
the *Partida* also notes that men who owe a debt of service to secular powers

are debarred from ordination thereby granting seigniorial control over the social groups from which the clergy may be drawn.

Taken together these strictures express a concern with the body, status, and the fallen, and potentially sinning, nature of the clergyman in the eyes of his parishioners. To be a member of the formal church hierarchy, the candidate must above all be male.[17] His body must be an exemplar of masculine integrity, morally and physically, and yet it must also be kept apart from the threatening and potentially polluting affects of association with women; this perhaps itself a tacit recognition that the danger inherent in priestly celibacy emanates from social anxiety about suppressed masculinity rather than from women themselves.[18] As I shall show below, these very tensions are dramatized in the figure of the Archpriest, protagonist of the *Libro*.

Some of the preoccupations expressed by these restrictions can be found in the implied relationship between sin, hunting, preaching, and minstrelsy. The Alfonsine legal codes, for example, prohibit the clergy from hunting wild beasts unless there is an immediate threat to the local community thus emphasizing the clergy's role as shepherd and protector of its flock.[19] This role is placed in clear contradistinction to murder, and to a third type of hunting of concern to the Church:

> ésta se faze por palabras de losenia e de escarnio e de remedijos e cae más en los ioglares e en los remedadores que en los otros omnes, ca estos atales son caçadores del diablo, e caçan por él las almas daquellos que se delectan en oyr las mentiras e los escarnios e las locuras que dizen e que fazen e les dan algo con que se mantengan e puedan usar deste mester malo. (I.vi.56)

> (this is done in words of flattery, scandal, or mimicry, and falls more to minstrels and to comic mimics than to other men since men such as these are the devil's huntsmen, and on his behalf they hunt the souls of those who take pleasure in hearing the lies, scandal, and madness, which they say and do, and of those who, with gifts, aid them in supporting themselves and practising this evil craft.)[20]

The implicit connection between hunting, inappropriate clerical activity, and minstrelesque practice is reiterated by Martín Pérez, who treats the prohibition against the clergy becoming involved in minstrelsy under the same title as that against hunting (II.79).[21] In this case, he seems concerned that both activities give rise to unwarranted bodily display and distraction from religious duties.[22] Taken together, these works reveal the general hostility of legal and ecclesiastical culture to the minstrel and other entertainers who fall outside their province of influence, and a concern that the preacher conducts himself in a seemly and dignified fashion. Some preaching

manuals, such as Thomas's, make explicit the dangerous proximity
between the art of the preacher and that of actor or minstrel, particularly in
the use of overemphatic gestures: "Thus it is clear that those who make
such gestures in preaching will be considered foolish, and will seem rather
to be actors than preachers."[23] As in the case of the sinning preacher or
hunting clergyman, the bodily nature of the preacher's representation gives
rise to anxiety about his moral status, potentially undermining the efficacy
of his message and leading to public scandal. The preacher whose conduct
draws attention to his fallen and bodily nature also raises awareness of the
denatured status of the celibate male as what R.N. Swanson has called
'emasculine' in the priest's renunciation of sexual masculinity and behavior
patterns that adhere in the social construct of male gender identity, such as
the expression of aggression, the achievement of reproduction, and related
patriarchal dominance over family or clan.[24] The liminality of the priest's
role is made manifest and is raised as a threat potentially polluting social
hierarchy through forbidden contact, social or sexual, with women.

However, not all minstrelesque activity was condemned outright.
Martín Pérez, for example, lists four categories of minstrelsy: traveling
actors who use costumes and props; itinerants who speak ill of others,
quack doctors, and fortunetellers; wandering minstrels who play instruments and sing songs, conjurors, and those who lewdly sing and perform
acrobatic feats without musical accompaniment; and, itinerant wild knights
who stage fights and take on all comers (II.135–38).[25] None of these groups
can be saved on account of the contaminating dangers it poses to the souls
of its members and audience unless penance is undertaken and more honorable trades or crafts adopted. Nevertheless, amongst the third category,
Martín draws attention to licit minstrelesque practice:

Si son tales juglares que cantan cantares de los santos e de las faziendas o de
las vidas de los reyes o de los prínçipes, e non cantan otros cantares locos que
mueven a los omes a amor mundanal, e cantan en lugares honestos e non en
lugares desonestos, bien podemos a estos tales juglares dar vagar a bivir de
tales ofiçios, tanto que se confiesen e bivan en otra manera de penitençia.
(II.137)

(If they are such minstrels as sing songs about saints and the deeds or lives of
kings or princes, and they do not sing other mad songs that move men to
worldly love, and they sing in decent places and not in scandalous ones, we
can well let such minstrels as these live from such crafts, provided that they
confess and otherwise live a life of penance.)[26]

The poets of the thirteenth-century *mester de clerecía*, some of whose work
was certainly known to Juan Ruiz, seem to have been aware of the dangerous

contiguity of ministry and minstrelsy, and take care to put clear water between their own artistic agenda and popular minstrelesque practice.[27] For example, the poet of the *Libro de Alexandre* (late twelfth or early thirteenth century) is at pains to point out the sinless nature and the benefits of his craft:[28]

> Señores si quisieredes mi serviçio prender,
> querríavos de grado servir de mi menster
> deve de lo que sabe omne largo seer
> si non podrié de culpa e de rieto (MS *P*: en yerro) caer
> mester (MS *P*: menester) traigo fermoso non es de joglaría (MS *P* janglería)
> mester (MS *P*: menester) es sin pecado ca es de clerezía
> fablar curso rimado por la quaderna vía
> a sílabas contadas ca (MS *P*: que) es grant maestría.
>
> (1–2)

> (Lords, if you wish to receive my service, / I should gladly serve you with my craft / man should be liberal with his knowledge / if not, he could fall into blame and treachery. / I bring a fair craft [MS *P*: duty or ministry], it is not minstrelsy / it is a craft [MS *P*: duty or ministry] without sin, it is of clerical learning / to speak rhyme and rhythm by the fourfold path / of counting the syllables it is very skilful work.)[29]

And Tarsiana of the *Libro de Apolonio* (1235–40) persuades a brothel-keeper who has bought her that her talents are better employed in licit minstrelsy than harlotry:[30]

> Señor, si lo hobiese yo de ti condonado,
> otro mester sabía que es más sin pecado,
> que es más ganancioso e que es más hondrado.
> Si tú me lo condonas, por la tu cortesía,
> que meta yo estudio de essa maestría,
> cuanto tú demandases, yo tanto te daría:
> tú habríes gran ganancia e yo non pecaría.
>
> (422b–23)[31]

> (Lord, if I were to be permitted by you to use / another craft I knew which is more without sin, / which is more beneficial and more respectable. / If you permit me, on account of your courtesy [or courtliness], / to get down to the study of such skilful work, / however much you request I should give you / you would benefit greatly, and I should not sin.)

In each of these examples, the poet's craft is described as skilful work, *maestría*, which is without sin, and contrasted with minstrelsy. Claire M. Waters summarizes the key difficulty underlying the tension between these two spheres of activity for the preacher, and both of which are exercised by the Archpriest:

> The overlapping categories of persona—body, self-presentation, gesture, deeds—are reminders that if a preacher's body is, as the theorists implicitly recognize, always an actor's body, then there is no way to know if he is an "actor of truth itself" or a mere *histrio*.[32]

The legal and confessional documents that I have been discussing point to a gap between the institutionally prescribed activities of the priest and the proscribed behavior of the minstrel whilst tacitly recognizing the potential for overlap. I should like to term the fissure between institutional legislation and individual performance as grotesque, and I shall return to the issue of clerical minstrelesque performance in relation to the *Libro* in my conclusion.

The origin of the term grotesque lies in the discovery and excavation of Nero's palace and Titus's baths and their frescoes in the late fifteenth century, and comes into English and Spanish from the Italian, *grotessche*; etymologically, "of grottos or caves." It was used specifically to refer to decorative marginal fillers used to frame a central image. Although condemned by Vitruvius, the frescoes' style had been described in classical sources such as those by Tacitus, Suetonius, and Pliny as a model of artistic absurdity, often containing mixed genus species.[33] To demonstrate the relevance of the term to medieval culture, Michael Camille, in his study of the marginalia of Gothic manuscripts, notes the application of the Latin *fabula, curiositates*, and *babuini* to describe such architectural and artistic sports of fancy, and I hold—with him—that the key concepts underlying the grotesque were available, in loosely if not coherently related forms in the period under discussion.[34] Prior to the rediscovery of Nero's palace, the depiction of hybrid creatures raised considerable discussion. For example, in his *Ars poetica*, Horace voiced the need to avoid hybridity, including composite species, since it introduces an indecorous note in the high style of poetry, which provokes laughter (ll.1–23). Bernard of Clairvaux's *Apologia ad Guillelmum* (1125; XXII.28–29) attacks grotesque art in the cloisters as a distraction from reading and proper meditation, with particular reference to animal figures, composite creatures and aggressive masculine activities barred to the clergy:[35]

> But apart from this, in the cloisters, before the eyes of the brothers while they read—what is that ridiculous monstrosity doing, an amazing kind of deformed beauty and yet a beautiful deformity? What are the filthy apes doing there? The fierce lions? The monstrous centaurs? The creatures, part man and part beast? [. . .] The fighting soldiers? The hunters blowing

horns? You may see so many bodies under one head, and conversely many heads on one body. On one side the tail of a serpent is seen on a quadruped, on the other side the head of a quadruped is on the body of a fish. [. . .] In short, everywhere so plentiful and astonishing a variety of contradictory forms is seen that one would rather read in the marble than in the books, and spend the whole day wondering at every single one of them, than in meditating on the law of God. Good God! If one is not ashamed of the absurdity, why is one not at least troubled at the expense?[36]

Bernard's account displaces Horace's concern about the contaminating presence of the low in poetry to the visual sphere, where its fascination to the eye and amusing nature gives rise to the sin of spiritual *acedia* in the monk. For Bernard the cloister is contaminated by the presence of distracting and indecorous images, of dirt, "any object or idea likely to confuse or contradict cherished classifications," which impinges on its moral codes and social status, and which arises from a breech of vows of poverty.[37] The institutionally ratified "systems of decorum" on which the Benedictine rule depends are threatened by the effect of sports of fancy on the minds of its brothers: there is a failure to "keep the low and the marginal in their places."[38]

Although focused on Antoine Rabelais's *Gargantua and Pantagruel*, Mikhail Bakhtin's seminal *Rabelais and his World*, originally written during the 1930s but not published until the mid-1960s, offers what is probably the most useful formulation of "the culture of folk humor in the Middle Ages and the Renaissance," which he saw as in opposition to serious official ecclesiastical and feudal culture, and in which the grotesque plays a central role.[39] Bakhtin discussed three forms of folk culture: ritual spectacle, in which hierarchical and social norms are suspended in a process of crisis, death and renewal; comic verbal compositions, often part of "legalized carnival licentiousness"; and the genres of billingsgate, such as insults, oaths, and curses.[40] The essential characteristics of all three forms are festive or carnivalesque laughter, which is communal, universal, and ambivalent, both triumphant and mocking, and "grotesque realism," which celebrates the "material bodily principle" in its cosmic and regenerative aspect through the themes of excess and increase, and dethrones official culture by translating its attributes to the bodily lower stratum.[41] Festive laugher therefore degrades and makes its object material. For Bakhtin degradation to the bodily lower stratum has two facets. First, official culture is literally revised downwards toward the earth, "an element that swallows up and gives birth at the same time," a translation that can also be applied directly to the body to map the head and face onto the digestive and reproductive systems.[42] Second, the material bodily principle simultaneously uncrowns and regenerates thus operating at a social, even cosmic, level. The grotesque body is therefore "an as yet unfinished metamorphosis, of death and birth, growth and becoming"; defying canonized aesthetics, it is a body of orifices and protuberances, without boundaries, "blended with the world, with animals, with objects."[43]

Horace's view of the grotesque is reflected in that of Geoffrey Galt Harpham, who notes that it is precisely the grotesque's indecorous and improper nature, as outlined by Bakhtin, that renders it humorous. Harpham argues that a grotesque image, such as a cross-species composite, causes an interval in the processes of cognition and recognition as the mind attempts to categorize it according to prior conceptual classifications before a "clear sense of the dominant principle emerges"; consequently it may be regarded as a psychological category or space arising from the "perception that something is illegitimately in something else."[44] I shall refer to the interval in cognition as a grotesque moment, particularly when it involves the dethroned subject in an apprehension of how he appears to someone else.

In my analysis, the medieval grotesque, as body or action, is situated in a primarily visual sphere. Medieval ocular theory was largely influenced by Aristotelian and Stoic theory as transmitted through the scientific investigations of Ibn Sina, known to medieval Christendom as Avicenna (900–1037), and Ibn al-Haitham, known as Alhazen (965–1039), into the physiology of the eye.[45] In the presence of light, the soul sends pneuma out through the optic nerve to make contact with objects in the visual field (extramission) from which it carries species, replicas thrown off by the object seen, back to each eye (intromission) to be presented to the optic nerve before being perceived and recognized by the intellective soul, which imprinted them as mental pictures, or phantasms, in memory. Although the view combining extramission and intromission, outlined here, formed the basis for thirteenth-century investigative natural philosophy, in fact, it competed with extramission, and—to a lesser extent—with intromission theory in various epistemological fields for some centuries.

Memory and the visual were inextricably linked.[46] The phantasm imprinted in memory is the final product of the entire process of sense perception, of whatever sort it may be; even material presented acoustically is turned into a visual image that becomes the site of mental *collatio*, or the gathering together in one place of various related strands. In Mary J. Carruthers' analysis, pictures, and by extension visual images, can be understood as a process akin to reading, involving an oral stage, *lectio*, followed by a *meditatio*, the commuting of substance to memory through re-presenting. Accordingly, a picture should be understood rhetorically as directly referential not to an object but to a text or image (*historia*) and thus to human memorative processes of reading and composition. The low plays an important role:

> No opprobrium of childishness or frivolity or obscenity or inappropriateness attaches to such image-making. The disgusting and the silly, the noble and the violent, the grotesque and the beautiful, the scatological and sexual are presented, one after another, and usually as part of the same scene, just as memory dictates. The one thing that cannot be tolerated is dullness or quietude or any failure to rivet the attention.[47]

Verbal tags, such as first lines of quotations, can also be used in memorization to cue longer passages where they were assigned to a position on an imagined grid or similar mnemonic picture. Although not necessarily indicating a mnemonic system, verbal tags such as "Da michi intellectum, e çetera" or "Intellectus bonus omnibus façientibus eum, e cetera" appear in the prose prologue to the *Libro*, where they are intended to recall the context of the Psalms from which they are taken (p. 105), through the use of a conventional cuing device "e cetera."[48] Elsewhere, Juan Ruiz employs a variation on the use of tags to evoke a memory of their context and meaning during a parody of the canonical hours (st. 372–87).[49] The parodic hours may be an attack on the tradition of the lover's mass; but the protagonist uses them to accuse the allegorical figure of Love of being responsible for the sin of spiritual sloth. The supplicant described fails to meditate properly on his devotions catching only tags whose appropriate association with context he misses to dwell instead on the obscene connotations of the language used. The scene displays *acedia* in action, "Con açidia traes estos males atantos, / muchos otros pecados, antojos e espantos" (388ab; And with sloth you bring so many other ills, / many other sins, whims, and horrors), but of course, the obscene connotation of the tags could potentially be put to excellent use in the memorization of the prayers appropriate to the offices, making feasible Juan Ruiz's claim in the *Libro*'s prose prologue not to write "por dar manera de pecar nin por mal dezir; mas fue por rreduçir a toda persona a memoria buena de bien obrar, e dar ensienplo de buenas constunbres e castigos de salvaçión" (p. 110; to give ways of sinning nor of speaking ill; rather it was to redirect everyone to good memory of good deeds, and to give an example of good habits and advice on salvation).

Juan Ruiz's *Libro de Buen Amor* presents the audience with a first-person narrator, identified with the author, who lays claim to the title of Archpriest of Hita, engages in a series of amorous misadventures, and who displays considerable erudition along with knowledge of the bawdy and profane. The narratorial persona enacts the fallen embodiment of the priest to whom scandal clings. In reality, relatively little is known about the identity and biography of the author of the *Libro de Buen Amor*, but at the time of writing there seems to be little grounds on which to reject the claim (19bcd, 575ab) that it was composed by one Juan Ruiz, Archpriest of Hita, since an individual of that name and title appears to have been active ca. 1330.[50] Of the many individuals sporting the common forename Juan Ruiz, two stand out as being identifiable with the author of the *Libro*: Juan Ruiz de Cisneros and Johan Rodrigues. Cisneros was a Christian born ca. 1295 in Muslim Alcalá la Real, who went on to enjoy a successful ecclesiastical career.[51] To date he has not been documented as having any connection with Hita, nor as having held the post of Archpriest, and, around the time the *Libro* was written, he held the higher office of canon. Nonetheless, he served the Archbishop of Toledo, Don Gil de Albornoz, to whom the "Cántica de los clérigos de Talavera" toward the close of the *Libro* alludes, and was therefore associated with an appropriate geographical location and ecclesiastical milieu. Johan Rodrigues was a choral master at the Monasterio de las Huelgas near Burgos, one of several Johannes Roderici whose compositions occur in the early fourteenth-century Códice Musical de las Huelgas. The choral master and the *Libro*'s author coincide in producing poetic compositions, and in demonstrating an interest in musical performance. The most reliable source of information about Juan Ruiz, therefore, is what can be deduced from the *Libro*.

The *Libro* comprises heterogeneous verse materials arranged around a loose (pseudo)-autobiographic framework. It opens with a short series of prayers and a prose prologue before moving into a discussion of authorial intention, the difficulty of interpretation, and the nature of humankind; the figures of author and protagonist are blurred. The first three amatory adventures, with women of different social estates, fail, and the Archpriest then berates the allegorical figure of Love, Don Amor, for inciting the deadly sins, which he endeavors to demonstrate through exemplary tales. In return he receives advice from Don Amor and Doña Venus about the successful pursuit of love affairs. Transformed into Don Melón without explanation, the first-person narrator seduces Doña Endrina through the offices of a go-between, and a stable relationship is established. In this, as in several other of the amorous adventures, the go-between also uses exemplary tales in a verbal seduction of the lady. From the advice from Don Amor to the completion of the seduction, this portion of the *Libro* reworks Ovid's *Ars amatoria*, and the pseudo-Ovidian *De vetula* and *Pamphilus de amore*. The adventure of Don Melón and Doña Endrina ends abruptly, and the identity of Don Melón is shed as the Archpriest chides women on the dangers of love. After a fifth attempted seduction and a brief encounter with an old bawd, he undertakes a journey through the *sierra* in which he encounters four peasant women: each escapade is related in narrative and lyric verse. Perhaps to make recompense for his misadventures, the narrator next offers two religious lyrics at the shrine of the Virgin at Vado. The narrator is drawn into a mock epic allegorical confrontation between Doña Cuaresma and Don Carnal, Lent and Flesh, of which Don Carnal is inevitably victor, and with Don Amor becomes Emperor. Like other religious, the Archpriest serves in the court of Love, but he exceptionally is favored by a visitation from Don Amor, and by sight of the interior of his lord's pavilion. Four further attempts at seduction come to abrupt and unsatisfactory ends before the death of the bawd, Trotaconventos, which is treated parodically and in grand style. A subsequent attempt to replace Trotaconventos and begin another affair fails; the Archpriest warns once again of the difficulties of interpretation, and the narrative thread dissolves into a series of end-pieces. This summary constructs a greater coherence than is actually present in the structure of the *Libro* since it elides heterogeneous elements, such as the sections on the Arms of the Christian and the benefits of small women, which follow the death of the bawd, and techniques such as the frequent use of parody on multiple levels, the juxtaposition of contraries, and extensive ambiguity, which together serve to obscure unitary meanings.[52]

The *Libro* is extant in three manuscripts—MS *T* (Madrid, Biblioteca Nacional Vitrina, 6–1), MS *G* (Madrid, Real Academia Española, 19), and MS *S* (Salamanca, Biblioteca Universitaria Antigua, 2663)—and a number of other testimonia.[53] The manuscripts were thought to represent two redactions, with MSS *GT* representing one branch, and MS *S*, a later, revised and expanded version, with little difference of substance between them other than the prose prologue, epigraphs, and opening prayers in *S*, and the slightly differing "jumble of end-pieces in *G* and *S*."[54] However, for the purposes of the present project, I adopt the one-version theory, current since at least 1913, which was lent support by Alberto Blecua's detailed argument, and which has currently achieved consensus.[55] I exclude the miscellaneous end-pieces after the second of two Joys of the Virgin lyrics since these seem to form a structural parallel with the opening pair, and the parallelism between the introduction of each suggests that the later ones are intended to mark the end of the *Libro* proper:

por que de todo bien es comienço e rraíz
la Virgen Santa María, por ende yo, Joan Roíz,
açipreste de Fita, della primero fiz
cantar de los sus gozos siete,

(19)

(because the Blessed Virgin Mary / is the beginning and end of everything good, therefore I, Juan Ruiz, / Archpriest of Hita, first made about her / a song of her seven Joys), and "Por que Santa María, segund que dicho he, / es comienço e fin del bien, tal es mi fe, / fiz le quatro cantares" (1626abc; Because the Blessed Mary, as I have said, / is the beginning and end of good, such is my faith, / I made her four songs).[56] Internal evidence suggests that composition of some episodes may have begun as early as ca. 1322, possibly as materials for oral performance, with the *Libro*'s arrangement completed in a single redaction sometime in the time frame 1330–43; but coming, by the time of Alfonso de Paradinas's copying of MS *S* before 1437, to be of interest to scholarly circles as a written text.[57] On the evidence of the *Libro*'s contents it is likely that Ruiz studied the school syllabus, and had some—possibly even extensive—knowledge of the university curriculum either directly or through teaching miscellanies, with particular proof of interests in law and medicine. As Archpriest, he would have been ordained as a priest, with the care of souls, and held particular responsibility for the ca. thirty-one curacies and benefices in Hita.[58]

In a survey of literature on the *Libro*, Louise O. Vasvári and I identified two significant gaps in Ruiz scholarship: an assessment of the function and techniques of his use of humor (a topic touched on in a large number of articles dealing with single episodes or aspects of humor but not systematically analyzed or contextualized), and the role of the visual. The aim of the current project is to address this gap.[59] I focus on biological sex and the social construction of gender; the role of priest as autobiographical narrator of amorous adventures and as tendentious joker; and, the tension between the protagonist's representation as a sinning Everyman and his empirical person as priest, a subject constituted through relation to the fallen body and the divine: the sex, scandal, and sermon of my title. The principle questions I shall be addressing relate Ruiz's use of humor to scholastic, memorative, and hygienic practice in the context of orthodox views concerning the vitiated and fallen human body and soul, to the humorous truancy and the place of the bawdy in sacred and secular contexts. Throughout I make reference to the visual. The monograph is the first to take such an approach to the *Libro*, the first systematically to approach Ruiz's use of humor, and the first extended consideration of the body and visual culture in relation to the *Libro* as a whole.[60]

I locate Juan Ruiz, despite the truant content of his book, as working within a broadly conservative, scholastic, official ideology; for this reason, it has been essential to begin with an examination of the relationship between the role of priest and scandal. I shall argue that humor and the visual are primarily memorial tools that the individual can actively appropriate according to his (or her) ability, disposition, and humoral balance. I also examine the charge of pleasure they produce in terms that reflect the homosocial tensions, as defined by Eve Kosofsky Sedgwick and discussed in chapter 2, residing in a strongly male-dominated hierarchical society.[61] In my analysis of humor, I shall make use of the accounts of tendentious joking by Sigmund Freud and Peter Lehman since their concern, implicit in Freud's case, was precisely the homosocial context in which Ruiz employs bawdy tales: that is, obscene joking offers men the opportunity to engage in sexual competition for dominance over one another. In considering the visual field, I draw on the terminology of Jacques Lacan's account of the mirror stage and the potency of the Other's gaze in constituting identity. Essentially Lacan argues that at the mirror stage the child begins to establish a relationship between the organism and its reality in a move through "the succession of phantasies that extends from a fragmented body-image to a form of its totality."[62] More explicitly, when the infant sees its own actions in a reflective surface or a parent's mimicry it sees itself as embodied, which forms the basis of its creation of a fantasy Ideal-I or *imago*, but it experiences an uncoordinated and vulnerable self. Consequently, the split between apprehension and experience means that the Ideal-I is itself a fantasy which our unconscious repeatedly challenges, and which is shored up by being regarded as an unproblematic and integrated whole by external objects, especially those objects whom we desire. The child's transition is a *méconnaissance*, a misconstruction and misrecognition in which the delusory image is adopted as representing its totality.[63]

In chapter 1, I shall propose that Juan Ruiz's prose prologue is not a parodic sermon, and that it positions him as a preacher or schoolman in a chain of learned authority whilst also displaying his double nature as a fallen individual. In it he establishes a disparity between the pre-lapsarian or grace-endowed operations of a healthy intellective soul, and the vitiated state of the fallen soul whose practice of *imitatio Christi*, cooperation with divine grace, and rightly directed love can counterbalance a predisposition to specific vices. Human cultural institutions and sciences arise as a function of the Fall to direct memory to good, but they are flawed since prefect memory and knowledge are available only to God, who exercises a panoptic gaze, to which I return in the conclusion. He then works out these ideas through the first humorous *exempla* directed by the narrator to the reader and the physical descriptions of the Archpriest and the seducible beauty to argue that individuals interpret and act according to their nature, disposition, and cultural competence.

In chapter 2, I take up the proposition, outlined in chapter 1, that the visual is a privileged domain since it has memorative and interpretative functions in the right direction of the faculties, and because it is used in the articulation of power and dominance. In the exemplary fabliaux to be discussed, the eroticization of the male body, its presentation as having an active role in labor in rightly ordered society, and images of contamination expose the polluting effects of desire. Nevertheless, Don Amor exploits the visual and humor to build homosocial bonds of solidarity with his interlocutor, luring him into a *méconnaissance* in which he constructs a fantasy of himself as wielder of a powerful phallic gaze. The descriptions of Alda de la Tablada and Christ represent the extreme poles of the human on the chain of being since Alda is bestial, even demonic, and Christ participates in the hypostatic union, and as in the descriptions of the seducible beauty and the Archpriest, the subject's body is disfigured, and rhetorically dismembered. As with the physical descriptions of the fallen human body, the beast fables open a discursive space for consideration of the unique position of man in the salvific economy as the only creature with a rational and intellective soul, and susceptible to salvation and damnation, and again the disfigured body is the focus of the humor of the indecorous. The cultural institutions whose existence is necessary to compensate for the diminished faculties of fallen humankind and to guarantee the symbolic order, the need for which the Fall caused, are necessarily also vitiated due to the participation in them of individuals whose disposition, cultural competences, and ethical and ontological status varies.

In chapter 3, I shall examine Ruiz's treatment of the amatory affairs from the perspective of René Girard's theory of mimetic desire to support the view that the affairs carried out in an urban milieu are realized within very narrow parameters, and that the Archpriest achieves no meaningful success regardless of whether the affairs precede or follow Don Amor's advice.[64] In the *sierra*, the Archpriest is subject to real dangers, and to those that emanate from customary practices in which women and their desire are not constrained, and consequently, the venial appetites dominate and he is emasculated and abjected. At the extradiegetic level, Girard's model reveals that although desire is mediated by different paradigms in the urban and mountain environments, the sexual drive is always governed by cultural practices as an effect of the Fall. The protagonist's clerical status as Archpriest raises the issue of scandal pertaining to the clergyman. His fallen nature as indicated by humoral characterology is confirmed by his representation as sick, threatened by death and personal disintegration, and in proximity to the dead, and thus he is abjected. The first-person narrator-protagonist's abjection is one of a number of characteristics that link the *Libro* as a performance-text to twentieth-century stand-up comedy, which I address in the conclusion.

# CHAPTER 1

## HUMOR AND THE HUMORS

One of the fundamental challenges that modern readers experience in handling the *Libro* lies in our desire to resolve the problem caused by the nature of the role that Juan Ruiz carves for his first-person narrator, the amorous Archpriest. I shall argue that this problem is posed in the opening portions of the *Libro*, in which Ruiz blurs the roles of author and narrator with those of preacher and poet. In contrast to the *mester de clerecía* poets who actively claim a position within religious orthodoxy for their minstrelsy, discussed in the introduction, I shall argue that Ruiz displays the double nature of the priest, and every human. This is supported by his treatment of Everyman's fallen body in the prologue, of the Archpriest and his appetitive nature in the physical description, and in his deeds in the later narrative portions of the *Libro*. In the opening too Ruiz makes clear the difficulties encountered in the interpretation of intention, and I shall have more to say on this issue, and its relevance to the *Libro*.

Ethically and spiritually, the difficulty for the Archpriest as narrator-protagonist, and, indeed, for Everyman, resides in the destructive and deformative effect of the Fall and first sin on human nature in body and soul.[1] In Eden, Adam and Eve were physically perfect creatures, whose constituent elements—the humors of their bodies and the faculties of their souls—were held to be in natural balance, if still subject to the exercise of free will. Sexual appetite and human reproductive function were present, but their impulses, and even the genitals themselves, were controlled by reason, and any pleasure resulting from sexual activity was without sin since lust and sexual desire were absent.[2] The Fall results in the degeneration of physical and psychic equilibrium, giving rise to characters dominated by humoral imbalance and spiritual weakness, whose salvation is facilitated by the operation of divine grace and their cooperation with it. Widely accepted amongst clergy and natural philosophers was the Augustinian theory that fallen human nature is transmitted by the vitiated seed from which the fetus develops and on contact with which the divinely created soul is corrupted. Nonetheless, since the Word became incarnate, all human endeavor unfolds within the context of the possibility of salvation through *imitatio Christi*, the struggle to collaborate with divine grace, and rightly directed love.

These tensions are first witnessed in the portion of the *Libro* that runs from the opening invocation through ten stanzas of *cuaderna vía* (probably comprising portions of two separate prayers), close to two folios of prose, two lyric poems on the Joys of the Virgin, and a *cuaderna vía* section on interpretation, including the famous *exemplum* on the Debate in Signs between the Greeks and the Romans (44–70; tale 1).[3] Ruiz is highly likely to have added the prose prologue and accompanying lyrics when the book was otherwise complete.[4] The tensions relating to status, human nature, and the body introduced in the opening sections recur in Ruiz's descriptions of human bodies, and the section of the *Libro* dealing with astrology and determinism. The prose prologue also supplements our understanding of where Ruiz positions himself in relation to contemporary intellectual and cultural traditions, and, as a consequence of this, provides some guidance as to the ideological structures that contain and shape the *Libro*, and which it has sometimes been read as resisting.

The opening strongly resembles a scholastic sermon, which normally began with the intonation of a *thema*, or Biblical versicle drawn from the day's liturgy, which provided its focus. The preacher would then introduce an *antithema*, also a Scriptural text, usually linked by word, sense, or both to the *thema*, to serve as a preface to the sermon proper.[5] His discussion of the *antithema* would again develop out of a verbal or conceptual link from it, and would move toward an invocation, usually in the form of a standard prayer, such as the "Ave Maria," for himself and his congregation. Discussion could be in either Latin or the vernacular, and, other than prayers and quotations, tended not to be in verse. The opening ten stanzas of the *Libro* only partially fit this description, and the extent to which they can be said to act as an *antithema* has been debated. Nevertheless, the implications of Ruiz's use of sermon technique have ramifications for his own ideological milieu.

There is a verbal link between the opening words of the *Libro*—the INRI, "Jesus Nazarenus Rrex *Judeorum*" (p. 101, my emphasis; Jesus of Nazarus, King *of the Jews*)—and the opening line of the *Libro*, "Señor Dios, que *a los jodíos*, pueblo de perdición" (1a, my emphasis; Lord God, who [freed] *the Jews*, people of perdition), and a conceptual link between the falsely accused and undeservedly imprisoned Christ, the motif of treacherous and unjust imprisonment as it is worked out in stanzas 1–7, and the supplicant who addresses God from a symbolic prison.[6] The content of these stanzas probably stems ultimately from the false Saint Ciprian's prayer, perhaps via the *Ordo commendatio animae* or related orations, recited in situations of mortal peril.[7] Prayers of this type have found wider uses than as entreaties for the moribund: first, as the *Itinerarium*, associated with an Abbot undertaking a journey; second, as ordeal prayers; third, as the *Inlatio*, an important prayer in the Mozarabic rite; and, fourth, more popularly, as a prayer of protection and exorcism, including in hagiography.[8] More directly, it belongs to the genre of medieval narrative prayers, familiar from French epic, and a range of peninsular sources, such as the *Poema de Mio Cid* (ll. 330–65), the *Poema de Fernán González* (st. 105c–113), and Gonzalo de Berceo's *Milagros de Nuestra Señora* (st. 453–65, 520–21, and 826–31) and *Loores* (st. 91–92).[9] In common with some of its Hispanic antecedents, "Señor Dios," uses the formula, "sacaste / libreste [. . .] saca / libra [. . .]," probably drawing on the *Ordo*'s "Libera, Domine, animam servi tui, sicut liberasti [. . .]" and—like other prayers in this tradition—it lists in nonchronological order those whose sufferings the Lord has succored.[10]

It seems possible that the *Libro* drew inspiration from the same tradition as the *Poema de Fernán González* where the Castilians use it to pray for guidance during the battle of Sangonera.[11] Interestingly, the *Libro* is the only Hispanic poem to use the prayer as an opening invocation, differing from its intra-narrative use elsewhere, and this may suggest architectural rather than literary antecedents.[12] Adriano Duque has argued that there is a strong similarity between the use of the prayer in the *Poema de Fernán González*, and the sculptural programs of the Gothic cathedral porticos, in particular that of Leon (ca. 1230), with the *Ordo* as an intermediary analogue.[13] The *enumeratio* of saints and Old Testament figures in the *Poema de Fernán González* draws on traditional Hispanic narrative prayers, but includes a new group of saints, such as Marina (Margaret), Catherine, John, Esther and Peter, which can be explained by analogy with cathedral porticos. Duque's argument is convincing in that he draws parallels between the ascending left to right spatial organization of sculptural programs in porticos, and the distribution through stanzas of those individuals mentioned in the *Poema de Fernán González*, and demonstrates the iconographical and symbolic prominence of the dragon or serpent in the visual representation of the holy figures and in the poem to show triumph over evil. The only weakness in his argument is his placement of Christ in a pivotal role in the *Poema de Fernán González* prayer, when it is addressed throughout to Omnipotent God, and turns to Christ only in the concluding two stanzas.[14] Nonetheless, the role Duque attributes to Christ fits with the spatial program he outlines, and is supported by Peter E. Russell's observation that it is a feature of such prayers, including Ruiz's, to treat the Creator and Incarnate Christ almost as a single figure. Duque goes on to suggest that just as the cathedral portico is a gateway from this world to heaven through Christ, which functions to focus the mind of the faithful before entry to sacred space, in the *Poema de Fernán González* the prayer sets up figural parallels between Christ and Fernán González, and marks a liminal or transitional moment in the history of Spain to a time of redemption. It is possible that Ruiz recognized the similarity of design between portico and the *Poema de Fernán González*, and consequently saw the prayer for this, and for thematic reasons, as discussed above, as appropriate for the opening to his book. If this reading were correct, the use of the INRI to open the book could be seen to correspond to the positioning of Christ at the apex of the tympanum in many Gothic and Romanesque porticos. It should come as no surprise, then, that the central space of the book contains the sacred and the profane, just as the decorative programs in the interior of Romanesque and Gothic churches do.[15]

After the first seven stanzas, the scribe left a slightly larger gap between lines in MS *S* than usually occurs between stanzas, perhaps indicating that he was aware of a lacuna in his exemplar or leaving space for rubrication: the three following stanzas change subject to deal with Mary and the Annunciation. Luis Beltrán's argument that stanzas 1–7 represent a complete prayer is quite feasible, although inconclusive. At seven stanzas, it is rather brief; however, the final stanza breaks with the *sacaste / libreste* formula described above, and makes an appeal for protection from treachery direct to the Lord thus ending in a similar way to some of the other lyric poems in the *Libro*.[16] Stanzas 8–10 emphasize the Virgin's role in Christ's incarnation, with a particular emphasis on her special status as conveyed through Annunciation (8cd, 9a) and through New Testament confirmation of prophecy concerning the Advent of the Messiah (8ab, 9ab); they close with a plea for her grace (9cd, 10a), consolation and blessing (9cd), and succor (10d). The final stanza reintroduces the theme of treachery, requesting that divine disfavor be removed from the supplicant, and turned against, "los mescladores" (10c; meddlers, enemies). Taken together the two prayers, in their extant form, present the supplicant addressing Omnipotent God and the Virgin, the latter as an agent in the economy of salvation who undoes the sins of the first fathers through her role in the Incarnation, to protect him from treachery, to liberate him from a figurative prison, and to aid him. In the opening stanzas of the *Libro*, Ruiz draws on sermon technique, particularly that of forging a verbal and conceptual link between an opening Scriptural authority, here the INRI, and its elaboration, in order to set up the principal group of themes—the salvific power of the Incarnation, and human need for divine succor—to be developed in the narratives of the *Libro*, and in the prefatory material.

I shall demonstrate that the thematic links between the opening prayers, and the petition that follows the prose prologue reinforce the latter's message. There is consensus about the affinities between the prologue and the sermon tradition, yet there has been considerable disagreement as to whether Ruiz's use of sermon technique is serious or parodic. Here I wish to put aside the argument that it is a parodic sermon and that it serves as a justification of the truant content of the *Libro*.[17] Instead, I shall argue that Ruiz has produced a hybrid prologue, uniting sermon technique and the scholastic tradition of prologues which use sermon-structure.[18] Beltrán has made this argument in part, insisting that it be read in context, and that the extent to which it conforms to sermon structure be determined, and I believe the importance of his observations has been largely overlooked. I aim here to redress that balance.[19]

There are two basic types of medieval sermon: the homily and the scholastic or university sermon. The homily takes a liturgically appropriate Biblical pericope as its *thema* or opening quotation, explains its context, tends to give an allegorical meaning, and then moves into tropological explanation and moral exhortation.[20] The scholastic sermon is based on a Biblical versicle or *thema* drawn from, or very occasionally merely linked to, the liturgy for the day, which is then developed using the principles of *divisio intra* or *divisio extra*.[21] In delivery, it was usual for the scholastic sermon to open, after the citation of the *thema*, with the elucidation of a second Biblical quotation as *antithema*, as discussed above. In practice, the *antithema* is infrequently recorded, and may not have formed a regular part of all sermons, particularly in the peninsula.[22] In *divisio intra* the *thema* is typically broken up into three grammatically coherent phrases, which the preacher then discusses, usually focusing on individual words. In *divisio extra*, the preacher divides the *thema* conceptually, and uses as proof a variety of different approaches and materials, including first-person experience, and *exempla* or comparisons, backed up by Scriptural authority. Preaching manuals describe these two principles of division slightly differently, or focus mainly on *divisio intra*, as is the case with the treatises edited by Th.-M. Charland, and this has led to some confusion on the part of modern commentators as to which method Ruiz was using. Recent studies of sermon practice show, in fact, that sermons often used both methods, and it seems that the measure of a good sermon was not the degree to which it followed the precepts of preaching manuals, but how appropriate its subject and method were for the audience addressed.[23]

The prologue opens with a quotation, "Intellectum tibi dabo et instruam te in via hac qua gradieris; firmabo super te occulos meos" (p. 104; I will give thee understanding, and instruct thee in the path that thou shouldst follow: my eyes shall be fixed upon thee), from Psalm 31 [32]: 8.

Thus the implied authorial voice is positioned, like the preacher, in a chain of authority that is divinely sanctioned, and transmitted in writing, "que es el [that is, *verso*] que primero suso escreví" (p. 104; that's the versicle which I first wrote above), even if expounded orally.[24] There is a mismatch between the apparent formal sermon structure of the prologue and its content. It seems to consist structurally of two portions.[25] The first constitutes the sermon, which comprises two developments, running from the introduction of the *thema* to its repetition (p. 110), a frequent closing device in sermons since the aim is to move toward a fresh and enriched understanding of the *thema*. The second consists of the application of the sermon development to the *Libro* as a whole, particularly with regard to intention and interpretation, and is therefore more in keeping with the traditional scholastic *accessus* or prologue.[26] However, the two parts overlap in terms of content, since a description of the matter of the *Libro* in the first person, and its *utilitas*, usefulness, for three categories of audience is introduced in the second development of the sermon material.[27]

Ruiz, in fact, seems to use the mixed method of division, deriving *Entendimiento* or understanding by word and concept from his first *divisio* of the *thema*, "Intellectum tibi dabo," but glossing the remaining two portions of the *thema* by concept alone, drawing on the Augustinian trinity of faculties of the soul.[28] As is proper to *divisio extra* he supports his arguments with appropriate Scriptural authority in the first part of the sermon development in which he focuses on the positive qualities of the faculties (to "E esta es la sentençia del verso que enpieça primero «*breve*»" (p. 107, editor's emphasis: And this is the meaning in brief of the opening versicle).[29] Thereafter, the sermon deals with the diminished faculties of the soul as a consequence of the Fall, and their effect on humanity's struggle against sin.[30] In this portion of the sermon, Ruiz draws on non-Scriptural authority, including the *Disticta Catonis*, and canon law codes, which he attributes, sometimes inaccurately, to "el decreto," taken to be Gratian's *Decretum*.[31] However, he was probably drawing on an encyclopedic source of authority, such as Geremia da Montagnone's *Compendium moralitum notabilium*.[32] As a practice, the use of encyclopedia to source authorities, including non-Scriptural ones, for sermon use was quite common; for example, a series of curial sermons were preached in Papal Avignon, mainly by canon lawyers, in the 1330s and 1340s, which drew extensively from the *Corpus iuris canonici*, especially sections of the *Decretum* on the sacraments and penance.[33] Of particular relevance, since it bears witness to the topicality of the *Libro*'s opening prayer, is the Good Friday sermon preached by the Dominican General Hughues Vaucemain in the house of Cardinal Pierre DuPréz on April 14, 1340, which used the examples of Joseph, Susanna, Daniel, and Christ as exemplary figures.

My discussion of Ruiz's engagement, in the prologue, with the debates of natural philosophy, and the theological issues that flow from them, will situate Ruiz intellectually as being fully cognizant of and able to reconcile competing theological and natural philosophical discourses about the nature of mankind, the soul, the effect of the Fall, and man's psychological and physical disposition.[34] The first sermon development comprises three divisions of the *thema*. In the opening *divisio*, Ruiz views the first phrase, or *rrazón*, of the *thema*, "Intellectum tibi dabo," as meaning that if the faculties are *buenas*, "good" or "healthy," the individual enjoys a hygienic effect on soul, body, and reputation—"traen al alma conssolaçión e aluengan la vida al cuerpo, e dan le onrra con pro e buena fama" (they bring consolation to the soul, they increase the body's longevity, and give honor with advantage and good reputation)—since from them will flow *timor Domini*, charitable love of God, the basis of all wisdom, "toda sabidoría" (p. 105).[35] The second phrase indicates that such salvific instruction of the soul takes place in a pure body, "cuerpo linpio," since the individual considers, loves, and desires, "pienssa e ama e desea," divine love and the commandments, causing the soul to abhor concupiscent love, "el pecado del amor loco deste mundo" (pp. 105–06). The development is linked to the *divisio* through the focus on instruction, "et instruam te," which is glossed as the informed and instructed soul, "informada e instruida el alma." The third *divisio*, comprising the remainder of the *thema*, is taken by Ruiz to mean that the soul, comprising three good or healthy faculties, chooses the good love of God. This choice lodges good love in the ventricle of the mind that houses memory so that through memory the body can be brought to good deeds, and the individual granted salvation on death; thus it can be said that on account of the good works carried out on the path to salvation, the Lord's eyes have been fixed upon the individual (pp. 106–07). In doing this, Ruiz is drawing the Augustinian trinity of faculties into relationship with the medical view of the mind as consisting of three ventricles that house the inner wits.[36] Memory becomes at once something that is proper to the soul, along with the other faculties, and proper to the body as part of the physical structures of mind:[37]

E desque el alma, con el buen entendimiento e buena voluntad, con buena rremembrança, escoge e ama el buen amor que es el de Dios, e pone lo en la çela de la memoria por que se acuerde dello e trae al cuerpo a fazer buenas obras por las quales se salva el omne. (106)

(And since the soul, with good understanding and good will, with good memory, chooses and loves the good love which is that of God, and stores it in the memory cell by which it is remembered and brought to the body in order to carry out good deeds on account of which man is saved.)

Here Ruiz clearly argues that it is corporal mnemonic storage that causes the body to carry out such deeds as lead to salvation. Memory will become important later in his development of this topic. Up to this point, Ruiz is describing the divinely created and intended state of the soul, which functions efficiently and effectively, through being positioned historically before the Fall or through cooperation with divine grace. This might initially be regarded as Augustinian voluntarism, in which will, the principal faculty, is permitted by grace to desire good.[38] Ruiz does not make this connection explicit but I believe that his insistence on the positive nature of the faculties and their operations implies it.

Having dealt with the positive meaning of the versicle from Psalm 31, Ruiz then introduces a contrasting negative example by means of the disjunctive connector, *Como quier* (p. 107), in the sermon's second development. He goes on to argue that sin does not proceed from good or healthy faculties but from human nature's weakness, "la flaqueza de la natura humana," which cannot be avoided due to the influence of the Fall. A subsequent citation, "Quis potest fazere mundum de imundo conçeptum semine?" (Job 14.4; Who can bring the pure from the impure seed?), makes explicit the fact that human nature's weakness refers to the taint of original sin.[39] This quotation is linked to questions associated with the Virgin Birth, declared an article of the faith by the Council of Letran (649), and provides a link to the two lyrics on the Joys of the Virgin that follow the prologue and those that close the *Libro* (st. 20–43 and 1635–49).[40] Beyond this Ruiz is clearly alluding to the theological notion that Original Sin is transmitted through the polluting effect of semen in human generation; an issue undoubtedly bearing on the Virgin Birth. Medieval theological views of the transmission of sin to the fetus through sexual generation are unrelentingly negative in the view they adopt of human nature, and the vitiation of human seed on account of original sin.[41] Peter Lombard, for example, takes the position that human intellect is not equally free to will good and evil: it is freer to will good only when blessed with divine grace and freer to will evil without the intervention of grace; in other words, the Lombard's position exposes a tension or contradiction in voluntarism that arises from the Fall.[42] Juan Ruiz's own position reveals just such a conflict.

The Psalms, Ruiz argues, state that man's thoughts are vanity, *vane* (Ps. 93 [94].11), and urge him be not like the mule and ass, which lack understanding. In this, Ruiz contrasts the sensitive and appetitive faculties, which humans and animals both exercise, with the full functioning of the intellective faculties, which only humans enjoy but which have diminished on account of the Fall. Impoverished memory prevents understanding from being appropriately guided to love and use good thus human nature is inclined more to evil than to virtue.[43] Commentarists in the Averroist

Aristotelian tradition distinguished between pathologically induced love resulting from an imbalance of the faculties and Neoplatonic love inspired by the sight of beauty, which are conceptually rather similar to the Augustinian notions of *recta amor*, rightly directed love that moves to the spiritual, and *mala amor*, concupiscent love whose objects remain worldly.[44] Animals, however, were created without the intellective soul, and were dominated by particular humors, according to their nature so that, for example, the lion was seen as having a choleric disposition, and the ass a melancholic one; thus appetitive drives are natural in them and not tainted by pathology or sin, as they are in man.[45] The emergence of humoral characterology from the late eleventh or early twelfth century led the four temperaments of fallen man to be linked with such animals as were dominated by particular humors, and consequently by specific sins and thus for man to yield to his appetite is for his nature to be bestial. I shall argue, in chapter 2, that this is an important concept for Ruiz in the development of the *Libro*, particularly in his description of the wild mountain woman, Alda de la Tablada, and in his use of animal fable.

It seems possible that Ruiz's use of legal rather than scriptural prooftexts in support of the argument in the sermon's second development underscores the need for custom and law in fallen man thus setting up a dichotomy between the pre-lapsarian or grace-endowed state of the soul, and the cultural, that is post-lapsarian, state of the soul. Ruiz's failure to mention grace in the prologue points more toward the contrast between before and after the Fall than to a concern with the salvific operations of grace. Written sources of law, exemplary teaching, moral philosophy, other learned disciplines, writing and visual representations were first used—he argues—because of the slippery, *desleznadera*, nature of human memory. The importance of this statement has been overlooked; in fact, it reveals the areas of cultural prestige that Ruiz encodes in his book, and whose doctrine he adeptly appropriates to cause humor. I shall discuss the implications of Ruiz's truancy in relation to audience and memory below.

Ruiz appears to be deliberately alluding to scholastic psychology or medical theory, such as the Galenic revival at Salerno and in the French schools, as taught by the natural philosophers on whose authority he bases his conceptual understanding of the *thema*, "entiendo yo tres cosas, las quales dizen algunos *doctores philósophos* que son en el alma" (pp. 104–05, my emphasis; I understand three things, which some *natural philosophers* say are in the soul), but as interpreted by theologians, such as Saint Augustine of Hippo (354–430), Peter Lombard (ca. 1095–1161), and Saint Bonaventure (ca. 1217–74), who argued that only after the Fall do humans become subject to involuntary movements of the appetitive functions, and thus are drawn more to ill than good.[46] This material, which focuses on the effects of the Fall, underscores a thematic preoccupation with salvation and mortality and their relation to sin in the first portion of the book, and not solely in the second, as has been previously proposed by Roger Walker.[47]

Ruiz continues his argument with a clearly theological dimension, drawing on *auctoritas* that he attributes to the *Decretals*:[48]

> Ca tener todas las cosas en la memoria e non olvidar algo más es de la divinidat que de la umanidad; esto dize el decreto. E por esto es más apropriada a la memoria del alma, que es spíritu de Dios criado e perfecto, e bive siempre en Dios. (108)

> (Thus holding everything in memory and not forgetting anything is more of the divinity that of humanity: the Decretals say that. And on account of this, memory is more appropriate to the soul's memory, which is created and perfect divine spirit [or spirit created and perfected by God], and lives always in Him.)

Only God is capable of perfect and complete memory and thus it is proper to soul, residing eternally in God rather than being proper to the transient human body. L. Jenaro-MacLennan suggests several possible interpretations of the ambiguous syntax.[49] However, vernacular analogues also make this assertion, with similarly erroneous attribution.[50] In the context of the prologue, Ruiz is clearly pointing to the two aspects of memory: physical corporal memory, which is located in the brain, comprises the physical storage space of memory and is necessarily mortal; and the faculty proper to the soul, which is necessarily immortal.[51] Ruiz may be referring here to the idea that individual phantasms or imprints of memory are proper to the sensitive soul, and not to the rational and immortal soul, in which reside quiddities; the abstracts, species, or intelligible forms by which we recognize, for example, that a mortal, rational individual endowed with the capacity for speech and laughter is human.[52] Whether Ruiz is differentiating between these two categories of memory or conflating them, he asserts the vitiated nature of physical or psychological memory and supports this assertion with *auctoritates* (Job 14.5 and 14.1), alluding directly to the transience of human life.[53] Ruiz is arguing that the human propensity for concupiscent love derives from the psychology of the soul, particularly in diseased memory.[54]

The arguments put forward by Peter Lombard in his *Sentences* exemplify the orthodoxy of the position taken by Ruiz.[55] He argues that, in order for post-lasparian humanity to desire good, free will must be supplemented by grace to become good will, which disposes the individual to virtue. Whilst the parents engender the child's flesh, already corrupted by the Fall and inclined to sin, its soul is God-given, and in fusing with the corrupt flesh of the child it too is vitiated. The Lombard contends that the central weakness inherited is a "depression of the will," but the other faculties and the body also bear the consequences of original sin, amongst which figure the corruption of sexual function through the actions of lust.[56] In this sense, Ruiz's diagnosis of the propriety of the fully functioning faculties of the soul to the sphere of the divine, and his concern that the stain of sin is an inescapable human weakness is fully justified.[57]

Ruiz next clearly moves away from sermon structure to introduce the first-person voice of the book's implied author with an expression of modesty:

> Onde, yo, de mi poquilla çiençia e de mucha e grand rrudeza, entendiendo quantos bienes fazen perder al alma e al cuerpo e los males muchos que les apareja e trae el amor loco del pecado del mundo, escogiendo e amando con buena voluntad salvación e gloria del paraíso para mi anima, fiz esta chica escriptura en memoria de bien, e conpuse este nuevo libro, en que son escriptas algunas maneras e maestrías e sotilezas engañosas del loco amor del mundo que usan algunos para pecar. (109)

> (Therefore, I, being of very little learning and of much and great ignorance, understanding how much good is lost to the soul and the body and the many ills which mad love of worldly sin prepares and brings them, with good will choosing and loving salvation and the glory of paradise for my soul, made this little writing in remembrance of good, and I composed this new book in which are written some of the deceitful ways, skilful work and subtleties of mad worldly love which some people use to sin.)

The implied author claims, despite his lack of learning, to will good and salvation and so to have composed his book in remembrance of good, and then he describes its contents as dealing with the dangers of worldly love; in other words, he claims to espouse good will. Ruiz then goes on to argue that the *utilitas* to the audience depends on its capacity to exercise the three faculties.[58] Those of good understanding on the path to salvation will reject worldly love, which is depicted in the book. Those of little understanding will see their intended sins exposed to public scrutiny, their memory will be roused, they will consider their reputation, and be moved to love themselves more greatly than sin. The sinner's protection of good name is a result of self-love. As rightly ordered *caritas* (p. 110; "la ordenada caridad"), self-love is its own beginning therefore the sinner, seeking to avoid tarnishing his or her reputation, will abhor disordered, concupiscent love, "loco amor, que faze perder las almas e caer en saña de Dios, apocando la vida e dando mala fama e deshonrra e muchos daños a los cuerpos" (p. 110; mad love, which causes souls to be lost and to incur divine wrath, shortening life, and bringing ill repute and dishonor and many other ills to the body). Finally, since humankind's very nature is vitiated, those who wish to sin will find ways of doing so described in the book. The *Libro*, therefore, is useful to all, whatever path he or she takes, whatever his or her disposition (pp. 109–10). At this point, Ruiz reiterates the opening phrase of the *thema*, a conventional closure in sermons, as noted above.

The concern with bodily pollution is in line with contemporary thinking, and will be expressed by Ruiz in relation to concupiscent love throughout the *Libro*. As noted above, medieval theological discourse explained the corruption of the body as a direct result of the Fall through the punishment of mortality, and the concomitant vitiation of semen. The Latin fathers, such as Jerome, cultivated the Biblical association of sin with sickness, which was developed by theologians, such as Saint Bonaventure, himself the son of a physician, and pseudo-Anselm of Loan, who appropriated the discourse of disease and applied it to the polluting effects of sin and the sacramental antidote.[59] Bodily status, integrity, and well being were all potentially contaminated by concupiscent love, and its threat is no more apparent than in medieval treatments of love sickness, such as the relevant sections of Constantine the African's († ca. 1087) *Viaticum*, and its commentaries. Likewise, the concern with self-love is similar to arguments put forward by the Lombard, drawing on Augustine, who sees the mind, its notice of itself, and its self-love, *mens*, *notitia*, and *amor*, as one the Trinitarian aspects of man.[60] Ruiz's treatment of self-love resonates also with the essentially Augustinian model, also taught by Bonaventure, amongst others, of the soul's capacity to ascend to God being dependant on "perception of the external world, and then of the mind itself, and finally the restoration of the trinitarian image within us."[61] Indeed, Pierre L. Ullman suggests that Ruiz may have known Augustine's work through an intermediary, such as Bonaventure, although closer knowledge of Augustinian thinking now seems possible.[62]

Ruiz's maneuver at the point under discussion could certainly be seen as parodic of the sermon form but only if it were taken out of context. Studies of the scholastic sermon tradition have shown how versatile the form itself was.[63] It might be adopted by a master to introduce a set text in the medieval lecture hall or by a new master to praise the discipline of higher study to which he had recently been incepted.[64] It had parodic performative uses, of course, but might also be used seriously to introduce matter seemingly antithetical to its original aim of Christian instruction, such as Aristotle's natural philosophy.[65] Academic works for circulation might also open with sermon-prologues, as did Peter Comestor's gospel commentaries (produced ca. 1159–78), which were widely disseminated, and adopted and adapted by his commentators, Peter of Poitiers and Praepositinus of Cremona.[66] Comestor's sermon-prologues are notable not just for their extensive diffusion but also for the fact that in them he admixed topics from the academic *accessus*, which governed content, with sermon structure.[67] B. Smalley observes that, although Comestor's sermon-prologues are the earliest extant, he makes allusions that suggest that he adopted the practice from a forebear, perhaps Abelard.[68]

It may be useful here to consider prologue conventions in more detail. A.J. Minnis has identified three broad types of medieval academic prologues.[69] The first type derives from the scholastic adoption of the introductory topics of ancient commentaries, and deals with questions of "by whom," "what," "why," "where," "in what manner," "when," and "by what means," including *intentio auctoris* (authorial objective), and *utilitas*. The second type, the "Aristotelian prologue" applies the philosopher's theory of the four causes, material, efficient, formal, and final, to exposition, and discusses the source material, the author, the external structure, and the end or objective of the work. The third type, derived from the Ciceronian topics, covered two broad approaches, both of which may appear in any given prologue: its intrinsic component introduced the work itself, and its extrinsic one described the work's place in conventional medieval epistemology. The extrinsic component also often dealt topics common to the first and second types, such as *intentio, utilitas*, the work's instructional value, and its external structure. Minnis himself discusses sermon-prologues but does not accord them the status of a separate category.[70]

The pursuit of love was used as *utilitas* in prologues without condemnation in the Ovidian tradition, and so such notions of *utilitas* would have been familiar to some of Ruiz's audience.[71] However, although the threefold *utilitas* fits in well with the content and elaboration of Ruiz's prologue, it sits uneasily with our expectations of the didactic intent of a sermon, and I contend that it is this clash of expectations that causes the modern reader to assume that there is parodic intent in the prologue. I should argue that if there were parodic intent, and I am yet to be wholly convinced on this point, then the target is the confused messages found in prologues, and the attempt by scholastic authors to acculturate pagan authors to a Christian message.[72] If this were the case, then it may be linked to the parody of the concept of *translatio studii* and the unfitness of the recipient of the tradition, which is an aspect of the Dispute in Signs, discussed below.[73]

Having addressed the question of *utilitas*, a rhetorical topic of prologues, Ruiz turns, in the final development of the prose prologue, to address *intentio*.[74] He urges readers to judge his words according to his intention, "segund derecho, las palabras sirven a la intención e non la intención a las palabras" (p. 110; as is right, my words serve my intention, and not my intention the words). God himself knows Ruiz's intention, which is to inculcate good memory leading to virtuous acts in everyone, and to give examples of living virtuously, and prophylactic stories against concupiscent love. Whilst the importance of this statement has been observed, I do not believe its meaning has yet been adequately qualified in the light of the context of the prologue. Ullman argued that this discussion is affiliated with Augustine's principle of voluntarism, in that "evil is in the eye of the beholder and not in the book, which therefore cannot block the path to salvation," and that will predominates over understanding, perhaps under-playing the role of memory.[75] In Augustinian thinking, memory is the main faculty to see things that happened and as they are in general; that is, as a faculty of the soul, memory has a key function in good decision-making.[76] However, Ruiz actually presents the contradictory view that an effect of the Fall is that memory lacks the reflexive power to correct pre-sent behavior on the basis of an accurate assessment of past behavior.[77] His willful misreading of Aristotle's statement that sustenance and reproduction are necessary to animal life as expressing man's continuous desire for union with a pleasing partner, discussed in chapter 3, and his use of it as an authority to excuse his concupiscent desire reveals such a failure of mem-ory, and the good or healthy operation of his intellective faculties. The humorous truancy of his statement is most apparent to those with an accurate recall of Aristotle.

The appeal for divine succor in poetic composition is common; how-ever, the specific request for divine guidance in being inspired and aided recalls both the sermon-prologue's description of the actions of the healthy or good rational faculties, and the stated intention of displaying the poetic arts. The narrator then moves on to introduce the first verse statement on interpretation, and it is this that links together the nucleus of following narrative units, and the prologue. The claims made echo those of the poets of *mester de clerecía*, discussed in the introduction:

> Non vos diré mentira en quanto en él [el rromanze] yaz,
> ca por todo el mundo se usa e se faz.
> E por que mejor de todos sea escuchado,
> fablar vos he por trobas e por cuento rrimado;
> es un dezir fermoso e saber sin pecado,
> rrazón más plazentera, fablar más apostado.
>
> (14cd, 15)

> (I won't lie to you about what lies in the poem / since it's what everyone uses and does. // And so that everyone may better listen to it / I shall speak in verse and by rhyme and rhythm; / it's a beautiful composition and knowledge without sin / a more pleasing argument, a more beautiful way of speaking.)

The *Libro* will depict current practice (14d) thus conforming to the cultural products that describe and advise about behavior, "de castigos e costunbres"

(p. 108), referred to in the prologue. It is pleasing to hear and itself without sin, as the prologue claims, although its form has been selected to appeal to a wide audience. In invoking Clementine and wisdom literature the *Libro* is clearly aligned with post-lapsarian cultural products created on account of the flawed nature of human memory, and by inserting the *Libro* in the chain of divinely sanctioned *auctoritas* its exemplarity is underlined. However, when it comes to dissemination, Ruiz's interest in *auctoritas* appears to wane:

> Qual quier omne que lo oya, si bien trobar sopiere,
> puede más ý añadir e enmendar, si quisiere;
> ande de mano en mano, a quien quier quel pidiere;
> como pella a las dueñas, tome lo quien podiere.
>
> (1629)

> (Whomsoever hears it [the book], if he knows how to compose poetry well, he can add more and amend there if he wishes; let it go from hand to hand, to whoever should ask for it; like a ball [thrown] to the ladies, let catch who catch can.)

This statement is often read, along with "faré / punto a mi librete, mas non lo çerraré" (1626cd; I shall put a full-stop to my little book, but I shall not close it), as indicating the open-ended nature of the *Libro*.[78] Even so, it is more directly related to widespread formal modesty topoi, inviting amendment by the general audience, able individuals, or the patron.[79] Ángel Gómez Moreno suggests its use may be comic and parodic, and Jeremy N.H. Lawrance links it to the convention's use in prose treatises, and reads Ruiz's treatment as parody, continuing:[80]

> By mocking aspiring improvers with the ludicrous image of their playing ball with it like women (compare Trotaconventos's invitation to the gullible Endrina to enter her house to play at ball and other foolish games, st. 861), Ruiz keeps control over his book: all can read it or enjoy it, but only experts can handle it (Zahareas 1964: 210). The rejection of closure in st. 1626–29 points to indeterminacy not of structure, but of interpretation.[81]

The image of women at ball play may contain a ludic allusion to the seduction of Doña Endrina and her, perhaps willing, failure to understand the *double entendre* of Trotaconventos's invitation, as Lawrance suggests, but such images of women at play are commonplace, and the emphasis may be more on the final hemistich of the stanza, and its implication that skill and chance play an equal part in success.[82] Nevertheless, the image may humorously transfer emasculinity, with its attendant threat of illicit access to women, from priests to poets at the same time as it asserts the author's identity as poet rather than priest (see the introduction).

Although the affiliation between stanza 1629 and amendment topoi has been observed, to the best of my knowledge no connection has yet been made between its particular form here and medieval reading and mnemonic practice. As Carruthers has shown, an essential component of medieval composition is the dissemination of material to an audience, which receives it, integrates it into its personal memory store, and then employs it as *auctoritas* by applying the sense to personally relevant situations. The invitation clearly alludes to this practice, which causes the promiscuous circulation of material through minds that are variously enabled to use it and which are likely to put it to different purposes.[83] However, it differs at the literal level since it is often read as referring directly to those skilled in composition, *trobar*; however, Ruiz uses *trobar* in a variety of senses, including that of 'to find,' which relates to the individual's discovery of meaning and capacity for memorization of ideas.[84] Language was held to comprise minimal sense units or periods, *sententiae* or *colae*, constituted by ideas rather than the words that express them, and that formed the basis of division for commentary and for storage in physical memory.[85] Taken in this way, the injunction is that whoever is skilled at the manipulation of words and, above all, of the *sententia* necessary in memory work, should use the *Libro* as far as possible to their own ends, and, in this way, the *Libro* will circulate widely; that is, become an *auctoritas*. The success of the invitation can be judged by manuscript annotation, and by the *Libro*'s subsequent quotation.[86]

Stanza 1629 reiterates stanza 70, which, if medieval reading practice and mnemonics are taken into account, clearly refers to memory storage by alluding to the medieval view that interpretation is in the mind of the recipient and the use that recipient gives to a text, whilst the author's intention is conveyed in the literal meaning, as discussed above:[87]

> De todos instrumentos yo, libro, só pariente:
> bien o mal, qual puntares, tal te diré ciertamente.
> Qual tú dezir quisieres, ý faz punto, ý, ten te;
> si me puntar sopieres, sienpre me avrás en miente.
>
> (70)

(I, Book, am related to all instruments: / good or ill, however you notate, that's what I shall say truly/ whatever you should wish to say, make a note there, pause there / if you know how to notate, you'll always have me in mind.)[88]

The reference to medieval reading and mnemonic practice is underscored by the use of *puntar* and *punto*, which implies the act of reading by division of *sententiae*, and the mental, and written, use of marginal and punctuation marks, *notae*, to aid memory storage and retrieval. However, Ruiz's comments on the issue of interpretation, and the propriety of the sign to the referent extend beyond this point, as an examination of Ruiz's final *intentio* in the sermon-prologue and episode of the Greeks and the Romans will show.

The Dispute in Signs has attracted a great deal of critical attention, at over a dozen lengthy discussions, partly because of its liminal position at the end of the preliminary materials, and partly because its focus on issues of interpretation has caused it to be viewed as a key to understanding the *Libro*. It begins at stanza 44, immediately after the first pair of lyrics on the Joys of the Virgin, and is generally taken to end at stanza 70, which consists of the *yo, libro* riddle, discussed above. It deals with a debate in signs contested when the Romans request access to Greek laws.[89] The Romans fear their lack of understanding of Greek learning will handicap them in the debate, and they select a ruffian, a *rribaldo* or *vellaco*, to represent them, either trusting to providence (51cd) or looking to avoid loss of face (52d). The two participants exchange two sets of signs before the Greek doctor judges the Romans fit to receive the law (58b), and the episode closes when each of the participants has given a different, but possible, interpretation of the meaning of the gestures (59c–60; 61b–63).[90] The outcome of the debate is not stated but the medieval theory of *translatio studii* is taken to indicate that the Greek's verdict was acted upon. Taking a broadly narratological approach, I shall focus on the way in which humor functions in the episode since the stanzas preceding the *exemplum* highlight its importance:

> Palabras son de sabio, e dixo lo Catón,
> que omne a sus coidados que tiene en coraçón
> entreponga plazeres e alegre la rrazón,
> que la mucha tristeza mucho pecado pon.
> E por que de buen seso non puede omne rreir,
> avré algunas burlas aquí a enxerir;
> cada que las oyeres, non quieras comedir
> salvo en la manera del trobar e del dezir.
>
> (44–45)

(They are words of wisdom, and Cato said them, / that amongst the cares kept in the heart / pleasure should be interspersed and reason cheered / since much sadness brings much sin. // And because no one can laugh at sound advice [or common sense] / I shall have to graft on some jokes here. / Every time you hear them, don't try to ruminate / except on their composition and how they're put.)

Here the Archpriest argues that since pleasure counters despair (44), and good sense, *buen seso*, does not incite laughter, he will graft on *algunas burlas,* which should be scrutinized, *comedir,* only for their poetic craft and expression. Notoriously, stanza 46 then mentions the issue of interpretation, and introduces the debate as a negative *exemplum.* His insistence on the hygienic effect of laughter to leaven the potential melancholy of the serious mind provides an important context for the episode under consideration, and for the *Libro* as a whole. Indeed the problem of pathological melancholy was a topic of serious discussion in moral philosophy and theology, with widely circulating discussions by John Chrysostom, Saint Jerome, John Cassian, Johannes Climaus, Isidore of Seville, Hugh of St Victor and William of Auvergne. It was particularly relevant to the monastic community, which took it as a test, revealing grace if it could be borne, and vice, overlapping with sloth, *acedia,* if not.[91]

Ruiz aligns the narrator and the audience with the Greek and Roman, and through the *doctor/rribaldo* dichotomy they are linked to the *cuerdo* and *non cuerdo* of the prose prologue:

Entiende bien mis dichos e piensa la sentencia;
non me contesca con tigo commo al doctor de Greçia (S)
con el rribaldo romano, e con su poca sabiençia, (S)
quando demandó Roma a Greçia la çiençia.

(46)

(Understand well my sayings and think about the *sententia*; / may the same thing not happen to us with as to the Greek doctor / with the ruffian, and his little wisdom [or knowledge], / when Rome asked Greece for learning.)

The debate concludes at stanza 64 where *Por* is used as a copulative to extrapolate from the *exemplum* to its message or *epimythium,* "Por esto dize la pastraña de la vieja ardida: / 'Non ha mala palabra si non es a mal tenida'" (64ab; That's why the bold old woman's saw goes, "No word is evil unless it's taken as such").[92] The proverb applies to the *exemplum* in order to point out that no ill arises from the ribald's signs since the outcome is successful for the Romans on account of the Greek's theological interpretation.[93] The Archpriest then goes on to develop the application of the *exemplum*'s message to the question of interpretation with a phrase (64d) parallel to its opening stanza (46a):

Verás que bien es dicha si bien fuese entendida.
Entiende bien mi dicho e avrás dueña garrida.
La burla que oyeres, non la tengas en vil;
la manera del libro, entiende la sotil;
que saber bien e mal dezir encobierto e doñeguil,
tú non fallarás uno de trobadores mill.

(64c–65)[94]

(You will see that good is spoken if it is understood as good. / Understand well what I say and you'll have a fair lady. / Whatever joke you hear, don't take it the wrong way; / understand the book's manner [to be] subtle; / you will not find one in a thousand poets / who knows good and evil speaking [or who knows good and speaks ill] as covertly or as pleasingly.)

The message that the Archpriest draws from the *exemplum* is at first clear: words in themselves have no negative moral value unless they are taken negatively. However, this didacticism is undermined by the promise that good understanding of the book will bring a *dueña garrida*. Immediately after this seeming contradiction, in 65a the Archpriest is quick to remind the audience not to take joking, *burlas*, amiss. Although the allusion to the *dueña garrida* is often seen as one of the Archpriest's humorously truant twists, Stephen Reckert suggests the line be amended to read *buena guarida*, 'good refuge.'[95] Reckert's solution is ambiguous, since the refuge may be concupiscent love or spiritual succor. If Reckert's amendment is wrong, it is possible, given the proximity of the Marian lyrics, that the *dueña garrida* whose favor the audience attains could be the Virgin rather than a worldly lady, depending on the audience's disposition and interpretation. Each of these interpretations is reinforced by Latin *explicits* associated with the Ovidian tradition in which a *pulchra puella*, 'beautiful girl,' or *paradisi gaudi amena*, 'pleasant joyful paradise,' is a reward for the exhausted scribe who has finished his copying or the reader who has read well, but which is ambiguous since, as John Dagenais notes, terms such as *puellarum pulcherrima* and *perpulchra domina*, 'most beautiful of girls' and 'very beautiful mistress,' were applied to the Virgin.[96] The Archpriest then warns that the book's meaning is subtle, and hidden. The lack of humor of good counsel set up in stanza 45 in the introduction to the *exemplum* appears to be echoed in stanza 67 in the interpretative position of *los cuerdos*:

En general a todos fabla la escriptura:
los cuerdos con buen sesso entendrán la cordura;
los mançebos livianos guarden se de locura;
escoja lo mejor el de buena ventura.

(In general, my writing speaks to all: / the wise with good counsel will understand the wisdom;/ let licentiousness young men protect themselves from the madness;/ let he of good fortune choose the best part.)

The apparent creation of two opposing groups in *los cuerdos* and *los mançebos livianos* recalls a similar dichotomy in the prose prologue:

E ansí este mi libro a todo omne o muger, al cuerdo e al non cuerdo, al que entendiere el bien e escogiere salvaçión e obrare bien, amando a Dios; otrosí

al que quisiere el amor loco; en la carrera que andudiere, puede cada uno
bien dezir: «*Intellectum tibi dabo, e çetera.*» E rruego e conssejo a quien lo viere
e lo oyere, que guarde bien las tres cosas del alma [entendimiento, voluntad,
memoria]: lo primero, que quiera bien entender e bien juzgar la mi
entençión por qué lo fiz, e la sentençia de lo que ý dize, e non al son feo de
las palabras; e segund derecho, las palabras sirven a la intençión e non la
intençión a las palabras. (110, editor's emphasis)

(And thus this, my book, can well say, 'Intellectum tibi dabo, etc,' to every
man or woman, to the wise and the fool, whoever understands good and
chooses salvation and does good works in loving God; further to whoever
desires mad love, on whatever path he or she walks.[97] And I beg and advise
whoever sees or hears it to hold unto themselves the three things pertaining
to the soul [understanding, will and memory]: chiefly, to wish to understand
well and judge well the reason why I made it, and the *sentençia* of which it
speaks here, and not to the ugly noise of the words; and, as is right, my words
serve my intention, and not my intention the words.)

Here the wise individual who understands good and chooses love of God
is contrasted with the fool who prefers *amor loco*. Nevertheless, these individuals have been endowed with the higher faculties and therefore can
decide their own paths. He then counsels the exercise of the faculties in the
interpretation of the *Libro* in which his own mastery of language means that
words are properly subordinate to intention, as discussed above. Stanzas
64–67 essentially repeat this point.

In these statements, the Archpriest sets up a series of homologous
relationships in which the audience is asked to set *cuerdo*: *buen sesso*: *entender
el bien* / *la cordura*: *escoger salvaçión*: *obrar bien, amando Dios* (wise: good counsel:
understand good / smartness: choose salvation: do good works, loving
God) against the series *non cuerdo*: *mançebo liviano*: *querer el loco amor* (foolish:
licentiousness young man: desire concupiscent love). The introduction and
conclusion of the *exemplum* therefore point to two aspects of the *exemplum*
itself that I should like now to explore further: the use of humor in the
*burla*; and, how the contrasting interpretative positions advocated in the
prologue square with the *exemplum* itself.

Vasvári has argued that in the agonistic gestural debate, the Greek
doctor fails to respond to an aggressive phallic insult in such a way that he
is rendered passive and thereby he, and learned culture, can be seen as the
net loser in the debate whilst the Roman displays dominant masculinity.
She shows that the ribald is traditionally figured as "a kind of talking penis,
with his bald head the *glans penis*"; this characterization allows him to use
"his whole body [. . .] to act out the insult to his adversary."[98] The comic
potential of the Roman's gestures as a parody of the use of signs as a com-
municative method amongst Cistercian and other monastic communities

pledged to observe silence is heightened further by their obscenity. The Roman may outdo the Greek in his masculine aggression but he too is the source of ridicule as he is aligned with the *non cuerdo* of earlier statements and represents the bluster of the ignorant impostor who has falsely usurped the mantle of learning, like the ignorant cleric who is one of the butts of Ruiz's satire in the *Libro*. The scope of Vasvári's discussion does not permit her to take the validity of both interpretations of the signs into account in her conclusion, and, although her reading of the ribald's gestures as expressing phallic aggression is convincing, I am not persuaded that it explains sufficiently the humor and tension that reside in this episode. In fact, the ribald's obscene and aggressive response illustrates the Romans' ignorance of Greek learning and of revelation, seen in the Greek's Trinitarian interpretation of signs. It is the Greek doctor's ethical or charitable reading—his refusal or failure to interpret the ribald's 'grotesque grammar'—that ultimately results in *translatio studii*, including knowledge of God.[99]

The comic technique arises from the careful narrative control of the solemn exchange of signs in which narrative voice directs attention in specific ways.[100] Both Greeks and Romans are seeking means to save face in a situation in which each party considers that the Romans deserve to lose. The Greeks propose a disputation to resolve the question of whether the Romans deserve or could understand Greek learning, "por se escusar" (48d; to get out of it); even if guilty of intellectual pride, the Greeks are right about the superiority of their learning as desirable cultural capital to which the Romans have no access.[101] Likewise the Romans recognize their inferiority, and the need to save face in the debate when they request the ribald's help, "escusa nos desta lid" (52d; get us out of this confrontation). However, the narrator tells the extradiegetic audience that the Romans' decision, "fue les conssejo sano" (51d; was sound counsel), and makes no such observation about the Greeks; thus an apparently foolish step in fact brings about a favorable outcome, perhaps, as Leo Spitzer implies, because of divine providence rather than chance.[102]

When the debate takes place, the Romans, a part of the intradiegetic audience of the exchange, are privy to the disguise, and the aggression and arrogance of the Roman ribald prior to the contest beginning (st. 53). The extradiegetic audience shares this knowledge but, notably, the Greeks do not. The Greeks are thereby set up as the butt of the ruse. In contrast to the aggression and bluster of the Roman, the Greek contestant adopts a scholarly solemnity, but this is undercut by the aggressive-defensive attitude the Roman brings to the contest. For the intradiegetic audience—the Greeks and Romans witnessing the debate—there are two interrelated semiotic codes to indicate the meaning of the signs that are deployed: the conscious

gestures that each participant makes, on the one hand, and the outward
signs of their emotions and states of mind, on the other. The intradiegetic
audience interprets the same semiotic systems as the combatants; but for the
Romans the prior attitude of the ribald is part of the context by which his
gestures would be understood; the Romans therefore have a privileged
position in the interpretation of the ribald's gestures. In marked contrast to
this, the narrator's implied audience have a doubly privileged position: first,
like the Romans, they are aware of the ribald's disguise and aggression; and
second, the narrator decodes the outward signs of the interior state of the
participants: the Greek is "sosegado, de vagar, [. . .] con su memoria sana"
(55a, 57b; calm, relaxed, of healthy [or sound] memory), and the Roman
is "bravo, de mal pagar [. . .] con fantasía vana [. . .] de porfía avié gana"
(55d, 57cd; wild, unhappy, with vain images in his mind, desirous of a
fight). Ruiz may be deliberately contrasting the Greek's soundly organized
memory store and healthy psychological state, "con su memoria sana,"
with the vanity and disorganization of the images impressed on the
Roman's memory store, and his psychologically diseased state, "con
fantasía vana."[103] Part of the humor, therefore, arises from the ironic contrast between the Greek's solemnity and the Roman's aggression.[104]
Despite what the extradiegetic audience knows of each of these figures, the
meaning of their gestures may remain enigmatic because, although what is
revealed about the Roman suggests an aggressive or scatological meaning,
the narrator has already commented that choosing the ribald "fue les conssejo
sano"; a statement whose irony can only be judged in performance and by
the disposition of individual readers and listeners.

   Excluding those members of the audience with previous knowledge of
other medieval versions of this *exemplum*, the difference in the demeanor of
the participants suggests that each will have a different understanding of the
signs. The extradiegetic audience's knowledge that the Romans trust to
providence supports the view that the Greek's reading of the signs is an
admissible one. The narrator and the audience familiar with the notion of
*translatio studii* enjoy foreknowledge of the ribald's success, and a privileged
interpretative position from which they learn each agent's interpretation of
his own, and the other's, action. Neither of the interpretations are exclusive
or definitive since meaning resides in the use to which signs and words are
put by the recipient, although their full sense and role in God's providential plan is known only to Him; only God enjoys the panoptic gaze.[105]
However, the solemn façade is broken down entirely in the Roman
ribald's explanation of the gestures as miming physical aggression. Of
course, the narrator has also prepared his audience for this by describing the
first of the Roman's gestures as "en manera de arpón" (56c; harpoon like),
and emphasizing his bluster, as discussed above.

In Freudian terms this joke is tendentious, in that it expresses both hostility and obscenity.[106] Within the *exemplum* itself, the extradiegetic audience is aligned with the intradiegetic audience of Romans as spectator or third party, and is gratified by the fact the ribald joker lifts inhibitions associated with genital or sexual display in the process of another's humiliation. The ribald gets the better of the learned culture that excludes him but has failed to show the necessary competence to enjoy his prize; nor does the doctor's understanding extend to the ribald's domain. The ribald's victory must then be an ironic commentary on the notion of *translatio studii* since it recognizes that learning and power may be transmitted through unfit agents.[107] The use of an *exemplum* concerned with the transmission of culture, particularly in the form of law, appropriately recalls the sermon-prologue's insistence that law is necessary because of the fallen state of humankind, and this context particularly calls to mind the subtext of *translatio studii* within the *Libro*.

Overall, the point is not the Augustinian view of the arbitrary relationship between signified and signifier, which is taken as understood; but rather it is that mutual miscomprehension results from the divergent dispositions and cultural competencies of the two contestants.[108] The Greek's sober exercise of his well-balanced faculties represents higher intellective function; whilst the Roman's aggressive obscenity presents the lower appetitive, defensive, and aggressive functions shared with animals. However, unlike the Greek and the Roman, the narrator reveals himself to be fully competent in both grotesque and theological grammar through his manipulation of the aggressive-obscene and religious ramifications of gestural semiotics. Only God enjoys full knowledge of the consequences of human action, and, in his wisdom, He may choose to use an agent who appears unfit to mortal man in His providential plan. More specifically, however, in this regard the *exemplum* also makes the point that, despite the fallen and unfit nature of Ruiz's narrator, the Archpriest, and much of the *Libro*'s content, *intentio* and final purpose can be to the good.

The joke-work extends outward from the frame. In MS *S*, the audience is first asked to compare the Archpriest to the Greek doctor, and itself to the Roman, and it is thus figured as taking the position of the dominant participant in the joke work who, as joker/ribald, is permitted self-exposure through the mimed oroanal rape of the Greek who, in his turn, remains ignorant that he is the object of the joke. When the Archpriest discusses the message of the story, the ribald nature of the joke's pleasure is turned against the audience who have allied themselves with the Roman who interprets the gestures' meanings aggressively: "Non ha mala palabra si non es a mal tenida" (64b; There's no evil word unless it's taken as such). The Archpriest then argues that the nature of signs lies in their use not in any individual's interpretation of them; an orthodox position as I have argued. In this sense he asserts that the Greek's interpretation is as valid as the Roman's. The audience has now become the butt of narrator's ruse since its aggressive and ribald interpretation has been revealed: the narrator is equally competent in the high and low spheres but the joke-work has manipulated the audience into assuming that the low and indecorous is superior. The analogy between the Greek and the Archpriest is false, since he and his audience can, if blessed with good fortune, adopt three interpretative positions.[109] The disposition of the audience has been revealed as a central aspect in interpretation, and, in order to extract the full benefit from the material, it must be willing to exercise humor: in this sense, the *Libro*'s meaning is *sotil*, or polyvalent.

In the application of the message, the narrator returns again to make the familiar point about ambiguity in stanzas 65 and 67 (both cited above). The Archpriest explains here that there are three categories of interpretation, depending on nature, culture, and good fortune thus adopting a pessimistic rather than wholly voluntaristic or deterministic position on the individual's capacity will to good.[110] The wise will see the wisdom in the book, like the Greek who reads the signs in relation to the theological, but he may miss or lack the hygienic ability to laugh, and will not draw all the good from the *Libro* other than the skill involved in its composition (45d). The audience might also adopt the dominant role of the Roman, as "mançebos livianos," but if so, it must also accept the labels *rribaldo*, *non cuerdo*, and follower of *loco amor*, like the Roman who interprets the gestures as referring to bodily action. The ribald may laugh, but his focus will not be appropriately directed to "la manera del trobar e del dezir" (45d), and he may miss out on the hygienic application of laughter and the utility of the content, just as the Romans doubt their ability to receive Greek learning. The blessed, "el de buena ventura," will choose the best, sharing the interpretative position that the Archpriest himself adopts in the Debate in Signs, showing cultural competence in all spheres, being amused by the *burlas*, but putting laughter to appropriate hygienic use in expelling despair about the human condition, and in putting the *Libro* to good use.[111]

If my reading of the Dispute in Signs were accepted, then it would resolve a seeming contradiction between the Dispute, and the parallel *exemplum* of King Alcaraz and the Astrologers.[112] The *exemplum* tells how the King seeks horoscopes for his newborn son from five astrologers, each of whom gives a different account of the son's premature death. The discrepancies between their predictions incite the King's disbelief, and he imprisons them all; however, the son dies in a hunting accident in which each astrologer's version accounts for only a portion of the calamity. God alone has the power to alter fate, and complete knowledge, which can be only partially revealed to human agents.

Importantly, the episode also touches on iatromathematics, or the medical and psychological effects of astrological influence, and the question of astrological determinism, and is a prelude to and justification for the Archpriest's defense of his conduct based on his own natal horoscope. The *exemplum* opens with the introduction of astrology as a science with ancient *auctoritas* (st. 123–24), which judges a natal horoscope "por sentençia" (123d). To the best of my knowledge, "por sentençia" is usually construed as meaning that the horoscope has a deterministic impact; however, *sentençia*'s alternative meaning of authoritative received and transmitted wisdom has not been taken into account.[113] It seems possible that this meaning is at the very least latent since *sentençia* is overdetermined in that it is the final rhyme word of the stanza, two of whose other rhyme words, *çiençia* and *sabiençia* (123ab), belong to the same semantic field (learning), and the following stanza goes on to introduce by name the authorities upon whom astrology resides, such as Ptolemy and Plato (124a). If my view were not accepted, stanza 124 would simply paraphrase 123. The effect of my interpretation is to place the emphasis on astrology as a branch of human learning at the outset of the *exemplum*, whilst maintaining the deterministic position that one cannot escape one's astrological fate by will alone. Being carried out by human agents, and having its full truth known only to God, astrological interpretation is necessarily fallible. This reading accords perfectly with the *exemplum*'s message that astrology is reliable (139d; de su astrología en que non avié que dubdar), and with the Archpriest's professed belief in this view:

> Yo creo los estrólogos verdad, natural mente;
> pero Dios, que crió natura e açidente,
> puede los demudar e fazer otra mente,
> segund la fe cathólica; yo desto só creyente.
> En creer lo de natura non es mal estança,
> e creer muy más en Dios con firme esperança.
>                    (140–41b)

> (I believe astrologers truly, naturally; / but God, who created Nature and external causes, / can change them and make them otherwise, / according to the Catholic faith; I am a believer in this. // It's not unorthodox to believe in Nature, / and to believe much more in God with unshakable hope.)

The position adopted by the Archpriest appears to echo the position of the theological compromise with astrology, adopted in Spain and southern Italy by Abelard of Bath (1090–1150), and his followers in the thirteenth century, who translated and popularized attitudes espoused by Arabic astronomers.[114] Arabic scientific views of astrological fatalism became increasingly combined with Aristotelian/Galenic medical ideas about the humors to give potency to notions of humoral physiognomy in scholastic medicine.[115]

The comparison, or *semejança*, Ruiz employs to give further support to this argument derives from the monarch or Pope's ability to overrule civil and canon law, respectively, in order to exhibit mercy.[116] Ruiz therefore shows how regal and papal authority reflect divine authority in microcosm, and points to both astrology and law as fields of human learning, *çiençia*, firmly located in a post-lapsarian world:[117]

> Veemos cada día pasar esto de fecho;
> pero por todo eso, las leyes y el derecho,
> e el fuero escripto, non es por ende desfecho;
> ante es çierta çiençia e de mucho provecho
>
> (147)

> (Everyday we such things come to pass; / however, despite specific laws, and the law, / and written local legal codes, they are not undone; / rather it is true learning, which is very beneficial)

Law and astrology are fallible, although not deliberately deceptive, being authoritative sciences (st. 150) that are, even so, subject to being overridden by higher powers. Further, the Archpriest's belief in astrology is based on direct observation of the *semejança*, and, in particular, of the amatory pursuits of those born under Venus, including personal experience. The Archpriest's comment about his inclination to love service, and his persistent failure in it is in keeping with his later physical description, as discussed below. Ruiz's character portrait of the Archpriest as a Venerean draws on a popularized tradition of Ptolemy and Plato, which was widely disseminated in the peninsula through Latin and vernacular translations of the work of Arabic and Jewish natural philosophers, with astrology being widely taught as a part of the medical university curriculum.[118] Ruiz's familiarity with such material accords well with the intellectual context that I have been outlining for him here.

The Debate in Signs shows the audience a microcosm of the available interpretative paths. There is slippage and uncertainty in the relationship between narrator and audience and the figures in the *exemplum*, between signifier and sign, between religious and obscene, and finally between joke subject, listener, and the object of the joke. I contend that Ruiz's point is that such slippage and indeterminacy is a direct result of the Fall, of which humankind's partial access to knowledge through diseased faculties is an aspect. The Fall has caused humankind to be cast into a realm of unlikeness in which its access to meaning is never complete.[119] In contrast, above and beyond this partial view, God exercises his providential plan for humankind and his panoptic vision of all events from eternity. This point is reiterated in the *exemplum* about King Alcaraz, in which the stars are shown to indicate character traits and dispositions that cannot be overcome or avoided through human will, but only through divine succor, which can be gained through religious practice (st. 149). In the prologue, Ruiz links the vitiation of the soul and the body as products both of first sin, and of Everyman's sin. Deformation of human disposition in soul and body can reduce man to the level of the beast, which has lacked, since creation, in perfect intellective function. If, as in the Debate in Signs, the fallen body's gestural systems yield a polyvalent semiotic code, the body may also be examined as a site of post-lapsarian pollution as a result of humoral imbalance, and astrological influence can be seen as one feature of this. Indeed, the body and its features as sign is a prominent aspect of the four descriptions in the *Libro*: Don Amor's *descriptio puellae*, Trotaconventos's of the Archpriest, and those of the wild mountain woman Alda, and the wounded body of the crucified Christ. Of these, the descriptions of the Archpriest and the *descriptio puellae* most clearly show the body as participating in fallen nature and influenced by its material constitution, and will be discussed here. I shall discuss the descriptions of Alda and Christ in relation to the grotesque in chapter 2. In composing his descriptions, Ruiz shows awareness and, I believe, a conscious manipulation of tradition, which has mistakenly been taken as the introduction of parodic elements; however, such manipulation could also be a deliberate adherence to strictures from rhetorical manuals that set pieces, such as descriptions, should be adapted for personal use in the construction of meaning.[120] Although I wish to rule out parodic intent, I believe that Ruiz's descriptions use deviation from normative ones in order to create meaning, which then, on the one hand, shows his familiarity with humoral characterology and physiognomy, and, on the other, sheds humorous light on the characters represented.

The *descriptio puellae* is part of the first lesson of Don Amor's *ars amandi* (st. 423–576) through which he teaches the Archpriest not to pursue inappropriate women (428) but to choose aptly on the basis of physical characteristics. It does not derive from the immediate source for this part of the episode, Ovid's *Ars amatoria*, but rather draws on *De vetula*, II.296–300.[121] The *descriptio* follows the scholastic model by working from head to foot, but is interrupted by a *digressio* on the selection of a female informant (436–43), "que la vea sin camisa, / que la talla del cuerpo, te dirá" (435cd; who can get a look at her without her undershift, / who will tell you the shape of lady's figure). The digression is absent from its model, but otherwise the description is structurally similar, being composed of two parts, the first dedicated to visible members, and the second to concealed body parts.[122] In the description, Ruiz controls the focus of the gaze of the voyeuristic reader or audience in a kind of striptease act, heightening erotic tension through the imposition of the digression on the go-between who has privileged access to the unknown body. The *descriptio* itself fetishizes the female body, and locates it "outside the (narrative) flow of the action and turn[s] her into an icon."[123] The intermediary figure of the go-between heightens the viewer's scopophilic pleasure, that is, the focusing of desire in the act of looking, through the fantasy of a mediator who, despite being female, has knowledge of the concealed and the power to grant access to it directly, and indirectly through description. The female go-between is at once a powerful figure as gatekeeper to the lady, and a powerless one, since she depends on male patronage, and, despite her knowledge of the unseen, does not enjoy sexual possession. As is the case with Ferrand Garçía (105–22), the male go-between, however, occupies a position similar to the priest's in that his free access to the desired object may become sexual possession.

In the main the description conforms to that of the ideal beloved; however, there are some significant discrepancies that have led to speculation that they may be drawn from the Arabic rather than Latin tradition; for example, that the beloved should be broad hipped (432d, MS *S* only; 445c; "ancheta de caderas"), have slightly damp armpits (445a; "los sobacos tiene un poco mojados"), and that her teeth should be "apartadillos" (434b; spaced; perhaps a reference to a diastema between her front teeth). Interestingly, the first and last of these discordant features have prompted scribal or editorial problems. In the first case, although this phrase is also found in the second part of the description (445c) in MSS *S* and *G*, in the first part of the description in *S*, the reference to her hips is given out of its proper place in rhetorical ordering, with her eyes (432d), perhaps the result of a *lapsus scribiendi*, whilst at 432d MS *G* gives "angosta de cabellos" (lit. narrow haired), accepted only by Beltrán and Morros, with various editors offering emendations for *cabellos*, such as *carriellos*, 'jaws,' or *tenriellas*, 'cheeks.'[124] Jacques Joset rejects the traditional emendation of *apartadillos* to *apretadillos* ("crowded together," possibly implying crooked) on the grounds that gappy teeth were associated with sensuality in Geoffrey Chaucer's description of the Wife of Bath and the Arabic tradition, whilst Morros observes the opposite trait in the Latin elegiac *comedia*, *De vetula*, a source of this episode.[125] Anxiety about the origins of these traits arises from the fact that they are out of place in the standard textbook description of a beauty, and, in some cases, out of place in the critics' own construction of what ought to constitute female beauty. However, it is essential to observe that Don Amor does not promise to teach the Archpriest how to seduce a beauty but how to select a woman susceptible to his advances, "Sabe primera mente la muger escoger" (430d; Know first how to choose the woman).[126]

More constructive in the analysis of Ruiz's rhetorical portraits to date has been Peter N. Dunn's study of the influence of disciplines associated with medicine and natural philosophy, particularly physiognomy and iatromathematics, in Trotaconventos's portrait of the Archpriest.[127] The application of physiognomy and iatromathematics assists the modern reader in reconstructing possible meanings of the out of place features that would have been available to medieval audiences familiar, as I have been arguing that Ruiz himself was, with natural philosophy. Following what I take to be Ruiz's instruction to his audience to consider polyvalence a feature of the *Libro*, I shall also take into account popular tradition. In discussing the *descriptio puellae*, I shall focus on the three discordant features mentioned above in order to show that, when read from a physiognomic perspective, the *descriptio puellae* reveals physical traits indicative of a nature inclined to lust.[128]

Physiognomists conceded with popular opinion that broad hips connote "repulsive fecund energy," which was a widely disseminated feature.[129] The description of Wife of Bath's attractive gappy teeth in Chaucer's Prologue to the Wife of Bath's Tale (1393–96) leaves little doubt about their connotations:[130]

Gat-tothed I was, and that bicam me weel;
I hadde the prente of seinte Venus seel.
As help me God, I was a lusty oon,
And faire, and riche, and yong, and wel bigon,
And trewely, as myne housbondes tolde me,
I hadde the beste *quoniam* myghte be.
For certes, I am al Venerien
In feelynge, and myne herte is Marcien.
Venus me yaf my lust, my likerousnesse,
And Mars yaf me my sturdy hardynesse;
Myn ascendent was Taur, and Mars therinne.
Allas, allas! That evere love was synne!
I folwed ay myn inclinacioun
By vertu of my constellacioun;
That made me I koude noght withdrawe
My chambre of Venus from a good felawe.
                    (ll. 603–18)[131]

Her boast vividly illustrates that being gap-toothed was, first, a physical sign indicating that she was born under Venus; and, second, possibly in keeping with the physiognomists' view, her facial characteristic is reduplicated else-where on her body at an appropriate place, her sex organs.[132] Thus the Wife of Bath claims that the bearer of the seal, or birthmark, of Venus enjoys a lascivious nature and is endowed with particularly pleasure-giving genitalia. If such astrological interpretation were rejected, there still remains the carnivalesque association between a woman's upper and lower mouths where the gap between the teeth may signify the accessibility and open nature of the vaginal orifice and the association between mouth and genitals may indicate appetite.[133] With regard to slightly damp or sweaty armpits, the suggestion may well be that the seducible lady's humoral bal-ance tends toward the moist. In general, the female body was held to be cooler and moister than the better balanced warm and dry male body. Such humoral characteristics indicate not only her physical imperfection, but her concomitant tendency to seek intercourse. Related to this notion, is the idea that through sexual intercourse the organism might purge excess humors efficiently.[134] If the *descriptio puellae* can be read in this way, it is clear that the description is not intended to describe a textbook beauty but rather to outline the physical features of an attractive woman of lascivious character.[135] Through the introduction of such physiognomic features into the description, Juan Ruiz presents us with a grotesque undercutting of a textbook *descriptio puellae*. However, the description is more than simply comic since those in possession of the appropriate cultural competences can read the unusual features as signs of the lady's sensual nature. The lewd connotations of some of these physical signs would be equally evident to high and low readings of the *Libro*; however, their slight deviation from normative descriptions makes them particularly memorable. Dunn makes a similar point about the readability of Trotaconventos's description of the Archpriest. The representation of grotesque features, that is, those aspects of the description that contrast with normative ones, is one of the ways in which the audience is prepared for the carnivalesque reversal of this description in the person of the wild mountain woman, Alda de la Tablada (1008–20), which I shall discuss in chapter 2.[136]

The Archpriest's character coincides with that indicated astrologically for a Venerean since, despite his active pursuit of women, he does not enjoy success (st. 153).[137] His physical description also conforms to that of a son of Venus. He is described as *trefudo* (1485b; stocky, thickset), black haired (1485d), large eared, nosed, and mouthed (1485d, 1486d, 1487b).[138] According to the physiognomist, M. Angellus Blondus, these are all fea-tures indicative of the influence of Taurus, a sign governed by Venus, and described by the Doncella Teodor as the sign of those who "adolescerán por su culpa y no ternán dicha en mugeres" (will fall ill on account of it and will be unlucky with women).[139] If my reading of the Archpriest's physiognomy were accurate, it accounts for Dunn's interpretation that the Archpriest's physique represents, "a man whose temperament promises success, but who is rendered helpless by some contrary influence."[140] The influence of the sign could be felt if it were either the sun sign or the rising sign at the nativity of the subject so such a physiognomy is not necessarily an indicator of the subject's solar zodiacal sign. The influence of Taurus would clarify two further, as yet unresolved, aspects of the description of the Archpriest. First, the complexion of the Taurean is typically *cetrino*, 'olive' or 'brownish,' from Late Latin *citrinus*, 'lime-like,' broadly equivalent to Ruiz's *baço*; a complexion sometimes attributed to the influence of Saturn.[141] Second, although Taureans tend to be melancholic in disposition thereby suggesting a conflict with the identification of the Archpriest as sanguine, under Taurus, "crece mucho la sangre" (blood increases a great deal), thereby suggesting that blood or sanguinity may come to play a part in the Taurean subject's humoral balance.[142] The twelfth-century Hispano-Arab Ibn Gālib attributes gaiety of character, also linked to sanguinity, to Venereans on the authority of Ptolemy.[143]

Elisha K. Kane has argued, in my view quite rightly, that a number of the features previously considered discordant in the Archpriest's portrait actually point to his virility.[144] He also notes that many of these features deviate from more standard schoolbook descriptions of a man; my analysis, however, supports the view of André Stanislav Michalski, Dunn, and Harriet Goldberg that Ruiz applies physiognomy to further the description's meaning.[145] Deviation from more normative descriptions gives those in the *Libro* a sense of being more ambiguous and difficult to define; for some twentieth-century readers, even a sense of the individuality of the portraits. The descriptions of the Archpriest and the seducible lady highlight their specificities in such a way that their natures as creatures susceptible— on account of their fallen natures and tainted flesh—to particular sin is revealed: the beauty is susceptible to lust, as is the Archpriest, whose complexion also reveals the amorous disappointments that await him. Although the *descriptio puellae* and that of the Archpriest move away from idealized schoolbook models of hero and heroine, such as those found in *De vetula*, they are informed by other models such as traditional association, and prevailing concepts of physiognomy and iatromathematics.[146]

Ruiz's adoption of the sermon-prologue and elements from the academic *accessus* at the opening of the *Libro* suggests his familiarity with the academic milieu or with the academic commentary tradition, and this view is strongly supported by the orthodoxy of the views expressed therein. Reading the prose section as akin to the sermon-prologue tradition resolves the ambiguities and explains the tensions that have caused the prologue to be taken as containing truant material. Such an opening, along with the accompanying invocations, situates the implied author as a preacher or schoolman in a chain of learned authority. The sermon-prologue establishes a disparity between the pre-lapsarian or grace-endowed operations of a healthy intellective soul, and the more usual state of the soul of fallen man. The opening invocations (1–10, 11–45) reflect these issues in references to the Incarnation, and by addressing the Virgin, and the Father God, whose unicity of knowledge is depicted in the prose-sermon, the Debate in Signs, and King Alcaraz and the Astrologers.

The ill operation of the vitiated faculties of the soul leads to contamination of the body, which would otherwise be kept clean. The lack of properly functioning faculties has a number of consequences. The domination of particular vices, associated with specific dispositions, leads to the dominance of the appetitive functions, and bestialization. The weakness in memory, in particular, gives rise to the need for the institutions of human culture, such as custom, law, and visual arts. This need is reflected in Ruiz's selection of mainly legal *auctoritas* in the second development of the sermon, and in his choice of an opening *exemplum* that deals with signs and the law, and most likely drawn from a legal source, Accursius's commentary on the *Digest* of Justinian, 1.2.2.24.[147] The possibility that "Señor Dios, que a los jodíos, pueblo de perdición" (st. 1–7) may draw on a cathedral façade underscores the point made in the prologue about the importance of cultural prompts to keep behavior ordered, and move the individual to good.

Ruiz draws the topic of *utilitas* from the *accessus* tradition, and uses it to highlight the diversity of audience dispositions to his material. He is thus able to develop the notion of the polluting effects of sin on the subject, and the theological idea of self-love as a factor in moving the individual to good. The topics of *utilitas* that Ruiz elaborates are not unusual in academic or pseudo-Ovidian prologues; however, their admixture is. Ruiz also adopts the category *intentio auctoris* from the prologue tradition, and uses this to stress further the unicity of divine knowledge, underscoring the panoptic gaze of God highlighted in the final division of his *thema*, "in via hac qua gradieris; firmabo super te occulos meos" (p. 104; in the path that thou shouldst follow my eyes shall be fixed upon thee). The representation of God as enjoying a panoptic gaze above mortal lawgivers is a commonplace of the illumination of legal manuscripts, and can be found in Gratian's *Decretum*, and the Justinian code. Folio 1ᵛ of the British Museum, Additional MS 20787, of the *Primera partida*, whose text is cited above, contains two such illustrations, the first in a miniature depicting Alfonso the Wise transmitting divine law to his scholars whilst God looks on, and the second in a historiated initial "A," which presents Alfonso kneeling and holding his book up to God. In each case, the Father is positioned centrally in the upper register of the image, and Alfonso looks up to him.[148] I shall examine Ruiz's treatment of the panoptic gaze in the conclusion.

The *utilitas* and *intentio auctoris* clearly espouse the scholastic view that interpretation and application are the responsibility of the recipient, and not the author, whose intention can only be fully known to God. Recipients are also responsible for their ability to use well what is read or heard, and to carry out appropriate memory work; however, the diminishment of the faculties, and personal disposition affect the individual's ability to do so. The Dispute in Signs reinforces this point, to show that God's providence exercises above and beyond the intentions of mortal individuals. It is introduced as the first comic *exemplum*, which forms a necessary part of the avoidance of sin caused through excessive sadness or scholarly melancholy. The *Libro* will provide such humor and polyvalence of interpretation. The *exemplum* of King Alcaraz reiterates the point that a multiplicity of interpretations is available, and explores the tension between divine foreknowledge and providence, and astrological determinism to show that determinism and the fallen nature of humanity strongly predispose the individual but that astrological interpretation is a fallible human science, whose ultimate truth is known only to God. Free will is possible but the vitiation of the faculties, and the fallen imbalance of the physical and psychological nature of humanity tend to move it to sin. This point is further strengthened through the iatromathematical discussion of the empirical person of the Archpriest as a Venerean, predisposed to failure in sexual love, and by the *descriptio puellae* whose body is marked by physiognomic indicators of a lustful nature. The two descriptions therefore support the overall pessimistic view of post-lapsarian humanity as marked by a propensity to sin.

# CHAPTER 2

# THE GAZE AND THE GROTESQUE

The body as sign is a prominent feature of the two rhetorical descriptions, discussed in chapter 1. Don Amor's *descriptio puellae*, and Trotaconventos's portrait of the Archpriest are both clearly predicated on a voyeuristic or scopophilic gaze whose pleasure resides mainly in treating the other as an object to be appraised, but which depends also on the tension between the dangers emanating from that object as unknown, unknowable, and threatening, and the potential to knowledge and possession of it transmitted through physiognomy. Such scopophilia is latent in most medieval rhetorical descriptions, and I should argue that it is actualized in the *Libro* in three ways.[1] First, the physical description is relayed by one character with access to higher-level knowledge of the object to another in an exchange intended as informative but embedded in an agonistic debate. Second, although the descriptions correspond to the broad outlines of standard rhetorical practice, they deviate from the norm in ways that convey physiognomic meaning. Whilst such meaning may be considered to individualize rather than objectivize, its function is in fact to create the fantasy that the intradiegetic viewing subject can possess the object without danger. In the case of the Archpriest, the seducible beauty will be sexually available and malleable, and, in that of Doña Garoça, the Archpriest represents a fittingly masculine figure, which, nonetheless, poses a limited sexual threat. Third, there is an emphasis in the prefatory material on the interpretative processes of medieval reading and mnemonic practices, and the role of the physical imprint of visual images in the faculty and ventricle that correspond to memory. The characters listening to the descriptions, and the reader or audience are thus figured as envisioning, and internalizing or incorporating the visual image of the body concerned in their own memory, and subjecting it to the meditative and recollective processes that produce meaning for the individual. The characters act upon that internalized knowledge by pursuing Doña Endrina, and accepting the

Archpriest's advances, respectively, whilst the audience enjoys a privileged gaze. Although human interpretation of natural and physiognomic signs is fallible, the panoptic gaze of God is located beyond this scheme as all seeing and all knowing. The audience or reader is invited to take up an interpretative position between the two poles, and reminded to stay aware of the subjective and contingent nature of all interpretation in the face of the inscrutability of divine intention. The act of conscious looking and the interiorization of physical signs involve wielding a powerful phallic gaze that possesses the object and renders it other, as susceptible to specific sin. Looking becomes mastery of the object and power for the audience in the same way that in the worldly sphere "the scope of the prince's gaze marks his public domain."[2] This maneuver brings literary culture, whether written or spoken, into proximity with the sphere of the visual.

In this chapter, I shall examine Juan Ruiz's treatment of the body in his representation of human characters, and of anthropomorphized animals in the Aesopic tradition. The human characters depicted in the three exemplary fabliaux occupy the terrain of the grotesque. As in the Debate in Signs, narratorial control and humor construct a space for the superior and voyeuristic position of the audience whilst permitting a complex interplay of pleasure that expresses and contains anxieties about masculinity. Grotesque elements also feature in the depiction of two bodies whose position on the chain of being is crucial to a reading of hybridity in the Libro: the wild woman, Alda de la Tablada, and the crucified body of Christ; the former has attracted much critical attention, whilst very little has been observed about the latter. Alda occupies the space of both the human and the animal, and the hypostatic union is clearly presented in the depiction of Christ, who consequently occupies the space of the divine and the human. Finally, I close the chapter with an examination of the three of the Libro's Aesopic tales that center on the figure of the anthropomorphized ass to argue that, however they are employed within the narrative frame, the fables blur the ontological, and hence ethical, boundaries between beast and fallen man.

All three of the exemplary fabliaux, the tales of the Young Miller (189–98; tale 6), the Two Lazy Suitors (457–73; tale 17), and Pitas Payas and his Wife (474–89; tale 18), occur in the debate with Don Amor.[3] The extensive secondary criticism on the three tales tends to consider their relation to analogues, to analyze questions of parodic intent and humor, and to treat them in isolation from context and individually even when more than one tale is discussed. Although some individual analysis is necessary, I intend to take the tales together in order to draw out their similarities and differences to show that the two characters draw on a shared ideology of love, revealed in their representation of the desiring male subject and his relation to the female in the tales, and in the similar range of imagery in their applications and epimythium. A necessary tool in this analysis is the use of psychoanalytical models of humor and the joke in order to explore the mechanisms that activate shared pleasure to create affiliative bonds between the characters.[4]

In the debate, the Archpriest attacks Don Amor, accusing him of causing all sin, drawing his matter mainly from the Biblical and Aesopic traditions, and using only one exemplary fabliau. In it, a young miller wishes to take three wives. His parents persuade him to marry first the youngest, and, then after a month, the eldest. Toward the end of the first month, they tell him that his brother wishes to marry just one woman, and he offers to share his own bride. Before he married, the Young Miller could stop the millstone with one foot, and afterward, when he tries to stop it, he falls over and lands with his legs in the air. He curses the millstone, in words that are now proverbial: "¡Ay molino rreçio! ¡Aun te vea casado!" (195d; Oh, tough mill, I'll see you married yet!).

Don Amor's response has been considered an *ars amatoria* rather than a refutation of the Archpriest's argument, and, whilst this is certainly its intradiegetic function, it also conveys the destructive effects of love. Don Amor uses two exemplary fabliaux in close proximity to one another. In the first, two lazy men want to marry the same woman, who mockingly tests them by offering to marry the lazier. Don Amor's treatment of laziness in relation to failure in love fittingly parallels the Archpriest's attack on the final capital sin, *acedia*, which dealt with the same topic but which focuses on spiritual torpor giving way to sensuality. The *Cojo*, 'lame one,' boasts that he acquired his impediment by being too lazy to lift his feet whilst descending a staircase, and became permanently hoarse by failing to open his mouth whilst swimming in the heat. The *Tuerto*, 'One Eye,' boasts that he failed to seduce a courtly lady because he did not wipe his nose after sneezing, and that he was blinded by not moving his position in bed when rain was dripping into his eye. The lady rejects them both. In the second tale, Don Pitas Payas, a painter from Brittany, marries a young woman who enjoys company. When he goes off on business, he paints a lamb on her belly, "por que seades guardada de toda altra locura" (476c; so that you may be protected from all types of madness). She takes a lover, who repaints the image when her husband returns after two years' absence. Don Pitas asks to see it and is astonished to discover that the little lamb has become an impressive dish: a well-equipped ram. His wife remarks that it is only natural for a lamb to become a ram in two years. These brief summaries reveal that especially prominent in the *exempla* is a focus on physical debasement and deformity. The gaze and the grotesque function together in these tales to represent a fragmentary and abject image of the male body.

In the Young Miller and Two Lazy Suitors, the protagonists are presented as desiring subjects, with a strong focus on the body. The Young Miller "quería cassar se [. . .] con tres mugeres" (189bc; wished to marry three women), and is described as:

> un garçón loco, mançebo, bien valiente;
> [. . .] atan rreçio,
> andando mucho la muela, tenían la con el pie quedo [. . .]
> Aquesta fuerça grande e aquesta valentía,
> ante que fuese casado ligero le fazía.
>
> (189a, 193cd, 194ab)

(a mad lad, young, lusty / so tough [that] / when the millstone was turning fast, he used to stop it with his stilling foot / This great strength and this great boldness / came easily to him before he was married.)

Before the match, he is depicted as possessing a healthy, active, and industrious male body. Nevertheless, there is a clear predisposition to priapism evident in his desire for multiple partners, and in the latent sexual denotation and symbolism, particularly in the use of *garçón* and *valentía*, which had this sense, and the reference to his ability to still the millwheel, very probably referring to his sexual prowess.[5] Don Amor opens the *exemplum* of the Two Lazy Suitors by introducing them as desiring subjects whose attentions are focused on the same object, but who are characterized by physical deformity:

> [. . .] andavan acuziossos;
> amos por una dueña estavan codiçiosos;
> *eran muy bien apuestos, e verás quán fermosos.*
> El uno era tuerto del su ojo derecho;
> rronco era el otro, de la pierna contrecho;
> el uno del otro avía muy grand despecho,
> *coidando que tenían su cassamiento fecho.*
>
> (457b–58, my emphasis)

(they were going around full of desire / both of then coveting the same lady / *they were very handsome, and you will see how fair.* // One was blind in his right eye, / the other was hoarse, with a deformed leg / each held the other in very low regard / *thinking he had the match made.*)

The irony of the final lines of each of these stanzas (emphasized) highlights humorously, and mockingly, each of the Suitors' self overestimation. They differ from the Young Miller in that their physical impediments are preexisting, but they share his misplaced self-confidence. In stanza 457d, Don Amor alludes to their perceived attractiveness, "muy bien apuestos," but ironically directs the gaze of his interlocutor to the reality of their physical appearance, "e verás quán fermosos." Each of the Suitors is then fetishized, in the sense that the audience's look is directed toward specific body parts—the blinded eye, and deformed leg (note that, despite the hoarseness, the leg is the physical attribute placed in rhyme position, parallel to the blinded eye)—which represent each of the Suitors; they are referred to throughout by these epithets. It may be significant that Freudian psychoanalysis has revealed that of all organs and limbs each of these is particularly linked to fears about castration.[6]

Each imagines himself as a welcome suitor whose success is assured but each is represented as abject object of the shared phallic gaze of the Archpriest and Don Amor, and perhaps the lady, as I shall argue below. The Suitors then are engaged in a *méconnaissance*; a misrecognition of their own integrity and a fantasy of ambition. They see themselves, and their potential to power, not as they are but as they would be, an attribute shared with the Young Miller.

In Pitas Payas and his Wife, the female antagonist is figured both as object of male desire, and as the center of narrative attention. However, although the focus dwells on her body, it is as a site of her husband's goods. Don Amor describes her initial disposition:

> muger moça, pagava se de conpaña [. . .]
> Commo era la moça nueva mente casada,
> avié con su marido fecha poca morada.
>
> (474d, 478ab)

> ([a] young woman, she was fond of company / Since the girl was recently married / she had not long lived together with her husband.)

When the two marry, the young woman is fond of company, ambiguously referring either to her husband or to company in general thus indirectly suggesting a degree of lasciviousness in her character.[7]

The structure of each tale contrasts the integrity of the protagonists' bodies before and after the main action of the tale through contrasting depictions. After the marriage, the Young Miller's attitude to sexual partners has altered radically, "tenía muger en que anbos a dos oviesen / casamiento abondo" (192bc; the wife he had could provide for him and his brother both / a satisfactory match), and his ability to stop the millwheel ceases, "Provó tener la muela commo avía usado: / levantó le las piernas, echó lo por mal cabo" (195ab; He tried to stop the millstone like he used to do: / his legs were tossed up, he was thrown to a bad end).[8] The young man's physical strength is also diminished:

A la muger primera el tanto la amó
que a la otra donzella nunca más la tomó;
non provó más tener la muela, sol non lo asmó.
(196abc)

(He love the first wife so much / that he never took the second bride / nor did he ever try to stop the mill wheel, nor even think about it.)

The sexual symbolism implies that his priapism and physical strength are sapped through his marriage, most probably as a result of sexual activity.[9] The overdetermination of the semantic field of milling in this tale brings to the fore its latent eroticization of labor linked to the production of food, particularly bread.[10]

Concomitant with this is, I believe, an eroticization of the male body, first as active and phallic. The overdetermination of the Young Miller's *pie quedo* through the unusual adjectival collocation may be significant since the foot has phallic connotations, and milling is connotative of sexual activity.[11] A reversal in the mode of eroticization comes about when the active male body is rendered passive and its phallus ineffective. This analysis is supported by the possibility that *mal cabo* evokes an image of the fallen Young Miller with his legs raised to his ears, and his buttocks exposed, reminiscent of the Romanesque architectural grotesque of the feet-to-ears acrobat or buttocks-exposer, one of a number of sculptural figures involved in genital display, and connotative of the sin of *luxuria* and *concupiscentia*.[12] The very indignity of this position, and its association with the lewd make of him a humorous figure, whose sexual desire and ambition is unequal to the demands of female sexuality; in short, his much vaunted masculinity is found wanting. Whilst warning of the dangers of finding too much symbolism in what may be a mechanical sculptural repertoire, Anthony Weir and James Jerman argue that such figures as the buttocks-exposer gave support to church teaching, and were probably regarded not so much as obscene as crude and vulgar, with satiric or sardonic humor.[13] Prior to his marriage, the young man engages in a fantasy of his priapism, a *méconnaissance*, but the reality of his physical capacity depletes his virility, and weakens and feminizes his body, which becomes the object of scornful humor. His humiliation forces a realization of his sexual insufficiency in the face of female appetite, and elicits the comic climax of the curse against the millstone. The humor of this *exemplum*, therefore, derives from its obscene exposure of fantasies of male potency, and from the slapstick of the Young

Miller's pratfall in which social and cultural expectations concerning the integrity and dignity of the male body as controlled and active are confounded.[14]

In the Two Lazy Suitors, the initially ironic description draws attention to the protagonists' failure to recognize their lack of suitability and the implausibility of their success. Nonetheless, these two improbable lovers are put to a suitor test in which a bridegroom is selected for a specific quality or variety of excellence.[15] In the *Libro*, however, the beloved's intention is malicious: she wished to tease and goad them, "queriendo los abeitar" (459c). Their misplaced self-confidence leads to their acceptance of the terms that she lays down for the test, and they engage in a boasting match about their laziness, in a parody of the commonplace of the epic hero's boast or *gab*.[16] They convincingly display their exemplary laziness, but the test is a deception designed to make fools of them and they are each exposed for what they are. Ironically, although no clear winner of the suitor test can be established, it serves its function by preventing the entry of unsuitable suitors into marriage. The exhibition of their deformed bodies contrasts markedly with appropriate forms of noble male display, such as in hunting and tournament, in which aggression and physical adroitness are key and thus contravenes the propriety and dignity of the complete man, as in the Young Miller.

In Pitas Payas, his temporary desertion of his wife has the consequence that "tomó un entendedor e pobló la posada" (478c; she took a lover and filled her roost).[17] The motif of the sexual insatiability of a woman, once her desire has been awakened is clearly invoked here. Vasvári's findings concerning its particular application to widows in the *Libro* might be fittingly extended to deserted wives.[18] "Pobló la posada" is a bawdy pun that alludes back to her pleasure in company, and to her sexual organs, as I have tried to show in my translation.[19] The alliteration on *p* evokes the 'erotic phonosymbolism' of the name "Pitas Payas," which perhaps jokingly alludes to the inadequacy of her husband's genitals, as discussed below.[20] However, it also calls to mind the name of the absent husband who should reside in her household and her bed; in this way Ruiz's poetry functions mnemonically for the audience as the lamb ought to for the wife.

In this *exemplum* the wife's body becomes a focal point before and after the main action of the tale; but here attention is drawn not to the body's members and quality, as in the Young Miller and Two Lazy Suitors, but to the husband's treatment of his wife as canvas. He paints a lamb, "un pequeño cordero," just under her navel, at the seat of desire in women, according to Isidore of Seville, Hildegard of Bingen, and Thomas of Cantimpré; a view possibly reflected in the Iberian practice of anointing the navel during Extreme Unction.[21] The image is rubbed out on account of her activities with her lover, "desfizo se el cordero, que dél non fincó nada" (478d; the lamb was undone, nothing was left of it), who replaces it with "un eguado carnero / conplido de cabeça, con todo su apero [. . .] un grand carnero con armas de prestar" (480ab, 483b; a mature ram / well-endowed with all his equipment / a great ram with excellent weaponry). The image of the ram equipped with weaponry calls to mind not only the implicit phallic imagery associated with cuckoldry and uncontained male libido, but also the aggressive representation of the penis as a weapon that penetrates the masochistic object.[22] On a literal level, the ram uses its horns against another male in the rutting season to demonstrate superior aggression and strength. Symbolically, on the one hand, the horns of the cuckold represent another's penetration and possession of the object that properly belongs to the husband, that is, his wife, and assures his possession of the phallus.[23] This is particularly well expressed in Pitas Payas where the ram and its horns are represented on the female body. On the other hand, it shows the symbolic phallic mastery of the rival over the husband himself through the disruption of his control of the goods that represent symbolic order, and of the smooth functioning of society through the managed exchange and control of woman. Like the ram, the lover displays superiority, and like the priest he can represent a threat to domestic order. However, the assimilation of lover and husband to the animal represents them both as debased.

Tales of cuckoldry, such as that of Pitas Payas, express the coexistence and interdependence of fantasies of unwitting submission and forced dominance.[24] Depending on the mise-en-scène, the audience may identify with the masochistic male forced into the position of submission whilst the narrative satisfyingly provides a disavowal of castration on account of the fact that it is the female object and not the male who is dominated directly; the tissue of disavowal is evident in the fact that it is the cuckolded man who is accepted as the object of the ruse. The tale of Pitas Payas dramatizes the grotesque moment of the subject's confrontation with the disavowal, and the momentary dissolution of subjecthood through Pitas Payas's loss of the mastery of language, and his forced confrontation with the falsity of the image of the power and integrity of masculinity in his own case. It is the grotesque moment that constitutes the comic climax in which Don Amor's interlocutor is permitted the possibility of masochistic identification with the humiliated subject. Through his epimythium and its application, Don Amor compounds the Archpriest's pleasure by using Pitas Payas as a negative *exemplum* thus affirming the disavowal of the castration complex, and creating a homosocial, even sadistic, bond between himself and the Archpriest as men who enjoy phallic power, and are able to circumvent the threat of symbolic castration inherent in cuckoldry. In the frame of the tale itself, the audience may also take pleasure in the dominant role of the lover or *entendedor* in a homosocial bond with the husband, as I shall argue below. The tension between the various pleasures that this tale affords leaves its traces in the somewhat perplexing application. On the basis of this analysis, it seems possible that the image of the lamb turned ram has a latent fetishistic function that at once admits the fearful spectacle of a castrated male character as the husband loses control of his wife as goods, failing to prevent her free circulation, and simultaneously permits the disavowal of the castration complex in the reader or audience through the restoration of the phallus to woman, and creates a bond between two interlocutors who therefore share a position of knowledge and superiority.

In the Young Miller, comic deflation is employed to create before and after images of masculine vigor. The initial situation in which the Miller desires three wives is contrasted with his postmarital condition through his response to his brother's wish to marry. The Miller's physical decline is demonstrated through the comparison of his capacity to stop the millstone prior to and after his marriage, with a comic emphasis on the after situation through the pratfall he endures, and his bitter and pithy address to the millstone. One of the characteristic registers of obscene language in the fabliaux, sexual euphemism is used in the grinding/sexual intercourse symbolic in which the sexual is displaced to domain of production and consumption of food, as is the case in Pitas Payas.[25]

The *exemplum* shows the pollution of the Miller's strong and active body through the demands of one wife; and thus may well draw on the misogynistic commonplace of the insatiable, and polluting, sexuality of women. Comically the woman chosen as the first bride is "la menor."[26] The significance of this woefully misguided decision is made apparent in a later section of the *Libro*, "De las propiedades que dueñas chicas han" (st. 1606–17; "On the qualities of small women"), which describes such women as more sexually uninhibited than their larger sisters (1611), as "frías de fuera, con el amor ardientes" (1609a; cold on the outside, burning with love). The Miller's initial madness and priapism, that is, his inability to govern his youthful appetite and his parents' misguided attempt to prevent his folly, lead to his failure to labor as effectively after the marriage as previously. The Archpriest's tale depicts a grotesque image of the physical limitations of the Young Miller, and his humiliation is powerfully depicted in the image of him thrown over by the millstone. In marked contrast to Don Amor's two tales, there is little emphasis on the role of the gaze other than in the depiction of the Young Miller as object of the shared gaze of the Archpriest and his interlocutor, to whom, however, the young man's fall is clearly attributed, "Ansí tu devaneo al garçón loco domó" (196d; Thus your pursuit tamed the mad lad).

In Two Lazy Suitors the motifs of the suitor test, and the epic hero's *gab* are displaced from more courtly and heroic forms into the world turned upside down, which features as an aspect of the grotesque in the tales of the Young Miller and Pitas Payas.[27] The mismatch between *veritas* and self-estimation makes them the butt of the lady's malicious joke. The incongruity between the suitors' estimation of their own likelihood of success, and grotesque description with its focus on the body as marked—to an exemplary degree—by the vice of laziness contributes to the humor. Within the rules of the world turned upside down each of the suitors reveals himself an exemplary tall-tale teller.[28] Nonetheless, their contest is not judged on topsy-turvy terms nor indeed on the terms that the lady deceptively lays down for them.[29]

Don Pitas Payas exploits comic development, and as in the Young Miller, the comic climax coincides with pithy words:

> "¿Cómo es esto, madona? O, ¿Cómo pode estar?
> Que yo pinté corder, e trobo este manjar."
> [. . .] "¿Cómo, monsseñer?
> ¿En dos anos petid corder non se fazer carner?
> Vós veniéssedes tenprano e trobaríades corder."
>                                     (483cd, 484bcd)

("What's this, my lady? Or, how can this be? / I painted a lamb, and I find this plateful." / "What, my lord? In two years a little lamb not become a ram?/ If you had returned earlier, you would have found a lamb.")

The initial situation shows that Pitas Payas and his wife operate competing codes with regard to their marriage: she expects to be remembered, whilst he places a prohibition on extra-marital sexual activity. In his introduction to and application of the tale to the Archpriest, Don Amor states explicitly that it deals with forgetfulness, "Del que olvidó la muger te diré la fazaña [. . .] desque te lo prometa, guarda non lo olvides" (474a, 485d; I'll tell you the tale of man who forgot his wife [. . .] once she promises it to you, take care you don't forget it). Naturally, well governed marriages would have depended on the operation of both of these rules, and not just one. Each of them experiences a failure of memory, which the visual image of the lamb should have prevented. Pitas Payas's request to see it on his return reveals precisely what it is that he has remembered, the image, her chastity, and what he has forgotten, the proper duty to tend to his wife and her needs. Her forgetting, however, is attributed to cunning and her feminine weakness, constructed as a natural flaw due to her inferiority to man, "Commo en este fecho es sienpre la muger / sotil e mal sabida" (484ab; As in such deeds woman is always / subtle and cunning), thus the responsibility is his.

Pitas Payas's euphemistic question about the image displaces the sexual to the realm of food imagery, as in the Young Miller, and his inability to name what he sees plays on the series of contrasts in the symbolism of the lamb turned ram. The most explicit level of symbolism is as a sign of chastity become cuckoldry, as discussed above. However, two further latent levels of symbolism may also be operative. Interpreting the lover's horned ram as a symbol of masculine aggression and assertiveness suggests that it is a phallic symbol whose size and strength is compared with Pitas Payas's lamb to imply the inadequacy of the husband's sexual organs. Such a reading lends further strength to my analysis of the *exemplum* as a joke that allows the listener the possibility of pleasure in experiencing sadistic dominance and superiority over the wife and husband, both of whom the *entendedor* marks with horns, and of simultaneously enjoying the masochistic pleasure of vulnerability to loss. In the context of male agonistic debate, the fantasy of sexual dominance over another man may have an accompanying latent homoerotic charge in permitting the imaginative contemplation of other men's penises. My conclusions here are very similar to those of Peter Lehman in his analysis of 1970s and 1980s Hollywood films directed by men in which female characters joke about penis size:

> The men who create and enjoy such jokes may be denying their vulnerability by positioning themselves as superior to the objects of the joke. Or, in heterosexual masochistic desire, they may be identifying with the male judged inadequate by the desired woman and thus enjoying that vulnerability. Or, in a disavowal of homosexual desire, they may be using the woman to deny their own homoerotic desires to look at and evaluate other men's penises.[30]

The parity in our conclusions is surprising since there are, of course, important domestic, sociological, and ideological differences between fourteenth-century Castile and twentieth-century America, which may have given rise to the operation of distinct psychological economies; the three most important being a radical shift in the experience and representation of sexual identities, particularly queer identity, of domestic and political structures, especially privacy, and in the male "experience and expectation of dominance."[31] I shall touch on some of these issues in my discussion of the *exemplum*'s epimythium.

Finally, the second latent level of symbolism is as a grotesque image of increase, linked to "pobló la posada," referring perhaps to fecundity and pregnancy, and bringing into play the latent link with the tale's analogues in the *De mercatore* tradition, as proposed by Donald C. McGrady.[32] This level activates a Bakhtinian grotesque realism in which the semantic fields of food, reproduction, waste, and death are inextricably linked to produce humor, and contain and express anxieties about sexuality, and gender and power relations.

The tale has already made use of comic diglossia in the characters' use of hybrid language to distance the characters, and make them ridiculous. However, a more serious point may lie behind Pitas Payas's loss of linguistic control, which is symptomatic of the effect of the Fall on humankind. It also situates him in the psychoanalytic state of *méconnaissance* at the mirror stage, in common with the Two Lazy Suitors and the Young Miller. In addition, it is characteristic of a series of fabliaux narratives in which what cannot be named is the penis, as in "L'Esquiriel" ("The Squirrel"), both male and female sexual organs, as in "Porcelet" ("Little Piggy"), and "La Dame qui aveine demandoit pour Morel sa provende avoir" ("The Lady Who Asks for Dobbin to Be Given Oats"), or the sex act itself, as in "La Damoisele qui ne pooit oïr parler de foutre" ("The Maiden Who Would Not Hear of Fucking").[33] In "L'Esquiriel," the girl is aroused not by frankly naming the male sexual organ, but its "improper designation as a squirrel" in a seduction by narrative consisting of a description of the body, foreplay, and intercourse through euphemistic designations.[34] In "Porcelet" and "La Dame," husband and wife agree to the misdesignation of sexual organs through recourse to the lexis of farming and food production: *porcelet*, 'piglet'; *son*, 'bran' and a paronomasia on *sens*, 'meaning'; *Morel*, a common proper name for a horse, such as Dobbin in English; and *sa provende*, 'food rations,' 'oats.'[35] The disjunction between signified and signifier, and the displacement of the sexual into narratives of food production heighten the wives' sexual appetites to the point of insatiability, and consequently sap their husbands' ability to produce semen. Like the three exemplary tales discussed here, the narrative in each of these fabliaux is preoccupied with the theme of castration through the fetishization and denaturing of sexual organs; however, of Ruiz's tales, only in Pitas Payas is there a link to the theme of naming, and to artistic creativity. There is, in addition, an important difference in the representation of desire in the two groups of tales: in the fabliaux discussed here, the center of the narrative is desire between a couple, whereas in the *Libro*'s tales, three parties are involved.

The psychoanalytic component of my analysis has revealed the complexities of the yield of pleasure produced by these tales of triangular desire, and the component that the visual plays in the humor. The love triangle has been used fruitfully as a category of analysis of desire by René Girard, who shows the necessary presence of a mediator in modern fictional representations of the desiring subject and his relationship to the love object.[36] There is an internal mediator, an obstacle to or rival for the object, whose presence increases its prestige; or, an external mediator, a model whose conduct or codes the subject imitates directly. Eve Kosofsky Sedgwick's analysis of Girard's work shows that the erotic triangle is historically contingent, and, as such, constitutes a powerful tool for analyzing the continuum of social relationships between men in relation to male traffic in and competition for women, which she describes as "male homosocial desire," and which is often characterized "by intense homophobia, fear and hatred."[37] Her analysis signals the importance of recognizing the role of homosexuality as a pole in the continuum of male homosocial desire that functions as a determinant law, or taboo, in male-dominated sociocultural order:

> in any male-dominated society, there is a special relationship between male homosocial (*including* homosexual) desire and the structure for maintaining and transmitting patriarchal power: a relationship founded on an inherent and potentially active structural congruence. For historical reasons, this special relationship may take the form of ideological homophobia, ideological homosexuality, or some highly conflicted but intensively structured combination of the two.[38]

Sedgwick's approach is particularly apt for my analysis since I have already shown that the pleasure arising from the three exemplary fabliaux owes its strength to tendentious humor with symbolic genital display as a component. The elegance residing in the Girard/Sedgwick approach is its capacity to permit the study of the contours of desire in relation to ideological structures, which I wish to analyze, and, in particular, to social codes, institutions, and power, upon which I shall also touch. It will prove useful to represent the various configurations of the love triangle in each tale diagrammatically.[39]

The Young Miller imagines a world turned upside down in which there is no social code against multiple brides (figure 2.1, triangle 1). Humorously his family follow this logic but impose their own restrictions: that the three

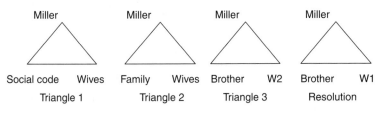

W = Wife

**Figure 2.1** The Young Miller.

desired brides should be married gradually over a period of time (figure 2.1, triangle 2). After a while the Miller's brother wants to marry "con una e con más non" (191c; with one and not with more), possibly a reference to his brother as rival for one of remaining two women (figure 2.1, triangle 3). The first son offers to share his own wife since the contagious effects of desire on his body render him physically incapacitated, correlating with the widely held medical view that masculinity is weakened by excessive intercourse. The Young Miller therefore posits rivalry as a necessary condition to satisfy his young bride sexually and enable him to maintain his strength and physical capacity to work (figure 2.1, resolution), thereby reversing operative social codes.[40] Ungoverned desire and priapism have significant, negative impact on the individual and, by extension, on social order, which depends ideologically, if not historically, on male dominance of the family unit and in male labor outside the household.

The erotic triangle in the Two Lazy Suitors is based on the rivalry of two individuals for one potential marital partner; each Suitor is the first mediating obstacle in relation to the other's access to the object (figure 2.2, triangle 1). Their courtship of her is governed by the literary code of the suitor test, which provides the second mediating obstacle (figure 2.2, triangle 2). It is treated parodically as a humorous and topsy-turvy version of a folkloric and romance convention, typically having two forms: first, serial testing in which the successful suitor is preceded by pretenders who meet a woeful fate, and, second, simultaneous testing in which the preferred candidate is chosen by the court or its representative on account of his exemplarity. In contrast, in the Two Lazy Suitors, the test is set by a beloved whose intention is malicious since she wishes to goad (459c, quoted above) not marry.[41] The conventions of the suitor test center on male identity and power, with the hero rather than heroine as protagonist.[42] Consecutive testing allows the reader or audience to identify with a male point-of-view that begins with a masochistic fantasy of failure and loss of the object, often accompanied by dismemberment, such as beheading, or imprisonment

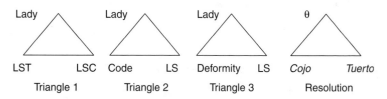

LS = Lazy Suitors;   LST = *Tuerto* as suitor;   LSC = *Cojo* as suitor

**Figure 2.2**   The Lazy Suitors.

prior to a pleasurable return to the status quo of male power in which the hero is victorious. Simultaneous testing allows for the coexistence of fantasies of failure and victory, with the hero being reassuringly rewarded.[43] Two Suitors attacks both of these models, annihilating the possibility of victory and "the experience and expectation of dominance" enjoyed by powerful male subjects, to render the protagonists as grotesque objects whose failure, on account of vice, to occupy appropriately the space of male subjecthood is exposed through desire.

Whether the Suitors interpret the lady's request as an invitation to topsy-turvy agonistic debate or take it literally, their desire and misplaced confidence blind them to her true intention and lead to the exposure of their faults (figure 2.2, triangle 3). The two subjects boastfully represent themselves as enjoying the "socio-economically privileged status that allows the leisured cultivation of desire."[44] The *Cojo* enjoys a summer dip, whilst the *Tuerto* describes a previous love affair, with attendant lyrical spring setting, and lying abed.[45] The representation of status contrasts markedly with the absurdity of their conduct: the hoarse *Cojo* is too lazy to lift his feet climbing the stairs and to open his mouth to drink whilst swimming; the *Tuerto* fails to wipe a runny nose in front of a lady whom he is courting and to roll over in bed to evade a drip falling into his eye: "It is the clash between the courtly milieu and their gross understanding of the rules of the game of love as well as the grotesquely dismembered description of their bodies which form the essence of the grotesque humor."[46]

Each of the suitors' bodies is marked through his practice of the vice of laziness, and as a result he ceases to be a complete man, and comes to lack the decorum that he appears to believe that he enjoys; as a result he becomes the despised "homo deformis et parvus" of Leviticus 21:17–23.[47] Each of the suitors undergoes a privation as a result of his inability, or unwillingness, to tend his body adequately, and, in particular, to pay mind to its boundaries through poor motor control (the *Cojo*), and the entry (both suitors) and exit (the *Tuerto*) of liquids. Debilitated motor control is also a feature of the Young Miller, whilst failure to control boundaries, domestic and sexual, is at issue in Pitas Payas. Such poor control of the body's margins and its integrity, and in particular the threat of the inappropriate penetration of its orifices, raises the specter of disgust as an always possible response to the disordered human body, which gives way to social and physical abjection, raising the proximity of death, and to the carnivalesque of Bakhtinian grotesque realism.[48]

As noted above, Don Pitas Payas and his wife articulate the social codes of marriage differently: he expects chastity and she requires that, "Non olvidedes vostra casa, nin la mi persona" (475d; Do not forget your house, nor my person; figure 2.3, triangle 1). The length of his absence puts him in breech

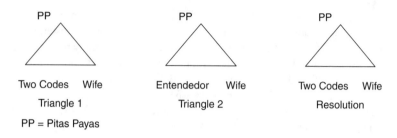

**Figure 2.3**    Don Pitas Payas and his Wife.

of her request, and she takes a lover, and in doing so breeches his code (figure 2.3, triangle 2). He has ignored the fact that a woman's sexual appetite, once aroused, is difficult to contain, and needs to be properly governed. His request upon his arrival represents the breech of both codes. He does not abide by the terms of her request, but expects his own to be honored: "Madona, si vos plaz, / mostrat me la figura e ajam buen solaz" (482ab; "My Lady, if you please, / show me the image, and we'll take pleasant solace together"). The lamb ought to have been a clear visual symbol ensuring that both codes be honored, and its transformation into a ram marks their breakdown (figure 2.3, resolution). Pitas Payas consequently loses control of his wife as goods, is unmanned, and his position as authoritative head of household is threatened. He is forced to face what he has feared, namely, another's knowledge and possession of his wife.

In the Two Lazy Suitors, the motifs of the suitor test, the courtly lover, and the epic hero's *gab* are comically deflated through the characters' base use of them. As argued above, they are displaced from other registers or genres into a world turned upside down. The tale's humor relies on the distance between Don Amor's representation of the Suitors in the frame, and their self-representation in the tale. A latent parody of the debilitating effects of love sickness may be present, and I shall return to this subject in chapter 3. The mismatch between *veritas* and self-estimation comprises the movement from *méconnaissance*, or fantasy of ambition and bodily power, to a forced confrontation with the image of the self as object of the hostile female gaze. The lady's judgment of the suitor test forces the two pretenders to regard and recognize their own fractured and deformed image since they are represented in language as objects of the (un)desiring gaze of the beloved. She forces each of them into a grotesque moment:

> "Non sé," dixo la dueña, "destas perezas grandes,
> quál es la mayor dellas; anbos pares estades;

veo vos, torpe coxo, de quál pie coxeades;
veo vos, tuerto suzio, que sienpre mal catades.
Buscad con quien casedes, que la dueña non se paga
de perezoso torpe, nin que vileza faga"
                              (466–67b)

( "I don't know," said the lady, "of these great [displays of] laziness / which
is the greater; you are both equal; / I see you, clumsy *Cojo*, on which foot
you limp / I see you, dirty *Tuerto*, who always look askew. / Look for
someone [else] to marry; the lady's not pleased / by clumsy laziness, nor
whoever acts vilely")

The lady's gaze could be described as phallic in two senses. First, she reduces
each of the suitors to the status of abject, rejected, and desubjectivized object
through repetition of "veo vos," and through an interpellation of the iconic
status of their deformities thus forcing a confrontation between the self constructed as desiring subject and wielder of the gaze, and the self as object.[49] In
fact, she forces them to see that each is the obstacle that stands in the way of
his own successful courtship of her, and removes herself as object from the
erotic triangle (figure 2.2, resolution). By doing this, her gaze is constructed
as phallic in a second sense. She takes upon herself a role traditionally attributed to the male domain: control of the circulation of and access to woman,
a legally and culturally determined prerogative of the patriarchal male. Her
position, of course, accords with the church view that the freely given con-
sent of each marital partner is all that is required. The *exemplum* conceals an
ideological rift between the courtship systems determined by secular and
ecclesiastical institutions, and raises the difficult—but for frontier society and
for the contemporary ecclesiastical establishment vital—problem of female
autonomy. In each case the desire for women implies a disruption of the
male-dominated social order that ratifies commonplace medieval misogynism, and shows that threats, literal or symbolic, to the integrity of the male
body are representative of wider social malaise since male labor, and control
of marriage and sexual reproduction are threatened.[50]

    In Pitas Payas and the Young Miller, women are depicted as objects of
desire that incite and contaminate the body and disrupt the proper ordering of the household, and of labor and trade. The Miller's desire is in itself
disordered, and it is through pursuit of it that his body's strength is
depleted, and, whilst Pitas Payas's wife introduced a lover and perhaps
illegitimate child into his household, his negligence of husbandly duties is
to blame, "Por ende te castigo, non dexes lo que pides; / non seas Pitas
Pajas" (485ab; Therefore, I counsel you, don't forget [lit. leave] what you
ask for / don't be Pitas Payas). In these three *exempla*, desire disrupts social
and literary models of conduct, and social order, particularly in the good

management of relationships. Regardless of which of the characters employs the exemplary fabliaux and to what ends he puts them, each tale encodes a negative message concerning the polluting effects of love. Indeed slippage between the tales' content and their intended function has often been noted as an aspect of Ruiz's truancy and humor.[51] This argument, in particular, has been used to show that the Archpriest's attack on love in the debate lacks conviction and persuasive value, is borne purely of his own frustrated desire, and is undermined by personal concern and ironic dissimulation: "he appears to be an indignant priest in his invective against the harms of physical love while making it apparent to his adversary that he is also something quite different, i.e., a frustrated lover."[52] Combined with this, the facts that Don Amor's advice is emphasized as measured (423a, 425a), and the Archpriest acts on it are taken as indicating that Don Amor has won the debate. I do not take issue with this reading of the narrative at the diegetic level and agree that Don Amor shows superior rhetorical skill, particularly in not attempting to rebut the veracity of Archpriest's attack; however, Vasvári's observation that "the narrator manages to outtalk Don Amor thirteen tales to three" should be borne in mind.[53] Indeed, I should argue that Don Amor circumvents the threat to the individual posed by love by constructing a fantasy image of the Archpriest's potential as an ideal lover that is contrasted strongly with the failed men of the exemplary fabliaux, thus building solidarity with his interlocutor. Nevertheless, Don Amor does not attempt a defence of love, and both characters present a view of desire in the exemplary fabliaux as polluting and dangerous.

As I have shown, the Young Miller presents the image of an active and energetic male body whose physical energy is experienced by the subject as a generalized sexual desire for woman. The body becomes depleted through union with the female. After the exemplary fabliaux, the Archpriest moves on to make explicit his assessment of love as a consuming contagion through an adaptation of the courtier image of passion as fire:

Eres padre del fuego, pariente de la llama:
más arde e más se quema qualquier que te más ama.
Amor, quien te más sigue, quemas le cuerpo e alma;
destruyes lo del todo, commo el fuego a la rrama
(197)

(You are fire's father, relative of the flame: / whoever loves you more blazes more and burns more. / Love, whoever follows you more, you burn him [up] body and soul / you destroy him totally, like fire does branch)

The *exemplum* is the first in the Archpriest's attack on Don Amor, prior to the Archpriest's *enumeratio* of the deadly sins, and his discussion of the way in which Amor is responsible for them all. Before the *exemplum* the Archpriest uses three separate word systems or image chains on which to base his opening tirade against Love; moral:

"mentiroso falso, en muchos enartar [. . .]," "con engaños e lijonjas e sotiles mentiras," "de commo las engañas" (182c, 183a, 188b)

(false liar, in deceiving many. . ., with deceptions and flattery and subtle lies, about how you deceive people)

trapping and hunting, including wounding:

"enervolas tus viras [. . .] fieres quando tires," "prendes con grand arrevatamiento [. . .] con maestrías çiento," "Desque los omnes prendes [. . .]," "do fieres de golpe" (183bc, 185bc, 186a, 187a)

(your arrows poison them, you wound when you draw, you take [them] quite suddenly [lit. you take them in a great seizure] / with a hundred ruses, Once you seize people. . ., where you wound suddenly)

and, medico-hygienic:

"salvar non puedes uno, puedes çient mill matar," "enpoçonas las lenguas," "traes enloqueçidos a muchos con tu saber: / fazes les perder el sueño, el comer y el bever [. . .] el cuerpo e el alma van perder," "lazar en tu mesnada," "do fieres de golpe, / non lo sana mengía, enplasto nin xarope," "como enflaquezes las gentes, e las dapñas," "tiras la fuerça." (182d, 183b, 184abd, 186c, 187ab, 188a, 188d)

(you can not save one, you can kill one hundred thousand, you poison their tongues, You drive many mad with your knowledge, / you make them lose sleep, and their appetite for food and drink. . .they are going to lose body and soul, to suffer in your retinue, where you wound suddenly, medicine, poultices and syrups cannot cure, how you weaken people, and harm them, you draw [their] strength.)

As this list shows, the greatest emphasis falls on the image of Love as contagion and sickness, and there is consequently a logical tie-in to the topic and thematics of the *exemplum* of the Young Miller.

It may be argued that the validity of the whole of the Archpriest's attack on Don Amor is undermined at the diegetic level by the fact that he is twice represented as angry; "sañudo, e non con vino" (181a; angry, and not on account of wine) and "con saña que tenía fui lo a denostar" (182a; with the anger I felt I went to challenge him). Strongly associated with *melancholia*, and sexual frustration, the anger displayed by the

Archpriest is in keeping with his humoral disposition as born under the sign of Venus, perhaps with the influence of Taurus. According to pseudo-Aristotle, melancholics are easily moved to both anger and desire. Such movements may be caused by digestive disturbances, such as in the immoderate consumption of wine, or by physiological processes, such as humoral imbalance in that their greater quantity of black bile, *colera negra*, gives rise to smoky fumes whose effects are similar to wine provoking lechery, and anger.[54] The Archpriest himself makes allusion to the effects of digestive upsets in his attack on the sin of gluttony, "Con la mucha vianda e vino, creçe la flema: / duermes con tu amiga, afoga te postema" (293ab; With much meat and wine phlegm increases: / you sleep with your lover, and you drown in puss). The Archpriest's insistence that his temper is provoked by anger and not wine may, in fact, together with 293ab, suggest Ruiz's awareness of this medical tradition, and indicate the similarity in effect of the *affectus* or emotion experienced by Archpriest and that produced by the consumption of alcohol to indicate that his anger is not to be regarded as righteous but as a result of his own imperfect physical condition. The Archpriest necessarily argues from the position of a fallen human subject but that does not undermine the validity of his statement.

The other two *exempla* under discussion occur consecutively, and are the first used by Don Amor in response to the Archpriest. Amor does not counter in the expected scholastic manner by refuting the Archpriest's proofs but rather offers a corrective to the Archpriest's prior inappropriate conduct. He targets two main areas: appropriate selection of both beloved and go-between, and the need for *mesura*, particularly in exercise of liberality, in doing good service, and in being assertive, avoiding laziness, and dressing well. In Two Lazy Suitors, the lady claims to reject both suitors because of parity in their extreme laziness, which has resulted in their physical deformities. The grotesque and abject nature of their sin is strongly emphasized, particularly in the *Tuerto*, whose failure to observe basic courtesy in wiping a dripping nose contrasts strongly with the courtly way that he introduces his encounter with a previous beloved, and in the association of the body parts affected with lower bodily functions. Like the Young Miller, the Lazy Suitors are physically affected by a vice that influences their behavior. The fact that the physical signs of sin leave a trace not only on the physical surfaces of the body, but also on the faculties becomes clear in Don Amor's own epimythium: "Por ende, mi amigo, en tu coraçón non yaga / nin tacha nin vileza de que dueña se despaga" (467cd; Finally, my friend, do not let lie in your heart / a stain or vileness unpleasing to women). Yet, in this *exemplum* it is the Lady who uses desire to cause the Two Lazy Suitors to lose all sense of shame, *vergüença*, and to act as she wishes, and not the reverse, as Don Amor implies:

Faz le una vegada la vergüença perder:
por aquesto faz mucho, si la quieres aver;
desque una vez pierde vergüença la muger,
más diabluras faze de quantas omne quier.
Talente de mugeres, ¡quien lo podría entender,
sus malas maestrías e su mucho mal saber!
quando son ençendidas e mal quieren fazer,
alma e cuerpo e fama, todo lo dexan perder.
(468–69)

(Make her lose her shame once / do a great deal to achieve this, if you want to possess her; / for once a woman loses her shame / she'll do more devilish things than man could want. / That's how women are. Whoever could understand it; / all their evil arts and their great ill knowledge! / When they are on fire and wish to do ill / soul and body and reputation, they'll let it all go to damnation [or they'll run the risk of losing it all].)

Don Amor then depicts laziness as representative of those vices that have a direct impact on the individual's constitution; however, the moral implications of such faults go unmentioned since he is concerned with the extent to which such vices offend women, and not God. The conduct of the two suitors is portrayed in terms of pollution, a *tacha* or *vileza* of the heart, which affects their status and desirability as husband. Don Amor maintains that desire's contaminating effects can be far-reaching but inverts the value of lack of shame in relation to women: what is folly in the lover becomes desirable in the beloved, so that she is willing to risk "alma e cuerpo e fama" (469d; quoted above). The precarious and threatening nature of desire—and the veracity of the Archpriest's earlier claims about it—are unambiguous in the *exemplum* in relation to the two suitors, and in the moralization in relation to women.

Don Amor then elaborates on the topic of women's lack of sexual inhibition to imply insatiability in terms that suggest the compulsive and infective nature of their desire through the images of gambling, singing, dancing, and weaving. This strategy appropriates and redeploys the Archpriest's own use of the image of the love as pollution. The language that Don Amor deploys makes the link explicit, as he develops a proverb whose subtext alludes to the sexual symbolism of the mill, and introduces the idea of love service, neglected through forgetfulness, to be developed in his second *exemplum*:

Non olvides la dueña, dicho te lo he de suso;
muger, molino e huerta sienpre querié grand uso [. . .]
Çierta cossa es esta: quel molino andando gana;

huerta mejor labrada da la mejor mançana;
muger mucho seguida sienpre anda loçana.
                    (472ab, 473abc)

(Do not forget the lady, I have already told you this above; / woman, mill, and orchard always need frequent use. / This is true: the mill earns when working; / a well worked orchard produces the better apple; / a much pursued woman is always merry.)

In the course of his treatment of this *exemplum*, Don Amor creates two out-groups, each of which has its positive corollary: man-as-object and phallic woman are contrasted negatively with woman-as-object and phallic man.

The promythium, subsequent elaboration, and epimythium make clear the fact that remembrance and constancy of love service is the intended subject of the *exemplum* (474a and 485d, both quoted above). The moral, echoing stanza 484, is that a man must guard his beloved, failure to do so will lead to the intervention of a third party, or *entendedor*, between the couple. The language that Don Amor uses to develop this idea recalls clearly the Archpriest's experience with Cruz and Ferrand Garçía, discussed in chapter 3:

Pedro levanta la liebre e la mueve del covil;
non la sigue nin la toma; faze commo cazador vil;
otro Pedro que la sigue e la corre más sotil
toma la. Este contesçe a caçadores mill.
Diz la muger entre dientes: "Otro Pedro es aquéste,
más garçón e más ardit quel primero que ameste."
                    (486–87b)

(Pedro raises the hare and flushes it from its form; / he does not follow it nor take it; he acts like a wretched huntsman; / another Pedro who follows it and runs it down subtly / takes it. This happens to a thousand hunters. // The woman says to herself, "This Pedro is quite different, / more of a lad and more able than the first one whom I loved.")

By introducing the figure of the rival, the *entendedor*, as a cunning and successful hunter, Don Amor offers the Archpriest the possibility of con-structing himself as wielder of the phallic gaze, capable of gazing upon and possessing the other as erotic object, and thus provides him with the fantasy of an integrated and powerful self. To achieve this the Archpriest must repress the threat of scandal, danger and contagion to body, soul, and estate that reside in desire, and, like the *dueña* of the Two Lazy Suitors, achieve power through regarding the other as object. He must disregard the civil and ecclesiastical institutions whose codes prevent the priest's access to desire, and whose laws are encoded in the Archpriest's earlier attack on

Love, as many of Juan Ruiz's peers did in fact. The Archpriest must also engage in a *méconnaissance* of his own, by seeing his potentiality in the image that Don Amor holds up for him, forgetting or repressing the previous amatory failures that would align him with the Two Lazy Suitors, and viewing his role as lover as bringing him into a competitive, and dominant, relationship with other men.

In using these rhetorical strategies, Don Amor constructs a shared social bond with the Archpriest in which he poses as wise advisor who is providing access to arcane knowledge to a privileged disciple or vassal. The knowledge that Don Amor purports to offer seems to give the Archpriest power over the threatening otherness of woman, and her potential to phallic power. In doing this, Don Amor reconfigures triangular desire so that the code through which the relationship between the desiring male subject and the love object is mediated is his worldly amatory code, and potential rivals are seen as inferior. The Archpriest, however, sees—or rather hears—only what he wishes since Don Amor himself exposes the dangerous and contaminating power inherent in desire. In this sense, Don Amor and his teaching stand in an analogous relation to the religious and secular institutions of medieval world as forces in the post-lapsarian world that hold the will to transgressive pleasure in tension with the laws that control desire and socialize man through language.

In the three exemplary fabliaux, depictions of the body and its potential contagion is a dominant theme regardless of whether the Archpriest or Don Amor use the tale thus exposing the shared underlying ideology concerning the personally and socially destructive effects of desire. The focus on the body as flawed and indicative of the subject's animic state can also be found in the Archpriest's narrative description of the wild mountain woman, Alda de la Tablada, and his lyrical one of the crucified Christ.[55] Gybbon-Monypenny's observation of the presence of nineteen of twenty-four features of the portrait of the seducible woman in that of Alda has lead to the view that the latter is indeed a deliberate parody of the former.[56] My recount, which includes Trotaconventos's description of the Archpriest, comes up with very similar figures. Of the seducible lady's twenty-five features, Alda has twenty (80%) and the Archpriest nineteen (76%), whilst the Archpriest shares seventeen of Alda's twenty-one features (81%). This high correlation between the features used in each portrait strongly supports the accepted view that Juan Ruiz was familiar with standard descriptions.[57] Nonetheless, it may also suggest that the three descriptions can be read against one another. Paired descriptions of the beautiful young woman and the hag are, in fact, common.[58]

As argued in chapter 1, the details of Ruiz's descriptions of the seducible lady and the Archpriest deviate from more standard schoolbook descriptions

by introducing grotesque features—that is, those that contrast with normative descriptions—to introduce physiognomic meaning. Ruiz's physical
descriptions blur the ontological integrity of his human characters in such a
way that their place on the chain of being as superior to and distinct from
the animal kingdom is called into question. This is particularly evident in his
description of Alda, and in the manner in which that description reverberates with the later one of the Archpriest himself, and with the book's animal
fables, especially those from the Archpriest's attack against love. The distortion in the *descriptio puellae* of Alda is seen not only in her grotesque features
but also in its neglect of the formal structure of schoolbook descriptions.[59]
Ruiz's description of Alda and its relationship with the two other human
descriptions in the *Libro* is productive of humor, whilst the contrast between
these and the beaten and broken body of Christ creates pathos.

The discursive space of the description of Alda opens with the Archpriest
lost in the Sierra de Guadarrama, without mount or sustenance. Despite the
early spring setting of March, he warns that he risks—and later undergoes—
exposure to snow and hail. The narrative setting is important not only
because it contributes to the humorous parody of the pastourelle activated
in the *serrana* section by contrasting the traditional *locus amoenus* with wild
and uncultivated space but also because it recalls a tradition in which cold
weather and the wilderness are associated with the diabolic.[60] Ruiz therefore
positions the Archpriest in a space threateningly aligned to the natural
world, representative of the appetite and the diabolic, and distanced from
culture, and its regulatory customs and laws. The Archpriest there encounters a series of four mountain girls, discussed in chapter 3, who subject him
to physical and sexual violence, and female-initiated courtship rites thereby
reversing the sexual and social roles of the two sexes in the urban contexts
depicted elsewhere in the *Libro*. Ruiz recounts the four adventures in narrative and then lyric meters, often with a disjunction in the action in each
form. The meeting with Alda is the last of his mountain adventures.

Alda is closely aligned to the animal kingdom: her size is compared to a
mare (1008d, 1012d), her ankles to a yearling cow (1016d), her feet to a
bear in MS *G* or a mare in MS *S* (1012d), and ears to a young donkey
(1013a). Ruiz employs simile for her ass-like or buckteeth (1014b), and
her hair and eyebrows, which are dark as a crow or a thrush, respectively
(1012b, 1014c). He also uses metaphor: she is a brood mare (1010b), with
a curlew's beak of a nose (1013c), and a mastiff's muzzle (1014a). If her
body is read as a sign indicating her nature, as Ruiz's rhetorical descriptions
of bodies in general suggests that it can be, then the fact that she comprises
features of or like these animals suggests that she also shares in their natures,
and positions her low down on the scale of being as in possession of a body
alienated from the image of God. In this case she is all sin: lust or

licentiousness (brood mare, bear, and ass or donkey), laziness (bear, thrush), madness (ass or donkey), avarice, envy, and servility (dog), and with a violent and diabolic nature (bear).[61] This characterization is partially borne out by her treatment in the lyric version of the encounter. Although drawing on rural courting practice (1027, 1034d–38), and both contradicting (1024c–e, 1026c) and reinforcing her portrayal as ugly (1040a), the lyric shows Alda as willing to trade nourishment and sexual favors for gifts (1027de, 1034d–38, 1040b–42) thus revealing her licentiousness, madness, and avarice. Further, the Aesopic tales in the *Libro* link some of the creatures from which her features are drawn with specific categories of sin thus reinforcing the possibility of a bestiary interpretation: the crow is associated with vanity and envy (285–90); the ass with laziness (239ab, 314d) and envy (1401–09); the thrush with theft (504d); the mastiff with greed (226–29), and the bitch possibly also lechery (1221d; "las alanas paridas en las cadenas presas" [the whelped mastiff bitches imprisoned in chains]).[62]

She is a creature not only of fallen nature but against Nature since her ontological status and sex are also in question. Although she is endowed with the feminine feature of breasts, hers are in stark opposition to the prevailing taste for small pert breasts in that their size is grotesquely exaggerated (1019), and they have more in common with depictions of the naked female damned, witches, and fertility goddesses.[63] More significantly, her large size, facial hair, formidable strength, and deep voice (1010cd, 1012d, 1015a, 1016–18) connote latent masculinity, which is made more explicit when the Archpriest's own physical characteristics are directly compared to hers. Her wrists are thicker and hairier than his own and her pinkie larger than his thumb. In addition, her long ears and nose (1013) are characteristics she shares with the Archpriest (1485d, 1486d), with folkloric and carnivalesque associations with male genitalia, which point to virility.[64]

If the comparison with the Archpriest calls into question Alda's femininity, then the corollary holds true for him. In his case, the lack of virility and a tendency to sensuality is also indicated by the features positive in woman but unfavorable in men that he shares with the seducible lady. Unjoined eyebrows (432c, 1486a) suggest a "lack of erotic vigor."[65] Small feet are indicative of (ef)femininity, and possibly also a lack of understanding and wit, despite a certain gaiety and a disposition toward fornication.[66] They both have red lips and gums (434cd; 1487abc), perhaps indicating a sanguine character and a passionate nature.[67] Don Amor's purpose in his discussion is clear, as shown in chapter 1. Similarly, Trotaconventos seems to be trying to convince Doña Garoça of the Archpriest's virility whilst, at the same time, suggesting that he will be incapable of presenting a sexual threat to her should they meet.[68] The humorous convergence of feminine characteristics with indicators of an appetitive nature doomed to dissatisfaction in the Archpriest

points again to the threats inherent in the priest's emasculinity, but in this
instance they are neutralized by his complexion and constitution. The sexual
residing in Alda's masculinity is much more of a threat to official culture, outside of which she dwells since she represents not just the extreme and
grotesque femininity of the wild mountain woman, but of all women. The
two *descriptiones puellae* stand side by side in that they depict, on the one hand,
all that is sexually desirable in a woman, and, on the other, all that elicits fear:
woman is frighteningly aligned with desire and death.

If Alda shares in the animal, aspects of her ontological status are revised
further down the chain of being. She also has diabolic characteristics seen
in her confused form, in her predominant coloring of red and black
(although these may also be humoral indicators), and the fact that she is
uglier than the demons from Revelation, a "fantasma" (1008c; specter,
fright), of whom the Archpriest comments "non sé de quál diablo es tal
fantasma quista" (1011d; I know not what devil loves such a fright); indeed,
elements from Revelations and from the folkloric tradition may be latent
throughout the description.[69] Don Amor's warning, prior to the description of the seducible beauty, to the Archpriest about what type of woman
to avoid can be appropriately applied in all its terms to Alda: "Guar te que
non sea bellosa nin barbuda; / atal media pecada el huerco la saguda" (448a;
Mind that she isn't hairy or bearded; / hell would shake at such a half-she-
devil!). Whilst demons are seldom noticeably female, her beak-like nose
may also be another indicator of a fallen and demonic nature.[70] Alda's
distorted form is both fearful (on account of its diabolic associations) but
more predominantly comic on account of her carnivalesque link to the animal world, sin, and the lower body.[71] Carnivalesque laughter is a feature
shared with many representations of devils and demons. Her deformed
physique makes her an object of scorn, and the emphasis on the fact that
her body shares more with the animal kingdom than with the human
underscores this. She occupies an ontological position on the scale of being
that aligns her more closely with the violent talking animals of the *Libro*'s
beast tales whose access to language gives shape to the question of whether
man's possession of the rational and intellective soul is unique, and to the
fear that it may not be immortal.

Alda occupies the space of the grotesque because she is a confusion of
categories, "un être diabolique et surnaturel, mi-animal, mi-homme."[72]
However, Alda is not merely rendered less human and more animal by this
description, the fact that some of her characteristics are shared with the
Archpriest positions his ontological status as partaking in her nature just as
she shares in that of beasts and demons: both have thickset frames (1008d;
1485b; *trefudo*), they are black haired (1012b, 1485d), large eared, nosed,
and mouthed (1013a, 1485d; 1013c, 1486d; 1014a, 1487b), and thick

necked (1013b; 1485cd).[73] His bodily status is feminized and revised down-ward in the size comparison with Alda, as noted above. Following work by Kane, Michalski, and Dunn, I suggested in chapter 1 that the Archpriest's physiognomy is indicative of a melancholy character with some disposition to sanguinity, most likely under the influence of Taurus, a sign governed by Venus and thereby fitting in with the Archpriest's earlier claims about his horoscope. The description of the Archpriest, then, shows his disposi-tion and complexion to be that of fallen man. The lack of animal features in his description renders him less debased than Alda but the comparison between the two revises his status as a creature made in the image of God down toward the fallen flesh subject to humoral influence rather than upward toward the spirit, and salvation. Despite these particularities, the Archpriest's body, his empirical person, is representative of the fallen, and physiognomically marked body of Everyman.

The bodies discussed so far are direct products of the Fall, and show the proximity of the body to sin, and to the animal. The *Libro*, however, also portrays a body that is simultaneously human and divine, that of the cruci-fied Christ described in the section immediately following the Archpriest's adventures with the wild mountain women. Elsewhere I have argued, with Margherita Morreale and Steven D. Kirby, amongst others, that the *serrana* section, and the two following lyrics, which treat the Seven Sorrows of the Virgin and the Wounds of Christ, should be regarded structurally as a pivot or bridge positioned toward the middle of the *Libro* between the Doña Endrina episode, and the Battle between Don Carnal and Lent.[74] The proximity of the description of Alda to that of Christ toward the *Libro*'s center highlights their ontological and spiritual significance as representing diametrically opposed poles of the human on the chain of being.

The first lyric, "Omillo me, Reína" (1046–58; I bow down, Queen), belongs to the "Obsecro te" tradition, depicting the torture endured by Christ during the Passion at each of the monastic *horae*, and the compassion of the Virgin in her aspect as coredemptriz. The Latin sequence may well have been intended for private devotion and meditation. "Omillo me, Reína" is a prayer directed to the Virgin petitioning, in the final stanza, for consolation and blessing. The opening refrain establishes the first-person supplicant as a sinner in its final line "oye a mí pecador" (1046d; hear me, a sinner). After two stanzas addressing the Virgin, the supplicant recounts the Passion in a linear narrative of Christ's betrayal by Judas, the arrest in the garden, trial by Pilate, judgment of the Jews, crucifixion, death, descent and burial, linking each event to the appropriate monastic hour, and directly invoking the Virgin as witness. It locates the Virgin spatially and temporally in two ways: first, as the recipient of the lyric in heavenly glory, and second as a privileged spectator at the crucifixion, witnessing her Son's suffering.

The second lyric, "Los que la ley avemos" (1059–66; Those who hold the law), is arranged around the themes of typological prefiguration of Christ's coming and the establishment of the new convenant through sacrifice as revealed to and known by the Christian community. The opening stanza functions as a refrain, whose rhyme scheme is reprised in the final two lines of each stanza, and in the final one. The first three stanzas deal with Old Testament prophecies concerning the Virgin Birth, the sacrifice of the Lamb, and the miracle of the Incarnation (Jeremiah 52:1; Isaiah 7:14; Daniel 7:13, 9:26; Psalms), and their meaning for the faithful. All three are aspects of Christianity whose nature is both shocking and moving. The middle stanza (1063) constitutes a formal and thematic axis to effect a transition by linking the hypostatic union of human and divine nature in the second and penultimate lines, whilst the intervening lines portray Christ as victim of Judas and the Jews. In the final section, His mistreated body parts and wounds become the focus of collective meditative attention further underscoring Incarnation. This thematic concern links it to the opening portions of the *Libro*, which treat the Incarnation, Virgin Birth, and Christ's embodiment.

In "Omillo me, Reína" a first-person singular supplicant voice functions at the diegetic level as the first-person narrator's voice but it is a feature shared by many affective lyrics in order to move those who read, speak, or listen to the prayer through *affectus* to contrition; a use of the poetic I, as described by Spitzer.[75] The supplicant makes an indirect approach to Christ's body through the protecting and spectral gaze of the Virgin so that the emphasis is not on what was visible but what the Virgin herself saw. Christ's body is positioned as object through linguistic structures, such as the passive; for example, "dando le Judas paz" (1051b; Judas giving Him the kiss of peace); "viste lo levando, / feriendo que lastima" (1052cd; you saw Him [being] carried / [being] wounded, alas); and, "Cristos fue judgado" (1053b; Christ was judged). In "Los que la ley avemos" knowledge of the Incarnation is achieved through the Old Testament prophecies, and more direct access to the divine body is possible through the contemplation of the Corpus Christi: "por nós todos morió, / Dios e omne que veemos / en el santo altar" (1062f–h; He died for all us, / God and man, whom we see on the holy altar).

The orientation of the supplicant and his interlocutor in relation to the body viewed differs markedly from the other bodies in the *Libro*. In the depictions of the seducible beauty and the Archpriest the descriptions permit the intradiegetic viewer to possess and have knowledge of the body viewed whilst containing the dangers that emanate from it. The act of viewing is encoded in the exemplary tales both intradiegetically and diegetically, but witnessing and participation are lacking. The lyrics under discussion depict the profanation of the sacred, the point around which all dangers coalesce, and access to it is achieved through the protecting and spectral gaze of the Virgin, and the contemplation of its presence in the host. However, unlike the exemplary tales, Christ's body is not represented before the action depicted nor is there any sense of a *méconnaissance* afterward. In "Omillo me, Reína," the contemplative moment is frozen in time and space, as the lyric closes by focusing attention on the Wounds of Christ:

> Por aquestas llagas
> desta santa pasión,
> a mis coítas fagas
> aver consolaçión
> (1058abcd)

(On account of these wounds / of this holy Passion, / may you grant consolation / to my sufferings)

Christ's body is rhetorically dismembered as each of the Wounds becomes a separate focus of veneration.[76] However, the passive and other structures that position Christ as object in the graphic description of the "master tableau" of Christ's torture in both lyrics largely efface agency and thereby limit the scope for sadistic pleasure within the scenario.[77] The spectral gaze of the *mater Christi* in the first lyric further invites affective identification. In the second part of each of the final three stanzas of the second lyric the gaze of the Christian community, a collective third-person plural located in the now of the present tense, is directed specifically to Christ's Wounds as a source of pleasure-in-pain in an experience of masochistic identification; a spiritual *imitatio Christi* that provokes contrition and appropriate *timor Domini*.

The contemplation of Christ's Wounds is positioned coeternally in the moment of Christ's crucifixion in its contemplation by the Virgin Mother and the Christian; a moment re-experienced with each Communion. The shedding of Christ's blood constitutes a sacrificial offering and the purging of the taint acquired through the Fall, and as such it becomes the redemptive and nourishing fluid consumed in Communion. Only because of the profanation of that most sacred body can salvation be achieved, and so it symbolizes a new convenant and community in the Church, one of the institutions necessitated by the Fall. The mistreatment of Christ's body is presented ideologically as permitting a radical restructuring of the symbolic order, abandonment of the old convenant with Judaism, and of humankind's relationship to the Other through a reoriented view of physical suffering in a religious register. Contemplation and consumption of Christ's body also permits the dissolution and purification of the sinning self and its incorporation of and in the body of Christ, *Ecclesia*.

Although there are earlier examples of veneration for Christ's broken body, in the main the adoration of the Wounds arose in tandem with the feast of the Corpus Christi from the thirteenth century onward.[78] For a contemporary audience, therefore, Christ's tortured and broken body is also a grotesque body. It is a body surprisingly portrayed as at once human and divine, a body that is as susceptible to brutality, to dismemberment—a most ignominious death in the Middle Ages—as Everyman's own, a body that was exposed to temptation. Psychoanalytically, Christ's patient acceptance of the pain of torture and his unambiguously male body—traditionally portrayed as bearded, naked with sinewy musculature but for a perizonium—redeems as a feminized site of penetration that simultaneously avows and disavows castration.[79] As God made in the image of humankind, in turn made in the image of God, Christ is the site at which anxieties about gender and temporal power converge and are dissolved for the medieval faithful.

Christ's body is dismembered by the anguished and compassionate gaze and does not provoke scorn or laughter since it is His body that bears suffering for others, and the only one whose contemplation, whose pursuit brings salvation.[80] Alda's body is a sign that points toward sin, and the fallen and essentially animal nature of sinners. Christ's body, in contrast, points beyond the fallen human to the possibility of salvation. The Archpriest's body is also a product of the Fall, and therefore of culture and it cannot endure the torments of nature and the promptings of its own flesh; its ontological status is revised down through its embodiment, the effect of the Fall, and contact with the feminine. The Archpriest, however, like all sinners was made in the image of God, an image now alienated from its former perfection and humoral equilibrium as a result of the Fall, and that gives him a stake in the divine. The Archpriest's body therefore is ambiguous in the etymological sense of driving both ways, simultaneously toward sin and toward salvation.[81] Christ's body embodies another ambiguity since he is both of the flesh and so human, and divine, and it is through Christ's sharing in the flesh, and through sharing in Christ's flesh in Communion, that salvation becomes possible. The preoccupation with bodily dismemberment and disfigurement, and the ontological status of the individual is carried through into Ruiz's treatment of the Aesopic tales. Although beast fables had serious uses, such as in sermon contexts, they were strongly associated with humor, and carried with them the stigma of being trifling and, frequently, truant.[82] Truancy flows from anthropomorphism in that the chain of being is disrupted when an animal speaks or appears to act rationally through means other than direct diabolic or divine intervention. Speech, and indeed laughter, is a sign of man's status as being of both the material and the spiritual worlds since it indicates his rationality, and thus difference from animals, plants and inanimate objects, and from the orders of angels, who do not need speech:

> Les animaux n'ont besoin d'aucun moyen de communiquer, puisqu'ils sont mus par le même instinct de nature, qu'ils ont mêmes passions et font tous les mêmes actes. Pour l'homme, mû par la raison diverse de chaque individu, apparaît la nécessité d'un signe rationnel et sensible lui permettant de communiquer: le langage. Les anges ayant "toute prompte et ineffable ouverture d'intelligence" communiquent par "le miroir de Dieu."[83]

Conversely, irrational or beast-like conduct in humans is a sign of an "ethical failure," and shows a renunciation of humanity, as Bernard of Chartres states:[84]

> Man is made beast whose rational and immortal nature was made as a lower soul, irrational and mortal, through temporal pleasure. Which has the greater animal soul when this is the definition of a beast? Which has the greater animal soul when he is a beast in nature yet has the form of a man?[85]

Clearly, then, talking animals and bestialized human characters call into question man's capacity to deserve or uniquely to enjoy the possibility of salvation.[86] The revision downward of the ontological status of Ruiz's characters indicates their low spiritual and fallen status, as has been shown. I contend that animal fables are deployed in the *Libro* to similar ends.

In Ruiz's fables, excessive violence and anthropomorphic behavior, which highlight the bestial quality of human conduct, is a characteristic strongly linked to humor, often carrying a latent charge of sexual euphemism. The fables themselves are always deployed to persuade another to act, generally embedded within a frame as part of an agonistic debate, in which their narrator draws analogies between the fable's content, its internal meaning, and, usually, its application to his or her particular situation. In addition, the extent to which the animal world of the fables is wholly independent of that of human actors varies, and different degrees of ontological separation from the human world are displayed. These points can be demonstrated with reference to the tales that deal with a particularly marginal and inharmonious animal, the ass, and its interaction with the horse (237–45; tale 9), the lion (892–908; tale 22), and the lapdog (1401–09; tale 27). All three are drawn from a common source, the Aesopic tales of Walter the Englishman (ca. 1200), which are imbued with wit and Ovidian wordplay.[87] The Archpriest uses the first in his attack on Don Amor, the second is directed by the Archpriest to women listeners, and the final one is addressed by Trotaconventos to Doña Garoça, the nun. Since speech, law, justice, and social and ontological hierarchy are at stake in animal fables, my discussion will focus on these aspects of the tales.

The *exemplum* of the Horse and the Ass is used to accuse Don Amor of being at the root of pride. The battle horse enters the lists in an implied judicial duel because its owner, a *señor valiente*, raped a lady. The lord's social standing and innocence of the charge is therefore at stake. The horse is proud of his demeanor and attire, and frightens the other beasts with his uproar. Significantly, like his owner he is *valiente*, whose sexual connotations have been discussed above. It is fitting that the horse, a preeminent phallic symbol, should share in his master's lascivious and lusty nature. As the *exemplum* develops, it becomes clear that the horse functions as a metonym for his master in the execution of justice. The horse's pride in his outward show is contrasted strongly with the fearful ass through a counterpoint in which the horse is described in lines a–c of the two introductory stanzas, and the ass is mentioned in line d of each (emphasized), before a contrasting description of the ass's demeanor, and the interaction between the two is described:

> Iva lidiar en canpo el cavallo faziente,
> por que forçó la dueña el su señor valiente;
> lorigas bien levadas, muy valiente se siente;
> *mucho delantél iva el asno mal doliente.*
> Con los pies e con las manos, e con el noble freno,
> el cavallo sobervio fazía tan grand sueno
> que a las otras bestias espanta como trueno;
> *el asno con el miedo quedó, e nol fue bueno.*
> Estava rrefusando el asno con la grand carga;
> andava mal e poco, al cavallo enbarga;
> derribó le el cavallo, en medio de la varga;
> *diz: "Don villano nesçio, buscad carrera larga."*
>                                   (237–39, my emphasis)

(The war horse was going to fight in the lists / because his lusty lord raped a lady; / wearing his cuirasses well, he feels very full of life himself / *much further ahead of him was the sickly ass.* // With his fore and hind legs, and his decorated bridle / the proud horse was making a great racket / which frightened the other creatures like a thunderbolt; / *the ass stopped dead with fright, it was no good for him.* // The ass was resisting under his heavy burden; / his step was slow and labored; and he got in the horse's way; / the horse knocked him down in the middle of the path; / saying, "Stupid peasant, go and look for the main road.")

The portrayal of the horse is reversed in the second half of the *exemplum* in which, despite its pride and ambition, it is brutally wounded, and its bodily integrity is destroyed, "en el cuerpo muy fuerte de lança fue ferido; / las entrañas le salen, estava muy perdido" (240cd; its body was very gravely wounded by a lance blow, / his guts come out, he was very lost). The horse is physically debased and brought down to the level of the ass to the extent that the following stanza describes him laboring in the field and at the mill wheel. The following detailed six-line description of his physical ruin is similar to canonical descriptions of an old horse. Nevertheless, its terms could fittingly be applied to the lazy and reluctant ass (238d, 239ab).[88] The physically abjected horse has been spurned from his social role as the marker of the nobility of his owner, and the sight of his fall causes a humorous reversal at which the ass laughingly mocks the horse. Ruiz draws the emphasis on the visual from his source material, but the expansion of the description and of the ass's ironic use of the *ubi sunt* appear to be Ruiz's own:[89]

> Diz: "Conpañero sobervio, ¿dó son tus enpelladas?
> ¿Dó es tu noble freno, e tu dorada silla?
> ¿Dó es tu sobervia? ¿Dó es la tu rrenzilla?
> Sienpre vivrás mesquino e con mucho manzilla;
> vengue la tu sobervia tanta mala postilla."
>
> (243d–44)

(He said, "Proud comrade, where has your pushing gone? / Where is your decorated bridle, and your gilded saddle? / Where is your pride? Your scolding talk? / You will always live as a wretch, and with much bitterness / your pride become so much evil scabbing.")

The horse's use of the honorific *Don* and formal *vos* contrasts with the ass's familiar *tú*, and the latter's including the horse within his own social sphere by referring to him as *conpañero*. The horse ironically raises the ass's social level to mock him, and the ass uses leveling language to emphasize the new parity between the two beasts. The carnivalesque reversal of the horse-become-as-the-ass portrays the prideful beast who acts against his nature and becomes the butt of his own vice. Direct speech is used to humiliate the other, here the horse, through an image of its own physical debasement. The emphasis on bodily decay and an alteration in the individual's position in the social hierarchy is in keeping with the Archpriest's insistence that the pursuit of love leads to physical, social, and spiritual falls manifest as contamination and pollution. At the most superficial level, the sexual sin of the owner is visited upon one of his possessions, his battle horse. The blow struck against the horse appears symbolic of his master's loss of the judicial duel, and its physical decline is indicative of his owner's loss of nobility, and consequently of status. As a phallic metonym of his owner, the blow to the horse's pride is a consequence of his owner's sexual sin, and the debasement and loss of the horse to labor marks the just lowering of the knight's own social prestige. The tale of the Horse and the Ass therefore shows the strong link between pride and sexual desire.

The tale of the Lion and the Ass is addressed by the Archpriest directly to lady listeners, "Dueñas, aved orejas, oíd buena liçión" (892a; Ladies, open your ears, listen to a good lesson), and warns such implied extradiegetic listeners that correct understanding will protect them from man and so prevent the same fate as the ass from befalling them.[90] The fable is thus a negative *exemplum* that warns against foolish behavior. As it opens, the ass's mutilation seems to be symbolic rather than actual, but as the fable unfolds the role of bodily debasement and mutilation becomes clear, and—as in Horse and the Ass—the punishment meted out is appropriately applied to the body as well as having a metaphorical component.

In the Lion and the Ass, the judicial element is not present, but a clearly ordered social hierarchy is, and speech is used deceptively rather than mockingly. The setting depicts a hierarchical social structure of animals, which is ruled over by the King. However, it immediately becomes apparent that the court in question is not well ordered since the tale opens with the King, the Lion, depicted as suffering from a headache for no reason. The social context in this fable is very similar to that depicted in the Lion's Share (82–89; tale 2), which the Dueña Cuerda uses to refuse the Archpriest's advances, and in the Lion that Killed Itself in Rage (311–16; tale 14), which the Archpriest addresses to Don Amor in the agonistic debate between the two to illustrate the sin of vainglory and wrath. In each of these fables, the lion, head of the hierarchy of animals, is particularly associated with anger, in keeping with its humoral disposition, and is in pain. In the first, despite his suffering, the lion is gladdened by visits from client-animals. To cheer him a feast is held, the animals invite the lion to choose one of their number to eat, and the wolf is placed in charge of dividing the carcass of the chosen animal. Foolishly, the wolf keeps the better part for himself, and is brutally beaten by the lion as punishment, "el cuero con la oreja del casco le fue arrancar" (86c; its scalp and an ear was ripped off). The fox is then placed in charge and gives the choice portion to the lion, which marvels at the fox's fairness, and asks an explanation to which the fox replies: "En la cabeça del lobo tomé yo liçión; / en el lobo castigué qué feziese o qué non" (88cd; I read a good lesson from the wolf's head / I learned from the wolf what to do and what not). In the second, the proud lion is the scourge of the other beasts, wantonly killing and wounding them until weakened by physical decay and old age, perhaps brought on prematurely as a result of his wrathful conduct. His previous behavior causes all the other animals to turn on him: the boar and the bull gore him, and the lazy ass saddles and kicks him on the forehead (314d, 315a; "el asno pereçoso en él ponié su sillo. / Dio le grand par de coçes, en la fruente ge las pon"). The ass's conduct shows that there is a reversal in the power structure in which vassal-beasts that were once subjected by the lion's anger now dominate the beast. In his fury the lion tears himself to shreds with his claws (315bcd), and, consequently, all of the animals act according to their natures. The lion's anger destroys him in three senses: first, his rage contributes to his debilitation and aging; second, it causes the other animals to take their revenge for his wrathful conduct; and, finally, he quite literally tears himself apart.

Of the lion's antagonists, the ass stands out since—unlike the other animals—not only its motivation but also its actions are anthropomorphized. The ass's saddling of the lion suggests the possibility of a symbolic or allegorical reading of the fable. If the animal court is seen as a model that reflects the human one, both are flawed since the person of the ruler suffers illness and decay, and the subordinate and weak come to dominate. Mary Douglas has observed that the body is particularly susceptible to symbolic interpretation as representing any bounded system, especially social structures.[91] In these fables the two systems, the body and society as measured through the conduct of its highest member, are mutually interdependent, and equally flawed.

The celebrations are marred by the unsuitable and disharmonious musical performance of the ass, inappropriately given the role of minstrel by his peers, "fezieron dél joglar" (894a). His inane attempts to perform anger the lion, which takes offence, "sentióse por escarnido el león del orejudo" (895d; the lion felt himself to be mocked by his long-eared subject), and the ass flees, only to return when persuaded to do so by the fox. The reference to the ass's large ears recalls the fool's hat and its long association with *ignorantia* in missals and on façades, but also brings into play the Pythagorean view that as a creature it singularly lacked bodily harmony, that its singing symbolizes inadequacy in performance, and that it represented carnal rather than spiritual man, "Asinus est populus gentilis" (Matthew 21:5), and commentaries on Romans 8:1–9, as presented graphically on a Zamoran misericord in which a friar who wears a hood with ass's ears kneels at a lectern, and crosses himself with one hand whilst making an obscene hand gesture with the other.[92] At Seville a misericord shows an ass sitting on its haunches and reading.[93] Isabel Mateo Gómez notes its similarity to another depicted in relief at Leon, in which an ass, on all fours and robed in what appears to be a monastic habit, also holds a document that it appears to read.[94] She considers the two images not to be related to the Ass and the Lyre tradition but to Friar Anselmo Turmeda's *Dispute of the Ass* (ca. 1418), in which a cleric and an ass debate the respective moral status of man and beast in relation to a series of sins, including avarice, pride, anger, and lust. This cluster of ideas contributes to the satiric humor in the presentation of the ass that attempts inappropriately to occupy a role to which he is particularly unsuited. It may be significant that the ass is also associated in the plastic arts tradition with inappropriately carnal conduct on the part of priests, and that the festivities take place at sext on a Sunday, when attention should more fittingly be accorded to religious than secular duties.[95] Misericords at Zamora, Plasencia, and Toledo show clerical lust: a friar inserts his hand into a penitent's skirts, a cardinal visits a woman, and a friar negotiates favors, respectively.[96] If this association is valid, it once again links the ostentatious display of the minstrel to conduct deemed inappropriate in priests. Indeed in the Old French *Roman de Renart* an ass cleric appears, and his name "Messire Bernart l'Archiprestre" is applied to the ass in one of the analogues of the Ass and the Lapdog in the French Aesopic tradition.[97] However, the Archpriest's application of the message of the *exemplum* to women also chastises foolish and ostentatious conduct in women, thereby linking women and priests as potential transgressors of a social order concerned with containing inappropriate sexual conduct. The accent on large ears and their association with lasciviousness in the physical description of the Archpriest and Alda strengthen this reading.

Two instances of deceptive language occur in the second part of the *exemplum* when the lion sends the fox to flatter the gullible ass, "creó falsos falagos" (899a; he believed false flattery), leading the latter into an ambush in which he is wounded, "abriol por los costados" (900c; its side was slashed open), and then imprisoned. The lion appoints the wolf as a warder, ordering "que lo guardase todo mejor que las ovejas" (901b; that he guard it all better than sheep). The wolf eats the ass's heart and ears, and when summoned before the irate lion defends himself with the argument:

> quel asno tal nasçiera;
> que si él coraçón e orejas toviera,
> entendiera sus mañas e sus nuevas oyera;
> mas que lo non tenía e por ende veniera.
>
> (903)

(that the ass must have been born like that; / because if he had had a heart and ears, / he would have understood [the lion's] wiles and listened to his news / but he didn't and so he came [to court].)

It is significant that the fox and wolf should be the courtiers who utter deceptive words since their diabolic natures had been well established, and they were strongly associated with insatiable appetite and the deceptive use of language to satisfy this desire; these facets of their natures are exploited in the court case between the two presided over by the ape (321–72; tale 15), which exposes their hypocrisy.[98] The lion's instruction to the wolf to guard the ass better than he would sheep calls this latent association to the fore.

The application of the message of the *exemplum* to women listeners is amplified in such a way as to emphasize the role of hearing and the heart in learning from example:

> Assí, señoras dueñas, entended el rromançe:
> guardat vos de amor loco, non vos prenda nin alçance;
> abrid vuestras orejas, vuestro coraçón se lance
> en amor de Dios linpio, loco amor nol trançe.
> La que por desaventura es o fue engañada,
> guarde se que non torne al mal otra vegada;
> de coraçón e de orejas non quiera ser menguada;
> en ajena cabeça sea bien castigada.
>
> (904–05)

> (So, noble ladies, learn the story: / be wary of mad love, so that it doesn't seize you or reach you; / open your ears: let your heart go out / in pure love of God; so that mad love doesn't break it. // Whichever lady unluckily is or was deceived / should be wary not to turn to the bad once again; / she should not wish to lack heart and ears; / on another's head let her learn.)

James F. Burke, in his study of vision in *Celestina*, notes that in some medieval treatments of the senses, the auditory was emphasized along with the visual as the primary portals to the mind, which is clearly the process that the Archpriest describes here.[99] The *exemplum* dealing with the ass with no heart and no ears creates a strong visual image of the fate of whomsoever succumbs to false words, and lady listeners are enjoined to internalize the message of the story, and learn from another's example so they do not endure a similar fate. Each of the animals that is portrayed as physically depleted or debased has a role to play in transmitting the lesson of the fable. The ass's ears and heart are fetishized as what is lost when proper understanding, and internalization, of another's desire is not achieved, and what is maintained when the self is well protected. The humorous treatment of the sick lion points to a weakness in his apparently all-powerful seat at the head of the hierarchy, since he can be outwitted in his designs if the lesson of correct interpretation is appropriately internalized and deployed. The potential socially disruptive action of the wolf in disobeying the lion's command in fact points to a weakness in a social order that permits the powerful to exploit those further down the hierarchy, such as the ass and the wolf. Through a sound understanding of the corrupt intentions of the powerful, the weak can outmaneuver the strong; thus the wolf is a positive example to lady listeners, despite the negative connotations carried by him, and his use of deceptive words. Ian Michael argues that the only point of contact between the fable and its application is that the ass's conduct and fate can be likened to those of foolish women; however, I have argued that the wolf in the *exemplum* has learned from the ass's example, and that lady listeners are similarly asked to learn from his deceptive words. I should argue that this maneuver is broadly similar to that found in the application to Pitas Payas, in which the wife's lover may be regarded as a positive *exemplum*. It may be that the application of this fable contains humorously truant misogynist content, which likens women, and their roles in courtship, to the wolf, and which may invoke the association between the term *loba*, and female sexual experience, cited earlier in the *Libro*:[100]

> fazes con tu grand fuego commo faze la loba:
> al más astroso lobo, al enatío, ajoba;
> aquél da de la mano e de aquél se encoba.
>
> (402bcd)

> ([Archpriest to Don Amor] With your great fire, you do as the she-wolf does / couple with the most wretched and ugly wolf / that's the one she takes by the hand, and she is covered by him.)

As such, women and Ruiz's wolf are like the powerful Reynardian characters of the wolf and the bear, which threaten the social and legal establishment when it suits them.[101]

The final of the three fables dealing with the figure of the ass concerns the ass and the lapdog, and is used by Trotaconventos in debate to persuade Doña Garoça to enter into a relationship with the Archpriest. As with the Lion and the Ass, the fable involves the ass in inappropriate and ostentatious self-display, which is subject to punishment, and like the Horse and the Ass, it contains latent sexual content, which augments the humor.[102] The only speech depicted is the ass's self-deceptive words. The level of ontological quarantine between the human and the animal is less even than that found in the Horse and the Ass as the interactions between owner and animal are clearly portrayed, and this has a leveling function.

On the second day of Doña Garoça's verbal seduction, Trotaconventos succeeds in drawing the nun away from her devotions, and into the more private space of the *estrado*, or reception room. Garoça's change of heart appears to be indicated in the lyrical stanza that precedes Trotaconventos's use of the *exemplum*, and which points to her succumbing to vice:

> Alegre va la monja del coro al parlador;
> alegre va el fraile de terçia al rrefitor;

quiere oír la monja nuevas del entendedor;
quiere el fraile goloso entrar en el tajador.
(1399)

(The nun goes gladly from choir to the reception room, / the friar goes
gladly from terce to the refectory: / the nun wants to hear news of her suitor, /
the greedy friar wants to get stuck in about the carving board.)

The tale is offered to Garoça as a negative *exemplum* of the treatment that
Trotaconventos should receive from the nun, but its playful and laughter-
provoking nature is referred to clearly, "diré vos un juguete [. . .] diré vos
la fablilla, si me dades un rrisete" (1400ad; I'll tell you a joke [or trifle. . .]
I'll tell you a yarn if you give me a laugh).[103] In it, the lady indulges her
lapdog, whose attentions flatter her, like a lover. The partial anthropomorphism of the dog's conduct, and the heavy use of physical phrases
humorously emphasize this aspect of their relationship, as in the dog's
mouthing of the lady's hands as if she were food:

con su lengua e boca las manos le besava;
ladrando e con la cola mucho la fallagava;
demostrava en todo grand amor que la amava.
(1401b–d)

(with his tongue and mouth he kissed her hands, / barking and with his tail
he flattered her a great deal: / in every thing he showed the great love he felt
for her.)

The oral eroticism of 1401b overdetermines the latent phallic euphemism
of the following stanza, "Ante ella e sus conpañas en pino se tenía; / tomavan
con él todos solaz e plazentería" (1402ab; Before her and her retinue he
raised himself up / they all took great solace and happiness with him), and
his oral attentions to the lady are rewarded with food and scraps from the
group (1402c). As in the wild woman section, and in fables in general,
there is a strong link between the two appetites.

The stupid ass, "asno de mal seso [. . .] el burro nesçio" (1403ab; the
wrong-headed ass [. . .] the stupid donkey), considers that he does their
lady greater service in carrying wood and flour for food than the lapdog,
and decides to mimic the dog's behavior, "pues tan bien terné pino e
falagaré la dueña, / commo aquel blanchete que yaze so su peña" (1404cd;
I'll stand right up and flatter our lady / like that little white lapdog which
lies under her fur). The ass fails to recognize the difference between his
nature and that of the lapdog, and so engages in a *méconnaissance* not unlike
that of the two lazy suitors. As a creature more fitting to noble circles the
lapdog enjoys privileged access to the lady and her entourage. Just like the

two suitors, the ass is involved in an erotic triangle in which he foolishly sees himself as a fit competitor for his mistress's attentions, rejecting the code that fits him, as a lowly beast of burden, for labor. Just as in the Young Miller, desire disrupts the body of labor. The latent sexual euphemism is also activated by the lapdog's access to the lady's lap. As is common in animal fables, the sphere of consumption and appetite is underlined in the treatment of the dog, and in the ass's reflections on the dog's privileged treatment.

The ass's access to seemingly rational, if ill-guided, thought is contrasted comically with the preposterous nature of his bestial behavior as he penetrates into the lady's *estrado*, and the sexual content of his desire is made plain by his comparison with the stud horse, known for its priapism, when mimicking the dog:[104]

> commo garañón loco el nesçio tal venía,
> rretoçando e faziendo mucha de caçorría;
> fue se para el estrado do la dueña seía.
> Puso en los sus onbros entranbos los sus braços
> (1405b–06a)

(like a mad stud the fool came on, / frolicking and acting very foolishly; / he went straight to the dais where the lady sat. / He put his forelegs on both of her shoulders)

The consequence of this action is that he receives a sound beating, whose sadistic brutality is comically slapstick, and which is delivered by phallic weapons connotative of male genitalia: "dieron le muchos palos, con piedras e con maços, / fasta que ya los palos se fazían pedaços" (1406cd, they beat him a lot with sticks, with stones and mallets, / until the very sticks themselves were broken into bits).[105] The inappropriate behavior of the ass is subject to criticism and sorely censured. Symbolically the actions of those who wish to act outside of their ordained sphere, such as amorous priests, are also attacked.

Trotaconventos then goes on to state in the epimythium of this tale that what God and Nature prohibit should not be attempted by the wise. The application is that Trotaconventos has endured such anger from Doña Garoça that she now dare not ask for the nun's response to her overtures on the Archpriest's behalf; that is, she fears to act like the ass lest the lady, Garoça, chastise her.[106] However, her behavior is more like the falsely flattering lapdog in that she panders to Garoça's self-representation as an unwilling beloved, and constructs Garoça social status as a noble, and potentially beneficent, mistress who conceals her own appetitive nature.

Like the lapdog, Trotaconventos secures access to the privileged space of the *estrado*. The debate between the two women turns on Garoça's apparent reluctance, discussed in chapter 3, to have her spiritual wealth threatened through the flattery of a insincere friend who will abandon her to deception, and Trotaconventos's praise of the value of worldly pleasure, and comfort, and her defence of herself as a humble servant capable of great service and loyalty.[107] As with others of the fables discussed here, there is a notable emphasis on food and consumption, which is in keeping with animal fables. Here, as in the Reynardian tradition, the link is used to introduce sexual euphemism. However, Garoça herself clearly brings an awareness of sexual symbolism into the discussion. Putting aside the possibility of there being latent sexual symbolism in her use of the phallic snake in her first tale, her application of the Town Mouse and the Country Mouse (1370–83; tale 25) carries sexual connotations, underscored by the parallelistic structure:

Más vale en convento las sardinas saladas,
e fazer a Dios serviço con las dueñas onrradas,
que perder la mi alma con perdizes assadas,
e fincar escarnida con otras deserradas.

(1385)

(There's greater worth in a convent in salted sardines / and serving God with honorable ladies / that in loosing my soul with roast birds [lit. partridges] / and being ruined with other fallen women.)

The references to fish and fowl in the first and third lines and their parallel with honorable and fallen women in the second and fourth lines suggest a marked contrast in the voluntary poverty of the spiritual, conventual life and the material comfort of worldly life. The noun *perdizes* was euphemistically applied to public women, and invokes bestiary lore concerning the capture of partridges through a manipulation of their lust, and so has strong associations with sexually licentious behavior.[108] The suggestion that Garoça is represented as aware of the sexual connotations of her debate with Trotaconventos is also supported by wordplay in the frame dialogue to the Ass and the Lapdog. Trotaconventos opens the second day's discussion with an offer to tell of an amusing trifle, a *juguete*, which has the connotation of play, particularly sexual. The sexualization of the semantic field of play may be developed when she describes the mistress and her dog, "Un perrillo blanchete con su señora jugava" (1401a; A little lapdog used to play with his mistress), and also when Garoça's rebuttal of the fable uses a form of expression, *mal juego*, that certainly carries with it associations of underhandedness, and sexual intercourse:[109]

Vieja, mañana madrugueste
a dezir me pastrañas de lo que ayer me fableste;
yo non lo consentría commo tú me lo rrogueste,
que conssentir non devo tan mal juego como éste.
                                                    (1410)

(Old Lady, you rose early this morning / to tell me tales about that business
which you spoke to me about yesterday; / I could not agree to what you
asked me; / nor ought I to agree to such poor play as this.)

In the Horse and the Ass, the horse's disfigurement arises from his own
pride. The metonymic link between the beast's phallic symbolism and his
owner suggests the knight is certainly guilty. His punishment for the rape
comprises the demise of his social and moral status as signaled by the
wounding of his horse on the field, and his loss of it to labor. The fable suggests that all prideful and lustful creatures, including the knight metonymi-
cally represented by his horse, belong to the same base and bestial level: that
of the foolish ass. The Lion and the Ass portrays the vulnerability of the
gullible and foolish to the predations of those more deceitful than themselves. Significantly, not only the ass but also the lion become victims, the
ass to those more powerful than himself, and the lion to powerful client-
animals under his dominion. Here all individuals are subject to the lack of
understanding and memory, thematized in the wolf's consumption of the
ass's ears and heart, regardless of their social position as near-outcasts or
rulers. As befits his character, the foolish ass is all too ready to presume to
act in a manner unfitting to his nature and station. However, the wrathful
monarch-lion's lack suggests the fallen nature of a society that grants the
deceitful, represented by the diabolic fox and wolf, sufficient power to
manipulate others.

The first level of humor in each of the fables discussed derives from the
truancy of animals that conduct themselves as if they were human whilst
still exhibiting bestial behavior. As Isidore observed, their content is against
nature: "Fables are things which have neither happened nor can happen
because they are against nature."[110] The lapdog may be regarded as an
exception to this since it is anthropomorphized to a lesser degree than the
other animals: its behavior, as described, is typical of its species, and it has
no access to speech. James J. Paxson's discussion of personification allegory
offers a parallel in terms of levels of ontological separation. For Paxson,
personification figures are simply described in the narrative and do not act
or speak whilst the characters of personification allegory, in contrast,
achieve voice and action.[111] In personification allegory—as, for example, in

visions—the main diegetic level in which human characters interact is separated, or ontologically quarantined, from the interdiegetic level in which the personification characters act and speak. The protagonist may witness the acts and speech of the personification characters, perhaps with the aid of a guide, or may interact directly with them but other non-allegorical characters will not do so. The fables discussed here are similar in that the characters that deploy them do not interact directly with the animal characters; however, within the tales the degree of relationship between human and animal characters varies as with the dream-vision protagonist who may witness or interact with allegorical characters. Drawing on Isidore's explanation of the Aristotelian classification of fables into Aesopic and Libyan types, Papias had already observed the existence of different levels of ontological quarantining in the eleventh century:[112]

"They are either Aesopic or Libyan" (Aristotle, *Rhetoric*, 2.20.2). They are called "Aesopic," from their inventor Aesop, when dumb animals or inanimate objects are feigned to have spoken amongst themselves. They are called "Libyan" when the exchange of words between man and beasts is feigned.[113]

The distinction between Aesopic and Libyan tales was "not widely observed."[114] Nevertheless, it does permit us to admit a contemporary awareness of the difference between fables in which animals alone interact such as in the Lion and the Ass, and those in which there is animal/human interaction as in the Horse and the Ass, and the Ass and the Lapdog.

In the Lion and the Ass, ontological quarantine between the human and animal worlds is maintained absolutely thus enhancing the allegorical relationship between the two spheres. The ass and the fox, however, are assigned the human roles of minstrels. Of all animals, the deceitful fox is particularly suited to play this role as conceived of by medieval clerical culture. The ass is exceptionally ill fitted to music by virtue of the traditional idea that he lacks the capacity to appreciate harmony, and his lack of guile renders him an unlikely minstrel. In addition, the frequent association of the ass and the fallen priest acts to intensify this impression, and to call to mind the injunctions on priests to avoid inappropriate bodily display. Like the ass in tale 22, the one in tale 27 fails to recognize its proper station, and act accordingly and, instead, assumes the inappropriate role of indulged pet. The ontological quarantining between animal and human is more complex in this fable since the lapdog's behavior toward its mistress is appropriate to its ontological status but the accent on the dog's phallic quality sexualizes it, casting it in the role of lover in a parodic and grotesque love triangle, with the ass as rival. The ass's attempt to cross species-specific behavioral boundaries is both comic and doomed to failure, and consequently, the lady's retinue justly punishes its impertinence in a *charivari*, as discussed in chapter 3. However, the sexualized language employed to depict relations between mistress and pet is then reactivated in the description of her retinue's sadistic punishment of the ass to suggest that the temperamentally imbalanced nature of animals extends to the human. Finally, in the Horse and the Ass, although the horse's owner is mentioned at the outset, the fact that the horse is a metonym for its owner indicates the fact that the human shares in the beast's nature.

Human behavior is only one aspect of the anthropomorphization of animals in the tales discussed. As in personification allegory, speech plays a significant role and, as a sign of the exercise of God-given reason, its use is especially significant in transmitting the humor and truancy of the tales. In the Horse and the Ass, the two animals misappropriate language to mock one another. The horse's brief attack on the ass is prideful and haughty; whilst the ass's ironic use of *ubi sunt* humorously draws attention to the dependence of pride on worldly status, which is easily lost, and presents the horse with an image of its fallen self. The speech attributed to the ass is similar in purpose to the lady's judgment of the two lazy suitors. In the Lion and the Ass, direct or reported speech is used by the two animals most associated with deception, the wolf and the fox, to that very end. Their use of language reveals the susceptibility of their interlocutors to false flattery, and thus self-deception. In the case of the ass this is stated explicitly: "Creó falsos falagos, él escapó peor" (899a; quoted above). However, the symbolic image of the ass with no ears and no heart as representing a failure of understanding and internalization of knowledge is equally applicable to the lion, the third animal in this tale to which speech is attributed. He uses deceptive language to plot the ass's return to the celebrations and punishment, and selects the female minstrel fox as go-between (896). Likewise, knowing of the wolf's treatment of the sheep that he guards, the lion entrusts him with the ass's carcass with a simple counter-command against its mistreatment. As in the Two Lazy Suitors and Don Pitas Payas, the tale ends at the point where he is presented with an image of himself, which reveals that he has been engaged in a *méconnaissance* of himself as all-powerful monarch. In the Ass and the Lapdog, the only words reported are the beast of burden's self-deceptive ones at seeing the favors received by the lapdog, which show him to be engaged in a *méconnaissance*. Speech in all three of these tales contributes actively to the humor.

Law and divine justice form the background to the fables, despite a lack of explicit comment. In the Horse and the Ass, the fact that the horse, as symbol of his owner's pride, lust, and social position, is so thoroughly debased reveals the importance of acting appropriately. In the Lion and the Ass, secular social order is flawed and this leads to a breakdown in ethical conduct, to category transgression in which the ass assumes an unfitting role, and illustrates the dangers of liminality. The ass transgresses behavioral boundaries and both eponymous beasts fail to internalize sensory data and interpret it correctly at physical cost: the ass loses its life, and its ears and heart are consumed, and the lion loses a portion of the carcass as foodstuff over which the animal hierarchy should dictate that he has absolute dominion. The fox and the wolf, however, receive no punishment. The words with which the lion charges the wolf with the ass's carcass humorously call attention to the latter's hypocrisy, and its reply is also humorous since its words can be fittingly applied to the ass symbolically and literally, and to the lion symbolically. In the Ass and the Lapdog, the speech uttered is self-deceptive, and the species confusion is between ass and dog, and human and animal behavior.

Sexual euphemism contributes strongly to the humor, especially as it implies the rupture of the taboo of bestiality. Whilst in behavioral terms all species and humans are leveled, those who cross boundaries inappropriately are punished, and consequently social mobility and breeches in civil status are attacked. Sex and consumption are strongly linked, and although the law is not thematicized, unfit behavior is roundly punished. Ontological separation appears to be linked to the importance of not seeking to cross boundaries of species, social category, and to ethical conduct.

In chapter 1, I argued that the visual is particularly important in the *Libro* in relation to memory, particularly in the generation of interpretation, and in creating the fantasy of power over the object. The combination of these areas invites the reader or listener to take up an interpretative position between fallible and fallen human knowledge as experienced in life and divine knowledge. The relationship between memory and the visual is a significant element in Ruiz's treatment of exemplary fabliaux, Aespoic tales, and the descriptions, especially those of Christ and Alda. The exemplary fabliaux analyzed in this chapter, like the descriptions discussed in chapter 1, focus on the incapacity and inadequacy of the fallen human body to act ethically.

The use of psychoanalytical theory has permitted me to argue that in all three exemplary fabliaux the abject human body, disfigured and fetishized, takes center stage as the butt of humor. The eroticization of the male body, and its connection with the spheres of labor, food production, and exchange in the Young Miller and the Don Pitas Payas link the tales recounted by the Archpriest and Don Amor. The two interlocutors in the agonistic debate exploit a similar range of images drawn not only from these spheres but also from those of contamination and pollution in their discussion of the impact of sexual desire on the individual. Despite the later development of the action, and the Archpriest's constant pursuit of sexual fulfillment, this cluster of images points to the existence of an underlying ideology of the destructive effects of sexual love. The analysis of triangular desire in the three tales supports this reading by permitting an examination of social codes and institutions, and power. The failure to attend properly to the integrity of the body and its boundaries, particularly through the pursuit of women, leads to its debilitation, and its ability to labor and to participate appropriately in the management and exchange of women; thus the effects of such action have a deleterious effect on society as a whole.

All three tales give a complex yield of pleasure to the interlocutor or reader/listener in which fantasies of domination and submission coexist. The tales' protagonists are all involved in *méconnaissance* or a misrecognition of their integrity and a fantasy of ambition to which they fail to live up; and it is precisely at this moment that speech intervenes to create a pithy climax. As I have illustrated, the focus on the visual is evident in all three tales but there is a much greater emphasis on the act of looking in the two tales deployed by Don Amor than in the Archpriest's Young Miller. The tales told by Don Amor use the visual and the language of contamination in order to create solidarity between himself and the Archpriest by raising the specter of an out-group of men who fail to dominate women appropriately, and constructing a fantasy image of the Archpriest as ideal lover. The Archpriest initially and temporarily rejects the possibility of finding an appropriate love object, but, on consideration, judges that he has always served ladies and followed Don Amor's strictures, and imposes the selection of love object on his heart (575–79). His adoption of the role of lover depends upon a *méconnaissance* of his own in which he disregards the institutions whose codes deny him active participation in the pursuit of desire, and forgets knowledge of the threat of contagion admitted by Don Amor, of the failure of the fabliaux protagonists, and of his own previous failures to construct himself as wielder of a powerful phallic gaze. The Archpriest's *méconnaissance* is achieved through the rhetorical effectiveness of Don Amor's discourse to create a veneer of solidarity between the two. Later, Don Amor privileges the Archpriest amongst all his disciples with a visitation (1259–63); I touched on this episode in the introduction, and shall return to it in the conclusion. In chapter 3, I shall examine the treatment of the Archpriest as lover in order to insist further that the Ruiz presents an image of the lover as a disorganized and forgetting subject.

In the tales discussed, physical disfigurement and abjection are outward signs of the fallen nature of man and the acts that are stains on the soul, warned against by Don Amor in Two Lazy Suitors at 467d, quoted above. Don Amor, of course, focuses on the particular flaws that are displeasing to women; however, in chapter 1, I argued that Ruiz's physical descriptions of the Archpriest and the seducible beauty reveal the flaws that incline them toward particular varieties of sin. The two remaining descriptions in the *Libro*, of Christ and Alda, are opposed in contemplative pathos and humor, respectively. The two descriptions contrast with each other, and those of the Archpriest and the seducible beauty. In chapter 3, I shall argue that the depiction of body of the wounded Christ is also played off against the lover's lament, in which the narrator describes the damaging effects of unrequited love in conventional terms.

As a subject, Alda occupies a low and degraded position on the chain of being in that her bodily and ethical status is bestial and even demonic, and she is prepared to trade sex and nourishment for gifts. The animal and demonic aspects of her description make of her the site of doubts about the human. The points of contact between the Archpriest, Alda and the seducible beauty embody his empirical person and reinforce the depiction of his emasculinity already established in Trotaconventos's description of him. He is a fallen Everyman subject to humoral influence, and whose relationship to *natura* should be shaped by his acculturation in the institutions designed to govern and save. Taken together the *descriptiones puellae* express anxiety about the threats of damnation and death residing in the feminine and in desire. The description of Alda is contrasted with that of the wounded body of Christ with which it appears in close proximity. That the two descriptions should be read against one another is reinforced by thematic focus on the Incarnation, Virgin Birth, and embodiment in the christological lyrics. Christ's body is subjected to a symbolic dismemberment in the contemplation of His Wounds. His role in the hypostatic union positions Him at the top of the chain of being; yet it embodies the ambiguity of being both divine and human.

Bodily dismemberment and disfigurement also feature strongly in animal fables, which form the majority of the *Libro*'s thirty-two tales. The use of animal fables for persuasive purposes formed a normal part of debate, and the similitude between animal and human behavior creates truant humor, which calls into question the fallen humankind's access to salvation. I chose to discuss tales in which the ass is protagonist since the ass was viewed as a particularly disharmonious and foolish beast, and is often the figure associated with lack of knowledge and the clergy in the pictorial and plastic arts. All three of the tales discussed are drawn from the Aesopic tradition, and manifest different degrees of quarantining between the animal and human worlds. In the Lion and the Ass, the relationship is purely allegorical, and the structure of animal society reflects the chain of being. In the Horse and the Ass, the animals are clearly depicted in a domesticated context, unlike the wild beasts of the Lion and the Ass, and no direct interaction with human characters is depicted; for example, when the horse is on his way to fight in the lists neither his rider, the Knight, nor the ass's drover is mentioned. In addition, the horse represents not only a type of human behavior but stands as a phallic metonym for his owner, and the disfigurement it endures represents the knight's loss of social prestige. In the Ass and the Lapdog, the dog's natural behavior in relation to its human mistress and her retinue is given a charge of sexual euphemism that hints at the appetitive nature of both dog and owner. The ass in turn ruptures boundaries of natural species-specific behavior to mimic the dog in an expressly sexualized manner, and it consequently receives a beating from the lady's retinue. In all three of the fables, animal speech is particularly linked to humor, and misappropriations of language to deceive and mock reflect the use of pithy remarks to conclude the exemplary fabliaux.

# CHAPTER 3

# THE STAND-UP ARCHPRIEST

In this chapter, I shall examine the ontological status of the Archpriest as narrator in relation to abjection and humor. In order to achieve this end, I study the ideological contours of the amorous affairs that provide a thread of continuity through the diverse materials that comprise the *Libro* to explicate how the former expose the narrator as a compromised Everyman character whose lustful activities and performative public confession call into question the very structures of the Law, in the Lacanian sense of those institutions and ideologies that should guarantee the place of the individual within social order. Although Juan Ruiz individualizes the Archpriest to present a seemingly empirical I, he elides the particularities of priestly identity, an issue to which I shall return later, and is at pains "to present his 'poetic I' as representative of humanity": "E yo como soy omne commo otro pecador" (76a; And I, as I am man like any other sinner).[1] I shall argue that the Archpriest is an abject character engaged in a continual *méconnaissance*, expressed through amatory failure and proximity to sickness and death. In this analysis, the advice of Don Amor and Doña Venus do not lead to a reversal in the Archpriest's fortunes in love. Consequently Félix Lecoy's suggestion in the conclusion of his *Recherches sur le "Libro de buen amor"* that the *Libro* is an *ars amatoria* cannot be borne out since, crucially, it does not show how to succeed in love but rather presents a series of indirect, failed approaches to the object.[2] The claim in the sermon-prologue, therefore, that "si algunos, lo que non los conssejo, quisieren usar del loco amor, aquí fallarán algunas maneras para ello" (p. 110; if some people, and I do not advise them to do so, should wish to practice mad love, they will find some ways of doing so here) can only be viewed as ironic since this *utilitas* is "una socarronería a costa del infeliz que se decida a emplear el *Libro* como manual 'del loco amor' (y a quien esperan, por tanto las mismas desdichas que al protagonista)."[3]

My analysis will reveal that the structure and development of the affairs show variation within a narrow paradigm, and that the amatory object remains elusive in all of them regardless of whether they precede or follow the advice of Don Amor and Doña Venus. In order to demonstrate this I shall once again have recourse to the paradigm of the erotic triangle, discussed in chapter 2, which will permit me to explore the treatment of the affairs comparatively. The model also has the advantage of not privileging any one of the affairs, such as the long narrative of the encounter between the Archpriest as Don Melón with his neighbor, Doña Endrina. I shall take the affairs together, and examine each stage separately in order to draw out the continuities and discontinuities in Ruiz's handling of them. I have found the paradigm of the erotic triangle to be an inadequate mode of analysis for the Archpriest's adventures with the wild women of the *sierra* at the intradiegetic level. When an individual pursues women outside of seeking legitimate marriage within a social order which relies on female sexual continence and honor to shore up its symbolic system, he must resort to secrecy, and thus scandal and exposure become keynotes in sexual relations, and, as I shall argue, it appears to be this process that leads to triangulation through rivalry, mediation, and obstacles in the *Libro*. Since a reversal in the male–female paradigm places the Archpriest as object in the mountain adventures, the model is inadequate. Nonetheless, poetic genres do serve as models, albeit inverted ones, and thus triangulation occurs at the extradiegetic level. I shall therefore treat the *sierra* episode separately. I shall conclude by examining the implications of the representation of the Archpriest as failed lover in the final section of this chapter.

By my count, the narrator engages in fourteen affairs, eleven after having received amatory advice from Don Amor and Doña Venus, and those with Cruz, and the Dueñas Cuerda and Ençerrada before that episode. Eight of the women are named: Cruz (112–22), Doña Endrina (653–891), Doña Garoça (1332–507), and Doña Fulana (1618–25) from the urban setting, and all four of the mountain women, La Chata, Gadea de Río Frío, Menga Llorente, and Alda de la Tablada (950–1042). The remaining six are referred to by epithets as the Dueña Cuerda, "The Clever Lady" (77–107), the Dueña Ençerrada, "The Locked-in Lady" (166–80), the Dueña Apuesta, "The Good-looking Lady" (910–44), the Viuda Loçana, "The Merry [or Lovely or Elegant?] Widow" (1315–20), the Dueña Devota, "The Devout Lady" (1321–31), and the Mora, "The Muslim Lady" (1508–12). Analyses of the amorous encounters have focused in the main on individual episodes, and those dealing with the mountain women, Endrina and Garoça, have excited most interest, with only four studies examining the *Libro*'s female characters as a whole according to different methodologies.[4] However, since my concern is the ideological treatment of the affairs, I wish to put aside the representation of the *Libro*'s female characters in their own right, and examine their treatment as amatory objects. I do not, however, wish to deny the value of an analysis, feminist or otherwise, of them.

The initial motivation provided for the majority of the affairs is, occasionally, to forget the suffering caused by the failure of a previous one and, more usually, to avoid loneliness since it is in man's nature to desire a mate. The failure of the affairs with the Dueñas Cuerda and Devota, and with Endrina and Garoça produce the state of loneliness that inclines the Archpriest to seek solace elsewhere with Cruz, Garoça, the Apuesta Dueña, and the Mora, respectively. The theme of loneliness is first introduced indirectly in the truant discussion of the Aristotelian precept that the primary drives of all animals are toward food and reproduction, which immediately precedes the encounter with the Dueña Cuerda (st. 71–76):

> Commo dize Aristótiles, cosa es verdadera:
> el mundo por dos cosas trabaja: la primera,
> por aver mantenençia; la otra cosa era
> por aver juntamiento con fenbra plazentera.
> (71)

> (As Aristotle says, it's true, / the world works for two ends: the first / to have sustenance; the other thing was / to have intercourse with a pleasing female.)[5]

Drawing on Aristotle's writing, particularly *De anima* (II.III and IV), Ruiz expounds with malicious humor the Stagirite's naturalist philosophy.[6] Aristotle's argument regarding the human sexual drive had been censured by Stephen Tempier, Bishop of Paris in 1277 as amongst other heretical theses currently being taught in the Faculty of Arts at the Sorbonne, now often referred to as Averroism or radical or heterodox Aristotelianism due to the use of the philosopher and his commentator as *auctoritates*. Tempier's 219 condemned propositions was one of a number of *Collectiones errorum* originating in Paris in the thirteenth and fourteenth centuries, and allusions to them in the oath of Bachelors of Theology and in philosophical and theological texts suggest that they circulated widely.[7] Heterodox Aristotelianism justifies sexual intercourse as being necessary, pleasurable, and even virtuous in order to ensure the survival of the species, consequently "simplex fornicatio, utpote soluti cum soluta, non est peccatum" (simple sexual intercourse, between an unattached man and an unattached women, is not sin).[8] There was certainly some familiarity with radical Aristotelianism in the peninsula prior to and contemporary with the *Libro*. In 1290 a work of necromancy, adopting the naturalist heterodoxy, and purporting to be by the Cordovan Virgil was presented at the court of

Sancho IV, and a contemporary of Ruiz, Friar Thomas Scott, disseminated such views.[9] In contrast, Ramon Llull wrote around twenty-one works attacking it, as also occurs in the *Libro del caballero Zifar* (ca. 1300–01), possibly by Ferrand Martínez, which Ruiz knew.[10]

The naturalist argument is reintroduced explicitly in the introduction to the encounter with the Dueña Ençerrada, when the affair is initiated on account of the difficulty of putting aside "la costumbre, el fado e la suerte" (habit, fate, and destiny); when habit as an aspect of *natura*, "la costunbre es otra natura" (habit is another form of Nature), inclines young men, *mançebos*, to seek solace by desiring a beloved (166–67). In the overarching narrative structure the fact that the Archpriest's mimetic desire arises from identification with young men may attach ironic humor to the narrator since archpriests, as ordained priests with the care of souls, would have been over the age of twenty five.[11] Andreas Capellanus's assertion that the appropriate age for the practice of courtly love is between eighteen and sixty years of age (I.5) runs contrary to the Iberian tradition in which older lovers are pilloried. The affair with the Viuda Loçana also arises as the result of a kind of mimetic desire. After comparing his own loneliness to the pleasure others take in company, the Archpriest calls the bawd, Trotaconventos:

> Día de Quasimodo, iglesias e altares
> vi llenos de alegrías, de bodas e cantares;
> todos avién grand fiesta, fazién grandes yantares;
> andan de boda en boda clérigos e juglares.
> Los que ante son solos, desque eran casados,
> veía los de dueñas estar aconpañados;
> pensé cómmo oviese de tales gasajados,
> ca omne que es solo sienpre piensa cuidados.
>
> (1315–16)

(On the Sunday after Easter, I saw churches and altars / full of joy, and weddings and songs; / everyone having a great celebration, having great feasts; / clerics and minstrels were going from wedding to wedding. // I saw those who were alone before, since they now had partners / being accompanied by ladies / I considered how could I have such pleasure / since the thoughts of a man who is alone are always care-ridden.)

Just as previously he had desired the Dueña Ençerrada in imitation of the habits of young men, the Archpriest's desire for the Viuda Loçana is prompted simply because he perceives others, perhaps the very clerics and minstrels who journey between weddings, to love.

In the case of the Dueña Devota, no initial motivation is given, and his desire is incited purely by sight, with the provision of no further textual justification. The episode's first line, however, parallels that of the

encounter with Viuda Loçana, which it immediately follows, by opening
with a formula alluding to a holy day, and with a reference to generalized
joy. The more secular celebration of marriage after Easter in the Viuda
Loçana episode is displaced to solemn processional in the following pursuit
of the Dueña Devota:

> Día era de Sant Marcos, fue fiesta señalada:
>   toda la santa iglesia faz proçesión onrrada,
> de las mayores del año, de cristianos loada;
> acaeçió me una ventura, la fiesta non pasada:
>
>                      (1321)
>
> (It was St Mark's day [25 March], it was a high feast day; / all of the holy
> church was making an honorable procession, / one of the most important of
> the year, praised by Christians; / an adventure befell me before the festival
> was over:)

Sacred space becomes the locus of desire as the Archpriest beholds the
Dueña in prayer. The opening of the passage in which the sacred and
profane spheres are blurred, initiated in the Viuda Loçana episode, is developed further by applying to the sphere of desire the lexicon of the salvific
economy, *rogar* (to beseech), *piadat* (compassion), *caridat* (charity). The
eroticization of the sacred finds its ultimate expression in the following
amatory adventure with the nun, Garoça.

The affair with Doña Endrina stands out since it is not begun expressly
for one of the reasons discussed above, and because the motivation for her
selection differs substantially from that in the other affairs. After meditating
on Don Amor's advice, the Archpriest is at a loss to understand his previous amatory failures since "en sus castigos sienpre usé bevir" (576d; I had
always lived according to his advice), and consequently he willfully imposes
a beloved upon his heart:

> Contra mi coraçón yo mesmo me torné;
> porfiando le dixe: "Agora yo te porné
> con dueña falaguera, e desta vez terné
> que si bien non abengo, nunca más aberné."
> Mi coraçón me dixo: "Faz lo e rrecabdarás"
>                      (578–79a)
>
> (I myself turned against my heart; / insisting, I said to it: "Now I'll give you /
> a promising lady, and this time I hold / that if I don't succeed, I'll never ever
> succeed." // My heart said to me, "Do it and reap rewards")

His action suggests that the reason for his previous disappointments lies in
his failure to choose an appropriate beloved, although he denies this, and

appears in keeping with Don Amor's advice; nevertheless, no information is given at this point about whether Endrina has the characteristics of the seducible beauty.

Whatever the initial motivation for seeking a beloved, the selection of love object is usually stimulated by sight as in the case of the Dueñas Apuesta and Devota, and the Viuda Loçana, or by the go-between's recommendation as with Garoça, the Mora, and Doña Fulana rather than on the qualities of the woman in question. Although Don Amor advises that the lover see the lady nude, "sin camisa" (435c), and that the bawd inspect the love object's figure as part of the selection process, this does not happen explicitly in any of the affairs but the latter may be implied in those cases in which the go-between recommends the beloved.[12] There are two exceptions: Endrina, as discussed above, and Cruz. The narrator implies that it is Cruz's characteristic of being "non santa mas sandía" (112c; not saintly but rather foolish) that renders her an appropriate object for amatory interest. The impetus for the choice of beloved is not mentioned explicitly in the case of the Dueñas Cuerda and Ençerrada; the Archpriest simply declares that "una dueña me prisso" (77a; a lady captured me) and that he took a new beloved (167d; "tomé amiga nueva").

The women's qualities are drawn from a limited set of around twenty character and physical traits, focusing primarily on conformity to social norms for female behavior, attractiveness, usually described in nonspecific terms such as *de talla apuesta, loçana, plazentera,* and *fermosa* (169ab, 581ab, 596a, 653b, 910b, 911ac, 912a, 1318a, 1322a; of an attractive figure, elegant, pleasing, beautiful), and social status indicated through allusion to birth, *de buen linaje* (168a, 912a), worth, *rrica* (582b, 911b, 1318b), and social affiliation, *fija dalgo, panadera, monja,* and *mora* (911c, 116a, 1332b, 1508c; noblewoman, baker, nun, and Muslim woman, respectively).[13] In contrast, Don Amor advises that the Archpriest choose a beloved on the basis of specific physical attributes that I have argued incline her toward sensuality. Particular concrete traits are mentioned only in the cases of Endrina, Garoça, and Alda, discussed in chapter 1. The former two, with whom the Archpriest enjoys most success, have the long graceful necks, "alto cuello de garça" (653b, 1499c; a heron-like neck) and fascinating eyes, "con saetas de amor fiere quando los sus ojos alça" and "unos ojos que paresçían candela" (653d, 1502a, respectively), of the seducible beauty.[14] Endrina's hair, small mouth, and complexion are praised without the mention of details whilst Garoça sports "color fresco de grana" (1499b; fresh deep-red color), and, in addition to connoting purity, the description of her as a white rose (1500b) may allude to her coloring; again, in each case aligning the lady with the seducible beauty without making any explicit comparison. The general qualities that Don Amor suggests, "muger

fermosa, donosa e loçana [. . .] non quieras amar muger villana [. . .] muger de
talla" (431ac, 432a; a beautiful woman, big-hearted and elegant [. . .] don't
chose to love a peasant woman [. . .seek] a woman with good bearing or a
good figure), are present in part in the majority of the love objects, including
the Dueñas Cuerda and Ençerrada, but notably not in Cruz the baker, whose
low social estate also contravenes Don Amor's recommendation.

Specific mention is made of a lady's wisdom or command of a particular
field of knowledge in the case of the Dueña Cuerda, an accomplished
needlewoman, Garoça, who as a nun has mastery of culinary and apothecary skills, and the Dueña Ençerrada, who is wise in the virtuous ways of
women; "todo saber de dueña sabe con sotileza; / cuerda e de buen seso,
non sabe de villeza; / muchas dueñas e otras, de buen saber las veza"
(168bcd; she knows all women's knowledge with subtleness / clever and of
good sense, she knows nothing base; / she teaches many ladies, and other
women, good knowledge). The Dueña Cuerda, in her rebuttal of the go-
between, allies herself with the prudent, "que el cuerdo e la cuerda en mal
ageno castiga" (89d; the wise man and woman learn from others' mistakes),
recalling the wise and foolish hermeneutic established in the immediately
preceding sections of the *Libro*, and showing an apparently wise women in
action. Her wisdom and common sense are then confirmed through Ruiz's
implication that she adapts and applies the Aesopic tale of the Earth's Labor
Pains (st. 96–102; tale 3) to her own case, "que le [a mi vieja] avía enbiada, /
esta fabla conpuesta de Isopete sacada" (96cd; that she had sent to my go-
between, / this tale taken from those composed by Aesop).

The Archpriest draws direct parallels between the failed affairs with the
Dueñas Cuerda and Ençerrada, "Así conteçió a mí e al mi buen mensajero /
con aquesta dueña cuerda, e con la otra primera" (178cd; Thus it befell me
and my good messenger / with this clever lady, and with the other, first one);
and, the attributes of the Dueña Ençerrada and Doña Endrina are almost
identical:[15]

De talla muy apuesta e de gesto amorosa, (, de gestos amorosa)
loçana (doñegil), doñeguil (muy loçana), plazentera, fermosa,
cortés e mesurada, falaguera, donosa,
graçiosa e donable (rrisueña), amor en toda cosa.

(169 (581))

(With a very attractive figure, and a loving expression (, of loving expression) /
lovely (elegant), elegant (very lovely), pleasing, beautiful, / courtly mannered
and restrained, pleasant [lit. encouraging, pleasing, flattering], generous /
elegant and gift-worthy (smiling), love in everything.)[16]

Although the parallelism may derive from oral compositional practices in
which each beloved is being portrayed in formulaic terms as the culmination

of womanly attributes, the effect in the written text is to de-emphasize the individuality of the female characters, objectifying them, and offering them as a series of types, whose identifying trait takes on a similar iconic status to the deformities of the Two Lazy Suitors.

In the narrative of the first mountain adventures, there is no physical description to compliment the narrative; however, the self-naming of the mountain woman, "La Chata; / yo só la Chata rrezia que a los omnes ata" (952cd; Snubnose; / I am strong Snubnose who attacks men) may be significant.[17] The name derives etymologically from the Latin *planus*, flat, plain, or simple, and its Castilian form is frequently applied to noses whilst the usual application of *rrezio* is to a wild animal. The conjunction of these two words together with the underlying phallic associations of noses suggests La Chata enjoys a male vigor and sexual potency, which is reinforced by the comic action. The names of the other mountain women may also act to interpellate aspects of their character: Gadea de Río Frío is named for Saint Agatha, whose feast day is associated with carnivalesque gender reversal thus highlighting the reversal in the power dynamic throughout the whole episode. Menga Lloriente's name indicates both her lack and alludes to her weeping. Alda may be an allusion to the wife of Roland in the *Chanson*, and associated therefore with courtly values, or to the *aldea* or village, and thus emphasize her rural environment. In this sense, Jacques Lacan's observation that "in the poetic field, the feminine object is emptied of real substance" is borne out.[18] Nonetheless, the twists that the Archpriest encounters in each affair differ subtlety, and the love objects are frequently granted voice, which is not typical of the courtly love lyric to which Lacan alludes.

In every case a mediator is employed, usually a *mensajera* or *vieja*, female messenger or old woman, as with the Dueñas Cuerda, Apuesta, Devota, and Garoça and the Mora, who, after the amatory advice from Don Amor, is frequently identified as Urraca or Trotaconventos.[19] Trotaconventos is employed to make the affair with Endrina progress only after the Archpriest has made the initial approach himself. Although no direct allusion is made to Don Amor's *ars amatoria*, during the attempted seduction of the Apuesta Dueña the Archpriest observes the ability of female hawkers to gain access to the love object in terms very closely parallel to those in the Endrina episode (st. 699–700), drawing on the field of battle strategy, "ya vos dixe que éstas [las que venden joyas] paran cavas e foyas; / non ay tales maestras commo estas viejas troyas; / éstas dan la maçada—si as orejas, oyas" (937bcd; I already said that these women jewelry hawkers prepare undermining and ditches; / no woman is as skilled as these old bawds; / they strike the hammer blow—if you have ears, listen).[20] Trotaconventos's intervention in the affairs with the Viuda Loçana and the Mora bring no joy since she fails to sway them. Likewise, the unnamed *mensajero* in the third adventure fails to break down the beloved's resistance. Indeed, all three of the male go-betweens employed by the Archpriest are unsuccessful. Ferrand Garçía turns rival and seduces Cruz, the love object of the second affair. The final adventure fails to develop on account of the gossiping of Don Hurón, appointed only after Trotaconventos dies, with a recklessly comic lack of concern for his unsuitability for the task. In fact, in the case of the Apuesta Dueña, Urraca, the loyal female go-between, is chosen in contrast to Ferrand Garçía (913) thus suggesting that the Archpriest selects the go-between on the basis of experience rather than drawing on Don Amor's advice. The first, third, tenth, and thirteenth affairs, therefore, are unsuccessful for reasons other than the failure to employ a verbally astute female go-between with access to the lady, but in the cases of Cruz and Doña Fulana the Archpriest's selection of an unreliable, male go-between leads to disappointment. Although the appointment of a male bawd may lead to failure, the corollary—that an appropriately selected go-between will lead to success—is not borne out, despite Don Amor's insistence on the centrality of the procurer to the lover's success.[21] Rather, a series of obstacles, such as the difficulty of access, the existence of a rival, and female resistance, impede the development of the amorous adventures to different degrees.

The first and the third affairs are hindered by obstacles, and linked by references to liberality and largesse. The first, with the Dueña Cuerda (st. 77–107), is stated to have stalled at the stage of social interaction in the opening stanza, "sienpre avía della buena fabla e buen rriso; / nunca ál fizo por mí, nin creo que fazer quiso" (77cd; I always had pleasant conversation and laughter from her; / she never did anything else for me, nor do I think that she wanted to do so) since the lady is jealously guarded, and cannot be bought, "non se podría vençer por pintada moneda" (79d; she could not be conquered by shining coin). Despite being a positive quality listed amongst other advantageous traits, the mere mention of buying the lady strikes a truant note, and is associated with the theme of liberality and largesse in seduction, developed later in the affair (as discussed below), and throughout the *Libro*, such as in the advice of Don Amor (st. 451, 508–12). In order to obviate the social and moral obstacle, the Archpriest employs a female go-between as mediator. As with Endrina and Garoça, the Dueña Cuerda uses an exemplary tale, here the Lion's Share (discussed in chapter 2), to ward off the go-between's advances and to show that she has learned from other's misfortune, "yo te mostraré commo el león santigua; / que el cuerdo e la cuerda en mal ageno castiga" (89cd; I shall show you how the lion blesses; / since the wise man and woman learn from other's misfortune). The obstacle that the lady cites is not in fact the social convention

concerning the protection of women, mentioned by the Archpriest, but
rather the dangers to which women subject themselves if they become
involved in amatory affairs.

The visual image of the Dueña Cuerda as lion punishing a creature
lower on the hierarchical scale is appropriate to the context at the
intradiegetic level; however, it may strike a truantly humorous note
beyond the fun normally associated with a beast fable at the extradiegetic
level since the lion's anger in this tale is not depicted as righteous. The
lion's dominant disposition of wrathful is transferred to the lady later in the
affair (94c) as she grows enraged at the lack of loyalty evident in suitors,
who fail to make good on their promises, "Los novios non dan quanto
prometen" (95d; Lovers don't give as much as they promise). Her application of the Aesopic tale of the Earth's Labor Pains elaborates this point:
"Quando quier casar omne con dueña mucho onrrada, / promete e manda
mucho; des que la ha cobrada, / de quanto le prometió o le da poco o
nada" (97abc; When a man wishes to court a much honored lady, / he
promises and commands a great deal; once he has procured her, / he gives
little or nothing of whatever he promised her). The Dueña Cuerda figures
courtship as a form of economic exchange in which the suitor effectively
pays for, *cobrar*, the beloved and thus the financial aspect of courtship,
whether or not it leads to marriage, is highlighted. This theme is further
elaborated on in the third affair in which the Archpriest ironically lists the
gifts he does not send before mentioning the songs he does offer the Dueña
Ençerrada. The Dueña's rejection of his song compares spiritual and physical
goods:

Non quiso rreçevir lo, bien fuxo de avoleza;
fizo de mí bavieca, diz : "Non muestran pereza
los omnes en dar poco por tomar grand rriqueza.
Levad lo e dezid le que mal mercar non es franqueza.
Non perderé yo a Dios, nin al su paraíso,
por pecado del mundo, que es sonbra de aliso.
Non soy yo tan sin sesso; si algo he priso,
'Quien toma dar deve', dize lo sabio enviso."

(172–73)

(She didn't want to accept it, she spurned wretchedness well; / she made a
fool of me, / she said, "Men show no laziness in giving a little to take great
wealth. / Take it back and tell him that poor [lit. bad or evil] dealing is not
largesse. // I won't lose God, nor his paradise, / for a worldly sin, which is
the shade of the alder tree. / Nor am I so without sense; if I have taken
something, / 'Whoever takes ought to give', the wise man in his wisdom
says so.")

*Bavoquía*, the abstract term sharing its root with the concrete noun, *bavieca*, belongs to the same semantic field as terms conveying foolishness, such as *locura*, and is contrasted with the group associated with wisdom, such as *cordura* and *seso*.[22] Ruiz opposes the foolish status of the narrator as *bavieca* to that of the beloved, whom he describes as *cuerda* thus aligning her with the Dueña Cuerda, who also rejects the Archpriest's suit, and with the wise hermeneutic. The rejecting beloved and the unrequited lover are therefore clearly aligned to two of the hermeneutic positions outlined in the *Libro*, and each is aware of his or her position. The Dueña Ençerrada couches her reproach in terms that contrast the worldly, particularly financial, values of exchange with the salvific economy, and within the dynamic of this adventure link each of the protagonists with the two poles. Within the threefold hermeneutic, which I have argued that Ruiz advocates, there is a third position in which the Dueña Ençerrada could be viewed truantly as engaging in bartering the price of access to body, and of her soul, particularly at 172d, as she is drawn into the verbal field. The relationship between money and access to the beloved is also alluded to indirectly in the narrator's description of the Dueña Cuerda, as discussed above, and adds a humorous element to the two women's self-righteous rejection of the Archpriest since it undercuts their protestations of virtue and points to received medieval misogynist views.

The development of the first affair differs in each of the surviving witnesses, neither of which is coherently or logically structured, with the inclusion of three stanzas (st. 90–92) in MS S that are absent from the other extant witness. In MS G, after the Dueña Cuerda uses the Lion's Share to tell the go-between that she has learned from other's mistakes (st. 82–89), the narrative recounts how *mescladores*, meddlers or gossips, claim that the Archpriest boasted about his conquest, causing her, through the go-between, to chastise and reject him and his songs, definitively (st. 93–104). In S, between these two sections of the narrative, the relationship is made public, the two cannot meet and the Dueña Cuerda orders the Archpriest to compose a sad narrative song, which she sings. In both versions, there is a clear taboo on there being public knowledge of the relationship such that the Dueña breaks it off when exposure is threatened. In the first affair, a go-between circumvents the initial obstacle of difficulty of access to the beloved. However, the breech of secrecy becomes a second obstacle, compounded by the lady's fear of the lover's dishonesty, phrased in terms of exchange. As depicted in MS S but not in G the affair may, perhaps, be seen as a partial success because the lady pays heed to the lover's suit but it develops no further than social intercourse. In the third affair, the theme of exchange and largesse is reworked so that the beloved expresses her fear of potential damnation for little recompense. In the intervening adventure with Cruz, the theme of largesse also appears in the lewd comparison of the Archpriest's offer of old wheat with Ferrand Garçía's gift of a rabbit. Liberality is one of the qualities that Don Amor particularly recommends the lover adopt, and the concern with gifts and exchange links the affairs to the adventures in the *sierra*, exposing them as operating within the same ideological contours regardless of the social status of or power dynamic between the partners.[23]

As is the custom, Doña Endrina (583b) and the Apuesta Dueña (912b) are largely confined to the family *domus*, under maternal vigilance, providing a social obstacle akin to the jealous guarding of the Dueña Cuerda.[24] In an amplification of the *Pamphilus*, Doña Venus also alludes to the figure of a protective mother (643–44), which is later raised as a potential obstacle in the affair with Doña Endrina (686, 844–45). The Archpriest makes his first approach to Endrina in public, but has to proceed with much caution under the subterfuge of taking a message from a female relative (655–59), and, when the relationship fails to progress, he follows Doña Venus's recommendation of a go-between to circumvent maternal protection (645). The go-between, Trotaconventos, is forced to address Endrina's fears of exposure directly (851), and successfully uses a *philocaptio* to heighten Endrina's interest, weaken her resolve, and lure her into an encounter with the Archpriest-Don Melón. Urraca is able to help the affair with the Apuesta Dueña progress but, when the Archpriest teases her (920), a temporary obstacle arises since she discloses the secret and the Apuesta Dueña is subjected to increased vigilance by her mother (922). John K. Walsh observes that "Don Amor (442–43) had warned the Archpriest that he must flatter and commend his go-between."[25] Trotaconventos, however, ably distracts Endrina's mother Doña Rama, and opens the way to access to Endrina. It seems likely that Trotaconventos cites Doña Rama as a false threat in order to raise the stakes in her negotiations with the Archpriest in a similar way to her threat of a rival, discussed below. After Trotaconventos's death, Don Hurón, with his fourteen faults (1620–21), causes the failure of the final affair since he makes public the content of the songs that the Archpriest had composed for Doña Fulana; the breech of secrecy leads her to deny the affair, "Tira te allá, pecado, / que a mí non te enbía, nin quiero tu mandado" (1625cd; Get thee hence, devil, / you weren't sent to me and I don't want your message). After exposing the affair with the Apuesta Dueña, Urraca, the go-between, employs a clever ruse to make herself a scandal thereby undermining her own authority, just as public knowledge of priestly scandal damages his (see the introduction). The Apuesta Dueña is no longer guarded, but soon dies, probably as a result of the *philocaptio* that Urraca gives her (941).[26]

In the affairs with Endrina and the Apuesta Dueña, the use of white magic brings about the seduction of each of the ladies. Nevertheless, neither is straightforward. The Apuesta Dueña dies "a pocos días" (943c), shortly after Urraca achieves success. No explicit mention is made of the Dueña's seduction by the Archpriest and thus emphasis falls ironically on the skill of the very go-between who may well have caused her death by poisoning. In the case of Doña Endrina, the Archpriest's disavowal of the experience as exemplary narrative, references to the source, and the confusion of his identity with that of Don Melón de la Huerta or Ortiz suggest that the episode is not to be regarded as experiential, even within the framework of the pseudo-autobiography, and is a good example of Spitzer's poetic I, discussed below. Further to this, Alan Deyermond argues convincingly that the whole episode from the appearance of Don Amor to the Archpriest's statement that the adventure did not actually happen to him (180–909), "dixe la [la estoria] por te dar ensienplo, non por que a mí vino" (909b; I told it [the Endrina story] to give you an example, not because it happened to me) may be regarded as a dream-vision experience.[27] Consequently, it may be argued that the Archpriest does not enjoy a single sexual conquest.

A rival prevents the Archpriest's access to the love object in the case of Cruz the baker and the Dueña Devota, and is muted as a possible hindrance in the development of the affair with Endrina, as discussed below. The Archpriest opens his narration of the adventures with Cruz by explaining that his male go-between usurped him, "puse por mi mensajero, coidando rrecabdar, / a un mi conpañero; sopo me el clavo echar: / él comió la vianda, e a mí fazié rrumiar" (113bcd; I chose a messenger, thinking to be successful, / one of my companions; he knew how to do me over [lit. stick the nail in me]; / he ate the meat, and he made me chew the cud), as related in a comic sacroprofane lyric, with obscene undercurrents.[28] The Dueña Devota, on the other hand, is a widow, "más val suelta estar la viuda que mal casar" (1326d; a widow is better off single [lit. is worth more] than ill married), as Urraca's words suggest, and whom she encourages to take a lover. Indeed, the go-between's proposition contains an element of fact since, in frontier society, a widow may have been able enjoy the benefits of comfort and autonomy.[29] Urraca's words also have a degree of irony for at the literal level they treat the widow as a good susceptible to valuation, and raise the issue of whom the recipient of the capital attached to the widow-as-goods is since, particularly in frontier society, a wealthy widow is undoubtedly marriageable. That the Dueña is a widow is also reflected in what Jacques Joset considers to be the lyric taken by Urraca to the Dueña, and which attributes to a turtle dove the words, "non avedes pavor, vós las mugeres todas, / de mudar vuestro amor por aver nuevas bodas" (1329bc; don't be afraid, all you ladies, / of changing your lover to remarry).[30] Ironically the dove is normally associated with chaste rather than wayward widowhood, and consequently these lines are usually interpreted as a question, "Aren't you afraid [. . .] of deserting your first love to remarry?"; however, given the fact that Urraca is engaged in persuading the lady to abandon her mourning weeds, I see every reason to read her words as giving a truant twist to the tradition of the faithful turtle dove in order to suggest that women, in keeping with actual frontier practice, ought to seek subsequent relationships.[31] The Dueña at any rate does develop a relationship with another individual, whom she marries, and as a consequence the nascent bond between her and the Archpriest is dissolved, "por non fazer pecado, o por non ser osada" (1330c; to avoid committing a sin, or because she does not dare). Although not made explicit, it would appear that the Archpriest may have enjoyed fleeting and partial success despite the affair's brevity. Consequently, there is an ironic contrast between the failure of the affair with the Viuda Loçana, and the willingness of the Dueña Devota to engage in amatory negotiations. Notably, Trotaconventos proposes that the Archpriest seduce a nun following the dissolution of the affair with the Dueña Devota since the social obstacle of matrimony to another is thereby obviated, and the affair will not be threatened by the risk of public exposure (1332c; "non se casará luego, nin saldrá a conçejo").

The lady's lack of receptiveness also poses an obstacle to the success of the affairs. The Dueña Ençerrada episode is described as misspent wild oats on that account, "senbré avena loca rribera de Henares [. . .] 'Quien en el arenal sienbra non trilla pegujares'" (170bd; I sowed wild oats on the banks of the Henares / "Whoever sows seed on the sandbanks will not thresh much wheat"). As in the lyric dealing with Cruz, Ruiz again draws on the field of food to convey sexual euphemism. Two of the affairs that follow the advice from Don Amor result in immediate rejections: those with the Viuda Loçana and the Mora, the latter of which—like the adventures that occur before Don Amor's advice—is announced as a failure in the opening stanza. Ruiz's depiction of widows, particularly Doña Endrina, draws on the popular tradition of the merry widow, who cannot be chaste once her sexual appetite has been aroused and who is therefore unable to pursue the life of chastity that the church deems appropriate for her.[32] The Viuda Loçana, however, flouts this expectation and instead rejects her suitor. The Mora likewise reverses stereotypes; this time of the lascivious Muslim woman, and rejects the go-between's advances outright through "buen seso."[33] The *Fueros* and Alfonso's *Partidas* prohibit interfaith marriages, and sexual relationships between a Christian woman and Muslim man, but to the best of my knowledge make no mention of men who conduct affairs with Muslim women although rape resulted in the payment of a bride price.[34] Indeed, relationships between Christian men and Muslim women seem to have been "a relatively minor issue" in frontier society.[35] The obstacle in this case is therefore the Mora's good sense rather than the religious bar. The diglossic dialogue between the go-between and the Mora reinforces the humor of the reversal of the stereotype of lascivious Muslim.[36]

As noted above, Trotaconventos proposes the seduction of a nun, Garoça, since she will not marry, and consequently public exposure poses no threat. The spiritual dangers emanating from the seduction of Garoça are put aside in favor of worldly ones as Trotaconventos describes the wayward nature of nuns, and her own familiarity with them (1333, 1338cd, 1339cd–42). Like the Dueña Cuerda and Doña Endrina, Garoça defends herself by entering into an agonistic debate with Trotaconventos in which she adduces exemplary tales. Garoça argues that the bawd cannot be relied on to return her friendship and trust but rather will lead her into a situation of moral peril through falsely flattering words.[37] Trotaconventos counters that the nun lacks gratitude and the appropriate respect for an old servant who seems no longer to be of service but may yet prove useful; Garoça's unfounded fears may cause her loss.[38] The debate concludes when Trotaconventos concedes Garoça's knowledge of exemplary tales, and gives her the assurance of not being left alone in the Archpriest's presence in the way that the devil abandoned his friend, the thief, at the gallows. The assurance contains a considerable degree of dramatic irony since the bawd had already abandoned Doña Endrina to Don Melón's predations, and because the *exemplum* quite openly equates the nun with a sinner, but denies the parallel between the bawd and the devil. Further to this, Trotaconventos's early identification of her as a wayward nun proves accurate when Garoça observes that a woman must test the go-between before talking of love: the debate between the two is a ritual means by which the nun protests her superior moral and rhetorical status before inevitable compliance.[39]

Whilst the question of access is resolved in spite of the nun's seclusion at the episode's opening thus privileging worldly concerns over the spiritual, at the close of the adventure the Archpriest raises the issue of spiritual bar:

> Pero que sea errança contra nuestro Señor
> el pecado de monja a omne doñeador,
> ¡Ay Dios, e yo lo fuese, aqueste pecador,
> que feziese penitençia deste fecho error!
> (1501)

(Even if a nun's sin with an amorous man / is an offence against Our Lord, / Oh God!, would that I were he, that sinner, / who had to do penance for this wrongful deed!)

The postponement of discussion of the moral status of a love affair with a nun and the implication that she affords the promise of great sensual pleasure "todo plazer del mundo e todo buen doñear, / solaz de mucho sabor e el falaguero jugar" (1342ab; all worldly pleasure and all good courtship / greatly satisfying solace and flattering play) heightens the erotic tension implicit in the depiction of a sexual encounter with a forbidden female since it points to her accessibility and confirms the misogynist commonplace that all women are sexually available. Dramatic irony structures the tale so as to create an expectation of the Archpriest's success. Despite this, the Archpriest claims that the love service between them is "linpio amor" (1503c) in which Garoça prays for him, and which is the only sort of love for which nuns are appropriate.[40] The erotic expectations of the audience are, therefore, defrauded by an unexpected turn toward spiritual well-being; however, Trotaconventos's affirmation of the longevity of affairs with nuns (1332d) is proven inaccurate when the affair ends after two months with Garoça's death.

In all ten of the amatory affairs, the Archpriest employs a go-between to obviate social obstacles, such as difficult access to the object as with the Dueñas Cuerda, Ençerrada, Apuesta, and Endrina. The Dueña Ençerrada, the Viuda Loçana, and the Mora reject the go-between's overtures outright; the latter two cases reverse received stereotypical misogynist views of female conduct, and their reactions are ironically contrasted with those of the Dueña Devota and Garoça, respectively. It may be that the possible Arabic etymology of the nun's name as beloved points to a contrast between her behavior and the Muslim beloved's.[41] The Dueña Devota, like Cruz, is lost to a rival, the threat of which is raised in connection with Endrina. Once initial access has been achieved, the Dueñas Cuerda and Ençerrada raise different moral and social objections to the development of the love affair using the language of exchange; however, each focuses on the dangers, particularly the potential loss of social and spiritual standing, which would arise were the affair to enter into the public arena. The threat of exposure is realized when it prevents an affair with Doña Fulana, and when Urraca makes public the Archpriest's attempts to seduce the Apuesta Dueña, leading to increased vigilance on the part of the Dueña's mother. Maternal watchfulness also poses a threat in the affair with Endrina. The go-between outwits the mothers of the Apuesta Dueña and Endrina to gain access to the beloved, and uses a love philter or *philocaptio* to sway the object, resulting in the death, most likely by poisoning of the Apuesta Dueña, and in the seduction or rape of Endrina. Since the Archpriest disavows the tale of Endrina he can be argued to have had only minor success in the affairs. Ironically, Trotaconventos recommends an affair with a nun to avoid the problems experienced in secular relations. Despite the promise of sensual delights, however, the Archpriest and Garoça enjoy the *amor purus* of an unconsummated affair. In short, the Archpriest fails to enjoy physical satisfaction more than fleetingly, if at all. The selection of an appropriate beloved, in as far as the embodiment of the seducible beauty can be found, and of a skilled go-between do not lead to amatory success. Consequently, Don Amor's *ars amatoria* offers no more than deceptive words.

The triangulation of desire in the amatory affairs takes place not simply at the intradiegetic level through the presence of mediators, rivals, and obstacles but also through the external mediation of the Aristotelian heterodox view of love as natural to the animal, and consequently without sin for humankind. For the Archpriest as amatory predator, the naturalistic heterodoxy represents an animal drive that overrides the power of culturally determined literary, social, and sacred codes of behavior that contrive to restrict free sexual access to women, and which shore up the institutions of marriage and the church. It is at the extradiegetic level that the adventures with the mountain women can usefully be analyzed according to Girard's theory of the mimetic desire. The *serrana* episode (st. 950–1042) forms a closed cycle in which the Archpriest undergoes a series of four misadventures with mountain women in a hostile environment. The relationship between the content of the narrative *cuaderna vía* and lyric versions of each adventure varies.[42] This may be due to the fact that the lyrics do not purport to retell the adventures related in *cuaderna vía* but to be lyric recreations of the events narrated. This is implied by the transitional phrases used to introduce them:[43]

> Fiz de lo que ý passó las coplas de yuso puestas. [. . .]
> Desta burla passada fiz un cantar atal:
> non es mucho fermoso, creo, nin comunal [. . .]
> De quanto que pasó fize un cantar serrano,
> éste de yuso escripto que tienes so la mano. [. . .]
> De quanto que me dixo, e de su mala talla,
> fize bien tres cantigas, más non pud bien pintalla;
> las dos son chançonetas, la otra de trotalla;
> de la que te non pagares, vey la e rríe e calla.
> (958d, 986ab, 996ab, 1021)

(I made the verses written below about [or based on] what happened there. // About this joke [I] experienced I made a song like this: / it's not very pretty, I think, nor typical. // From everything that happened I made a mountain song / this one written below that you have under your hand. // About everything that she said to me, and her bad [or evil?] figure / I made as many as three songs, but I couldn't manage to portray her well; / two are little *chansons*, and other is a dance song [or about sex?] / whichever does not please you, see it and laugh and shut up.)[44]

The juxtaposition of two different verse accounts of a broadly similar story embedded in a sequence of four heightens awareness of the poetic level over message content. The privileging of the poetic level in turn emphasizes Ruiz's artistry and virtuosity in contrast to the physical debasement his narrator undergoes. The counterpoint between narrative and lyric meters offers Ruiz as poet the opportunity to work through various configurations of the encounter between an itinerant male character and a female peasant whilst pointing to the external mediation of the literary codes between the Archpriest and the mountain women. The Archpriest's encounters with the *serranas*, therefore, are not triangulated by intradiegetic factors such as the rival, the obstacle, or the mediator but rather by literary models of desire. However, the relationship between the mountain adventures and their intertexts, such as the pastourelle tradition, in which a knight encounters a peasant girl in an idealized rural landscape, and courtly love, drawing on Andreas Capellanus's *Ars amatoria*, particularly the sections on bought love, love of peasants, and the easy obtainment of the object, is not straightforwardly mimetic.[45] The pleasure offered by the pastourelle lies in the sexual charge of a man encountering a woman, usually of lower social estate, alone in circumstances that would have been regarded as taboo in urban circles and in courtly literature, and in which she would have been seen as potentially vulnerable to attack. The nature of the encounter ranges through the purely voyeuristic to acceptance or rejection of sexual advances, and it is usually couched in a courtly idiom. Ruiz inverts the pastourelle tradition and the role of predator in the game of love to expose male vulnerability, and to reveal the true nature of human desire.

In the first adventure, the mountain woman is named as "La Chata" ("Stubnose," discussed above) in both sections, but her geographical location seems to vary between "Loçoya" and "Malangosto." Malangosto, however, may have been chosen for its meaning, "Evil Narrow," as much as for its proximity to Locoya. The Archpriest is struggling through the adverse weather when he meets La Chata who threatens violence if he fails to pay the toll at the mountain pass. He promises her a pendant with a broach fastening and rabbit skin, and she throws him over her shoulder to carry him. The narrative closes with a humorous associative connotation based on two senses of *cuesta*, "e a mí non me pesó por que me llevó a cuestas; / escusó me de passar los arroyos e las cuestas" (958bc; and it didn't weigh upon my conscience [lit. worry me] that I weighed upon her [lit. that she carried me]; / I avoided crossing streams and hills). The concluding image of a weary traveler carried across a river on strong shoulders is a grotesque and carnivalesque displacement of the traditional representation of Saint Julian in the visual arts as carrying a leper on his shoulders across a river. The Archpriest's invocation of Saint Julian the Hospitaler against "La Chata endiablada" (963ab, quoted below) points directly to this reversal, and also links the Archpriest himself to the sick outcast.[46] To the best of my knowledge, the fact that Saint Julian is patron saint not only of travelers and pilgrims, but also of traveling minstrels has passed unremarked, and suggests the dual nature of the Archpriest's identity as itinerant priest and poet. The humor is compounded by La Chata's sex, the implied gender reversal of strength and dominance, and the fact that she is motivated by financial gain not charitable love. The lyric develops the action further than in the narrative by giving different dialogue, loaded with euphemistic language relating the fields of exchange, food and struggle to the sexual in a description of a shared meal, and implying that sexual intercourse took place to the mutual satisfaction of both parties, "ove de fazer quanto quiso; / creo que fiz buen barato" (971fg; I had to do everything she wanted; / I think I did a good deal).

The second adventure is linked to the first in that there are two references to the fact that the Archpriest does not intend to keep his promise of taking gifts to La Chata (972b, 974b). The second mountain woman, a cowherd in both narrative and lyric, is named only in the latter as Gadea de Río Frío; a toponym reminiscent of the pass of Fuent Fría mentioned in the narrative. The narrative and lyric broadly share the content of the first lyric—encounter, exchange of dialogue, implied sexual intercourse— although Gadea makes mention of her lover or husband, Ferruzo (980a) or *el vaquerizo*, "cowherd" (992f) in the narrative and lyric, respectively; the only allusion to a potential internal obstacle in the mountain adventures. In both versions of the second encounter, Gadea complains that it has been unsatisfactory:

Rogó me que fincase con ella esa tarde,
ca mala es de amatar el estopa, de que arde;
dixe le yo: "Estó de priessa, sí Dios de mal me guarde."
Assanó contra mí; rresçelé e fui covarde.

(984)

(She asked me to spend that afternoon with her / as it's bad to dampen a burning stove; / I said to her, "I'm in a hurry, as God may protect me from evil." / She got angry at me; I became afraid and was a coward.)

mas escotar me la [vianda] fizo;
por que non fiz quanto manda,
diz: "¡Roín, gaho, envernizo!
¡Commo fiz loca demanda
en dexar por ti el vaquerizo!
Yot mostraré, si non ablandas,

cómmo se pella el erizo
sin agua e sin rroçío."
                (992b–i)

(she made me pay for it [food]; / because I didn't do everything she asks, / she said, "Wretched, ugly, sickly man! / What a mad quest I undertook / by leaving the little cowherd for you! / I'll show you, if you don't yield [lit. soften], / how to peel a hedgehog[47] / without water or dew.")

Gadea evaluates the Archpriest's masculinity—conveyed through the reference to his wretchedness and to the possibility of his softening or wilting—in comparison to her rustic partner, and finds him wanting. The virility and sexual vigor of the Archpriest is thus called into question, confirming his physiognomy, and his earlier description of his own fear and cowardice at the mountain woman's anger reinforce this view. Gadea's use of the phrase *loca demanda* links her response to the narrator's evaluation of his experience in the mountains in the sequence's first stanza, as discussed below.

The third woman, named in the lyric only as Menga Lloriente, is encountered at Cornejo in both versions.[48] The four-stanza opening gives a cursory introduction describing how the mountain woman believes the Archpriest to be a shepherd. Commentaries on the episode normally take this statement at face value but its intense irony adds a comic note to the following lyric since *pastor*, "shepherd," is a positive epithet traditionally applied to members of the priesthood. If read in the context of the opening narrative, the Archpriest permits Menga's self-deception to continue as he engages in courting her, boasting of his knowledge of rural practices. His actions provide an example of the deceptions of love. His self-proclaimed proficiency in country lore in the third lyric is in direct contrast to his lack of familiarity with the mountains, and their customs in the first episode and second lyric, as discussed below, and points to the protean nature of the protagonist's character as Everyman. Taken out of context, the lyric demonstrates Ruiz's knowledge of rural practice and a particular lyric genre, corresponding to his claim in the prologue to show how to compose poetry, and "dar ensienplo de buenas constunbres" [p. 110; give example of good habits], as underscored by Menga's reference to good understanding, "casar me he de buen talento / con tigo, si algo dieres; / farás buen entendimiento" (1002cde; I shall willingly marry / you, if you give something [a bride price]; / you will have a good deal [lit. understanding]), which recalls the phrase's use in the prologue. Anthony N. Zahareas and Oscar Pereira consider Menga to be motivated by materialism, and hold the view that the reference to understanding recalls the prologue with malicious humor.[49] It is possible that the Archpriest's interactions with Menga are intended to be read as the knowing adoption of a false persona to deceive a simple rustic character, whose ignorance and low social estate render her a comic butt, in keeping with Capellanus's advice on the seduction of peasant women through guile.[50] However, the reading strategies advocated throughout the *Libro* permit the coexistence of contradictory interpretative stances dependant on the audience point of view, sophistication, and disposition, clearly differentiating between Ruiz as poet, and his protagonist, the Archpriest.

In the opening narrative, there is a strong emphasis on Menga's wrongful thinking and her forgetfulness of the danger of losing what has been achieved by seeking out unknown future gains. In the lyric, however, it is the narrator who claims to be seeking a bride or a mistress. If taken alone the lyric is generically "a traditional rural courting song," "with little grounds for reading coarse materialism into [Menga's] lines."[51] R.B. Tate rejects María Rosa Lida de Malkiel's contention that the rustic content would have proven humorous to an urban audience due to its focus on the lower estates and their interests.[52] Each of these views has merits. If taken in the context of the other mountain adventures and the *Libro* as a whole, it is likely that the rural and its arcane skills would have been comic to an urbane urban audience, whether secular or religious, due to its association with the debased and lack of decorum. However, were the lyric performed alone, or had it been an independent composition prior to its use in the *sierra* episode, Tate's view would hold since the lyric is a clever pastiche.

The lyric itself depicts the verbal interaction of a rural suitor and peasant girl, using the first-person voice, with little description apart from the opening stanza, which sets the scene. The suitor describes his talents in the varied work and leisure of the active rural male (999c–1001). His masculinity is displayed verbally through a literal domination of and superiority over the animal, particularly the mare, wolf, greyhound, cow, bull, and unbroken colt, and through the production of cream, wineskins, and sandals, mastery of music, dance, and wrestling, and in the song itself. I suggest that the skills of which he boasts should not all be read at the denotative level since aspects of them contain latent sexual content such as his claims to ride mares bareback and, most particularly, to churn milk and make cream. Butter and cream production are traditionally female activities; however, churning may allude to sexual intercourse, and *natas*, "cream," is a well documented euphemism for ejaculate. Indeed Monique de Lope discusses precisely this connotation of cream in relation to the feast offered to the Archpriest by La Chata but not in the context of the third lyric.[53] The lyric ends, as do the previous two, with the narrator undertaking a journey; here—as with La Chata—claiming that he will fetch the promised goods, "que ya vo por lo que pides" (1005g).

The third narrative and lyric do not contain descriptions of violent physical action as seen in the previous two adventures; however, the humorous contrast between court and country continues in the *enumeratio* of rural activities of which the narrator claims knowledge. Tate has observed that this is a feature of rural courting songs, and queried the extent to which such a list would have been seen as funny. In my analysis, however, other than the simple breach of decorum, one further aspect of the context supports the reading proposed by Malkiel. There is a notable contrast between the narrator's claimed knowledge of and skill in rustic practices, depicted through the verb *saber* in the lyric *enumeratio*, and the repetition of the verb *coidar* (to think or believe), in the opening narrative. The mountain woman is depicted as making erroneous assumptions twice in st. 994 through the use of *coidar*, where it is linked to forgetfulness, and the verb is repeated in the following stanza:

> Preguntó me muchas cosas, *coidós* que era pastor;
> por oír de mal rrecabdo, dexós de su lavor;
> *coidós* que me traía rrodando en derredor;
> olvidó se la fabla del buen conssejador
> que dize a su amigo, queriéndol conssejar:
> "Non dexas lo ganado por lo que as de ganar;
> si dexas lo que tienes por mintroso *coidar*,
> non avrás lo que quieres, poder te has engañar."
> (994–95, my emphasis)

> (She asked me many things, *she thought* I was a shepherd; / she left off her work to listen to a worthless message / *she thought* that she had me courting her; / she forgot the good adviser's words // spoken to a friend, wishing to advise: / "Don't lose what you've got for what you have to gain / if you lose what you've got on account of wrongful *thinking* / you won't get what you want, you could be deceiving yourself.")

The friend's counsel outlined by the Archpriest echoes his observation in the opening narrative that "quien busca lo que non pierde lo que tiene deve perder" (951d; whoever seeks what he has not lost must lose what he has), which expresses the conservative ideology found elsewhere in the *Libro*, and links the book to the importance accorded to curiosity as a danger prompting sin in monastic practice.[54] The contrast in erroneous thinking and knowledge in the third episode supports the propositions outlined in the prologue in that both erroneous thinking and the need for and knowledge of cultural practice is an attribute of the Fall. Ruiz therefore exploits the contrast between a rural lyric genre, the courting song, and the more courtly pastourelle, which traditionally exploits an idealistic rural *locus amoenus*, and whose interest lies in the contrast between the court and the country, to show that the split between court and country is false since the conventions of each are necessarily post-lapsarian, that is to say that they

are cultural products, only necessary to humankind because of our ontological status as fallen and imperfect. Despite the veneer of courtesy that
covers courtly affairs, they are motivated by the same animal drives. This
point is supported by the emphasis on the lack of Archpriest's knowledge
of the customary practices of the mountain range, as discussed below.

The fourth woman is named and given a toponym, Alda de la Tablada,
only in the lyric version. There may be a link to the second encounter in
that the narrator refers to his proximity to Ferreros in each. The narrative
and lyric differ more than any of the other pairs. The opening two stanzas
of *cuaderna vía* set the scene of mortal danger in which the narrator finds
himself exposed to wild weather at the peak of the mountain pass, and
thirteen of the fourteen remaining opening stanzas give a description of the
mountain woman's ugliness (see chapter 2). The lyric depicts similar
weather conditions but the woman encountered is first described as "fermosa, loçana / e bien colorada" (1024de; beautiful, merry / and of good
color), and the Archpriest addresses her courteously, using the formal *vos* as
opposed to *tú*, as occurs in the second episode, and calling her *bella, fermo-
sura*, and *amada* (1025b, 1026c, 1028e; beauty, comeliness, beloved), until
she refuses him, when she is described as *heda* (1040a; ugly), indicating an
attitudinal shift.[55] It is she who propositions the narrator, who, despite
being married, agrees to take her as a mistress, and receives a poor meal—
in marked contrast to that described in the first lyric—in return. She then
suggests that whomsoever gives her gifts will receive food and board from
her such that "nol coste nada" (1033e; it won't cost you a thing) so he
invites her to ask for "la cosa çertera" (1034c; something specific). As
Vasvári notes, the use of a noun without a specific referent, like the neuter
pronouns *lo*, "it," and *esto*, "that," and the Latin noun *res*, "thing," may
euphemistically and humorously create an expectation that she will allude
to the male sex organ or sexual intercourse. However, reminiscent of the
third lyric, Alda lists a number of items of clothing (1035–38); once again
the narrator promises to bring the goods, but she refuses to do business
without payment, and it is she who utters the closing words.

The sequence opens with a partial citation of I Thessalonians 5: 21–22
("Omnia probate, quod bonum este tenete / ab omni specie mala abstinete
vos"; Prove all things; hold fast that which is good. / Abstain from all
appearance of evil) as an *auctoritas* justifying the sojourn in the mountains:

> Provar todas las cosas, el Apóstol lo manda:
> fui a provar la sierra e fiz loca demanda;
> luego perdí la mula, non fallava vianda;
> quien más de pan de trigo busca sin seso anda.
>
> (950)

(Prove all things, the Apostle commands it: / I went to prove the mountains and I undertook a mad quest / then I lost my mule, I could find no food; / it is senseless to seek for what cannot be had [lit. for more than fine white bread].)[56]

The quotation of the tag in the stanza's first hemistich is a twofold memorative cue. It calls to mind the full Biblical versicle, and its context, in which Paul exhorts the Thessalonians to abstain from evil, and prays for their spiritual well being, and it may also allude to the Archpriest's earlier introduction of that authority in the discussion of the nature of man as animal (st. 71–76) prior to the first amatory adventure:

E yo como soy omne commo otro pecador,
ove de las mugeres a las vezes grand amor.
Provar omne las cosas non es por ende peor,
e saber bien e mal e usar lo mejor.

(76)

(And I, as I am a man like any other sinner, / have at times had great love of women. / It is therefore not worse for man to try things, / and to know good and ill and to use the best.)

The Archpriest misappropriates the Pauline dictum by glossing it to include knowledge of good and evil, "saber bien e mal," without any indication of how to select the best from knowledge of good and evil, or whether the best is understood in a spiritual or worldly sense or both. Further, the first hemistich of 76d may be interpreted as an admonition either to recognize good and evil, for example, through the operations of the faculties, or to gain personal, experiential knowledge of them, and points to the body/soul dichotomy that Ruiz sees in the faculty of memory, as discussed in chapter 1.

The opening stanza makes clear the link between unconsidered experience and the theme of loss through the juxtaposition of the allusion to the Archpriest's missing mule and its elaboration at 950d, and the syntagm *loca demanda* (950b) and its repetition in the third lyric. Ruiz underlines the point through a similar reiteration of *provar* in the narrative of the second encounter where the contrast in the verb's two senses, drawn out in the earlier misappropriation of Paul's authority, is exploited to comic effect by being applied to a banal, secular context in which the Archpriest is physically attacked:[57]

*prové* me de llegar a la chata maldita;
dio me con la cayada en la oreja ficta.
Derribó me cuesta ayuso e caí estordido;
allí *prové* que era mal golpe el del oído.

(977cd, 978ab, my emphasis)

(I *tried* to approach cursed Snubnose, / she hit me hard on the ear with her staff. / She knocked me downhill and I fell down stunned; / there I *proved* that a blow to the ear is a bad one.)

Stanzas 983–84, present only in MS *S*, contribute further to the thematization of *provar* in the second narrative as they introduce a proverb, "Agora se prueva / que pan e vino juega, que non camisa nueva" (983ab; Now it is proven / that bread and wine make play, not a new shirt), which applies *provar* to a venial context. The proverb may be a variation on "[. . .] que non moço garrido" (not an attractive young man) in which the sexualization of *jugar*, latent in 983ab, and discussed in chapter 2, is more explicit.[58] The proverb, in both versions, reflects the medico-hygienic view that excesses of food and wine predispose the individual to sexual desire, and is borne out by 970b–g, discussed below.[59] The variation of the proverb employed in the *Libro* asserts that the actions of food and wine in inciting sexual passion exceed not merely an attractive partner but even gifts and monetary influence, on which Don Amor had insisted (st. 488–514), and which have an important role in the adventures in the *sierra*, in particular.[60] In the first adventure in the *sierra*, unconsidered action exposes the Archpriest to violent attack, and to lust prompted by wine and food. In the second episode, the association of violence, food, and sexual intercourse made by the repetition of *provar* places them as keynote of the *sierra* adventures.

The description of the mountain adventures as *loca demanda* and *sin seso* at the opening of the episode recalls the contrast in the three interpretative positions discussed in the opening portions of the *Libro* (see chapter 1) linking the episode with the ribald's actions, and prepares the audience for the episode's carnivalesque and sexually scabrous content.[61] The second hemistich of 950b, however, suggests that, in recounting the experience, the Archpriest engaged in evaluative memory work, of the sort outlined in the prologue (pp. 109–10; discussed in chapter 1), permitting him to qualify his misadventures as *loca demanda* even although his curiosity in undertaking the trip had not been curtailed by the good actions of his higher faculties.[62] This view is born out by Ruiz's manipulation of *ver/verse* in the first episode. The use of the reflexive *verse* (to find/see oneself) locates the action in a moment that is subject purely to experience and the actions of the senses:

> En çima deste puerto *vi me* en grant rrebata:
> fallé una vaqueriza çerca de una mata [. . .]
> desque *me vi* en coíta, arrezido, mal techo [. . .]
> yo, desque *me vi* con miedo, con frío e con quexa
>             (952ab, 954c, 957c, my emphasis)

(On the peak of this pass *I saw myself* in dire straits: / I found a little cowherd near a bush [. . .] / since *I saw myself* in trouble, frozen with cold, and sickly [. . .] / I, since *I saw myself* [seized by] fear, cold and in difficulty)

When La Chata threatens him, also using *ver*, the Archpriest's passivity in the face of current action is emphasized further "el que non quiere pagar, priado lo despojo. / Paga me, si non verás commo trillan rrastrojo" (953cd; I'll rapidly strip whoever does not wish to pay. / Pay me, if not you will see how the chaff [or stubble?] is threshed). The allusion to threshing recalls the overlap between the sexual and alimentary fields in the *Libro*. A number of later traditional lyrics use the image of threshing, and the rhythmic movement that accompanies it with clearly sexual connotations. At four occurrences in nine stanzas, *ver/verse* occurs with a greater frequency in the first narrative than elsewhere in the mountain episode thus pointing to a deliberate increase in usage, and reinforcing my analysis of the use of the visual field to focus on the gap between experience and evaluative memory work.[63] If I am correct, the Archpriest's engagement in evaluative memory work suggests that, although judgment of the mountain adventures is achieved after the fact, they occur under the sign of the fallen flesh. In addition, it alerts the audience to the failure of the narrator's faculties of understanding and memory to operate effectively to correct will and prevent the journey. The second mountain woman, Gadea, also uses the phrase, "fiz loca demanda" (I undertook a mad quest), when she regrets her desertion of Ferruzo for the Archpriest. Her experience applies the notion of losing what one has in the pursuit of potential future benefits, introduced in the first two stanzas of the episode, and prominent throughout it, to a specifically sexual context.

The Pauline *auctoritas* is reprised in the final stanza of the sequence: "por dineros faze / omne quanto plaze, / cosa es provada" (1042cde; on account of money / man does as much as he pleases; / [this] thing is proven [or tested]). The use of *provar* echoes the opening stanza, and suggests that the test or trial proves that money can buy anything in an echo of Don Amor's advice on the importance of money in love (st. 488–514). As in the second narrative, the *auctoritas* is applied to truant worldly content. Nonetheless, when the episode opened, the Archpriest was testing no specific hypothesis but was simply prompted by curiosity to visit the *sierra*. However, within the hermeneutic dynamic established earlier in the *Libro*, a foolish reader would take the adventures and this conclusion at face value, perhaps assuming that its attribution to a female character makes its application to sexual relations particularly apposite. For a wise reader engaged in active memory, the use of the authority in its shorter form would act as a memorial tag to the broader Biblical context, ". . .and hold unto yourself that which is good," implying that the sense of good is spiritual, and that curiosity and the vain seeking of potential future gain should be put aside. The fact that a wild woman, associated with sin and desire, rather than the narrator, utters the phrase would further strengthen such a reading. The blessed reader would necessarily recognize that there is truth in Alda's assertion, however truant and sinful it may be; use the material, including the lesson about curiosity and future gain, as appropriate as memory work; and enjoy Ruiz's poetic virtuosity and the humorous content.

The risk to bodily health, particularly in the first and fourth episodes, and the second narrative, grounds the adventures in the *sierra* in the real dangers experienced by the unprepared traveler in a physically threatening environment, and contrasts with the idealistic literary treatment of the rural as *locus amoenus*, and with the outcomes of the serial adventures undergone by the questing knight or spiritual traveler.[64] Indeed the inclement weather and the difficult terrain or ease of getting lost are mentioned repeatedly.[65] The emphasis on food and drink in the adventures therefore evokes the fantasies of those who are deprived of sustenance, and correlates with basic physical needs for survival. The link between the threat of death, sex, and food is a prominent characteristic of the carnivalesque, causing de Lope to link it to the Battle between Don Carnal and Doña Cuaresma (st. 1067–314).[66]

The Archpriest's anxiety about hunger, introduced in the opening stanza, "non fallava vianda" (950c; I could find no food), depletes him physically, and undermines his masculine vigor temporarily in the first adventure but more seriously in the second where the threat to his priapism is mentioned to comic effect: "más querría almorzar, / que ayuno e arreçido, non omne podría solazar; / si ante non comiese, non podría bien luchar" (982abc; I'd rather have lunch, / since a man can't enjoy solace when he's hungry and frozen with cold, / if I don't eat first, I won't be able to wrestle well; see also 964efg, 970abc, and 1032–33). La Chata's offer of bread and wine (965d) becomes a veritable feast of rich country dishes, some of which have sexual connotations.[67] Their consumption restores the Archpriest and appears to incite desire in both parties:[68]

fui me desatiriziendo;
commo me iva calentando,
ansí me iva sonrriendo;
oteó me la pastora,
diz: "Ya conpañón, agora
creo que vo entendiendo."
(970b–g)

(I thawed out / [and] I smiled / as I warmed up, / the shepherdess eyed me / she said, "Alright my friend, now / I think I'm starting to understand.")

The euphemistic language of warming latently suggests the Archpriest's arousal in a comic exposure made manifest by La Chata's visual apprehension of it, and its unveiling in her uninhibited suggestion that "Luchemos un rrato: / lieva te dende apriesa, / desbuelve te de aqués hato" (971bcd; Let's wrestle for a while / get up from there quick / get those clothes off).[69] In the second adventure, however, the encounter between the Archpriest and Gadea leads only to failure and disappointment (992). Sustenance also plays a prominent role in the fourth lyric, where the meal Alda offers (1030–31) is a qualitatively inferior reversal of that given by La Chata, just as the narrative description of Alda is a parodic reversal of the seducible beauty. The role of the active rural male in food production becomes the focus of the third lyric, as discussed below.

The menace of peril, anger, and aggression toward the traveler increase in the first two adventures and contribute to the dangerous aura of the mountain adventures; but the fact that the dangers emanate from women and the environment further belittles the male protagonist, and forms part of the matrix of unexpected reversals that contribute to the humor. The lowering and abjection of the male protagonist in a space dominated by aggressive women is conveyed through the exploitation of the visual field for humorous effect to feminize and bestialize him. The humor is increased since his misadventures come about because of his own stupidity both in undertaking the escapade in the mountains, and in confronting the mountain women in the way he does. The comic sexual reversal in which La Chata is strong enough to carry a man on her shoulders, "Echó me a su pescueço por las buenas rrespuestas" (958a; She threw me over her shoulder on account of my polite [right?] answers) is intensified in the lyric, where she physically attacks him, before picking him up after he offers her gifts:

> La Chata endiablada
> (¡Que Sant Illán la confonda!)
> arrojó me la cayada
> e rrodeó me la fonda,
> enaventó me el pedrero.
> (963a–e)

(Possessed La Chata / (may St Julian [the Hospitaler] confound her!) / hurled her staff at me / and swung her catapult around / and pitched a rock at me.)

> Tomó me rrezio por la mano,
> en su pescueço me puso,
> commo a çurrón liviano,
> e levom la cuesta ayuso [. . .]

Pusso me mucho aína
en una venta con su enhoto
                    (967a–d, 968ab)

(She took me brusquely by the hand / and put me over her shoulders / as if
I were a worthless pouch, / and carried me downhill [. . .] / She put me very
quickly / in a little hut, in comfort [or with great energy])[70]

In the second encounter, the violence also involves a blow from a staff.
Gadea's verbal threat is played out as action that floors the narrator:

"quiça el pecado puso
esa lengua tan aguda.
Sí la cayada te enbío".
Enbió me la cayada,
aquí tras el pastorejo;
fizo me ir la cuesta lada,
derribó me en el vallejo.
Dixo la endiablada:
"Así apiuelan el conejo.
Sobar te," diz, "el alvarda
si non partes del trebejo.
Lieva te, ve te, sandío."
                    (990g–91)

("Perhaps the devil gave you / that very sharp tongue. / So I'll throw my
staff at you." // She threw the staff at me / [it hit] here behind my shoulders /
it knocked me sideways [?] downhill / right into a ditch. / The possessed
woman said, "That's how to string up a rabbit. / I'll hit your saddle / if you
don't leave off this game. / Get up, go away, fool.")

As the Archpriest becomes an empty, valueless pouch or a snared rabbit,
ethical and ontological boundaries are blurred to render him grotesque and
abject. The violence to which he is submitted in the first two episodes, and
which he fears in the fourth narrative, reifies and dehumanizes, casting him
as a worthless pouch, and as captured prey, rendering him the comic butt
of its slapstick, and denying him status as a subject.

The presentation of Gadea and La Chata as violent and dominant, and
of the former as angered (990b), presents an image of a much disordered
female body. The gigantism alluded to by de Lope is an impression created
through the ease with which the first two dominate the Archpriest, physically attacking and lifting him, and confirmed in the *descriptio puellae*
through comparison with Alda's larger physical characteristics, despite relatively little physical description of the other mountain women, and of
Alda in the lyric.[71] The strength of La Chata and Gadea make them physically

repellent, which also plays an important role in sexual humor since "men laugh at ugly women in relief because they are not threateningly different."[72] Part of the humor of the mountain women episode relies on the tendentious. Both La Chata and Gadea wield a phallic implement, a staff, against the Archpriest, and coerce him to perform sexually, and this contributes to the humor ideologically and psychologically. The weapon they use marks their social status as rustic peasants, and so forms part of the ideological matrix of humor in which the rural, and its deviation from urban and literary norms, is the target. In my analysis, the humor of the third narrative and lyric is predicated almost entirely on this basis. The *serranas*' use of the staff also signifies the threat of the enforced submission of the male subject to symbolic castration, and—by endowing the female with a phallic weapon—mitigates the horror by providing a replacement for its threatened loss so that, as in the tale of Don Pitas Payas, discussed in chapter 2, avowal and disavowal of castration take place simultaneously with transferal to a fetishistic object. As with the complex charge of humor in the exemplary fabliaux, in these two episodes, the audience may take a superior and voyeuristic position in which it views the physical abuse of male subject with a phallic weapon at the hands of physically powerful women as rendering the male protagonist other and abjected, a passive and submissive object, and take sadistic pleasure. In other words, part of Ruiz's parody of the pastourelle involves a queering of the genre so that the vulnerable object of the scopophilic gaze is not female but male. However, once again, the audience has the option of taking pleasure in a masochistic identification with the object of the abuse or the sadistic identification with the abuser, a phallic female.

Although there is a contrast in how the Archpriest evaluates his performance in the first two encounters, it is implied that he endures sexual coercion in each since, in effect, he exchanges sexual intercourse for sustenance. The strong association between the appetitive lower bodily urges recalls the misappropriation of Aristotle from the *Libro*'s opening portions, discussed above, in which the received notion of an instinctual animal drive toward procreation becomes a truant desire for an attractive object. In his dealings with the mountain women, the Archpriest is bestialized since he operates at the level of the Aristotelian animal, which encompasses man's sensitive soul but not his rational one, being driven first by the need for sustenance in order to survive, "mantenençia" (71c), and becoming capable of sexual performance only once his primary need is met. The sexual drive is secondary in the mountains, where the female partner often initiates the encounter; however, in the urban context, where comfort and nourishment are come by more easily, almost no mention is made of them, and the sexual drive prevails. Finally, there is no mention of the need to attend to spiritual health, to which the context of the Pauline versicle cited at the episode's opening points. In the topsy-turvy environment of the mountains, where women dominate the environment, work, the domestic sphere, and cultural expressions of life, courtly and urban conventions concerning conduct are irrelevant. Courtship and the circulation of women cease to be an overt operation of male culture threatened by liminal men and women with easy access to private, domestic space, such as priests, minstrels, and old women hawkers, and become the domain of the women themselves who, like the go-between, move without restraint outside. In this environment, when female desire and identity may be freely expressed, *cupiditas* and the lower bodily appetites, venial and sexual, explicitly come to the fore in sexual politics.

The mountain adventures show the various contours of such appetites through the desire for food and sex, and the need to attain a partner, be it through marriage or concubinage. Female dominance itself forms part of a grotesque and humorous reversal of gender politics linked to spring festivals, including fertility rites, which are associated with Saint Agatha's day on February 5. Gadea may be named for Agatha, whose phonic similarity to Romance *la cata* or *la gata*, "cat," led to her being known as the cat saint, and on which Ruiz may pun for La Chata's name.[73] Burke takes this argument further to argue that the allusion to Agatha, and, particularly the cat, may locate the *serrana* adventures as *charivari* or *cencerrada*, a popular ritual punishment beating executed to censure a privileged individual for exploiting public and temporally limited carnivalesque license for sexual transgression.[74] The mountain adventures are therefore humorous in their grotesque reversal of male and female sexual roles. As a wild place, where normative urban and literary values are not upheld, the mountain range carries a concomitant charge of danger; however, it is not fully aligned with nature but has customary practices with which the Archpriest, but not Ruiz, is unfamiliar. The emphasis on custom recalls the reliance of the Archpriest on aspects of heterodox Aristotelianism to justify his own sexually predatory practices, particularly the allusion to it in the affair with the Dueña Ençerrada (st. 166–67).

Custom, *usanza*, is introduced explicitly by both interlocutors in the first mountain episode; attributed to the Archpriest in the narrative, "Dexa me passar, amiga, dar te he joyas de sierra: / si quieres, di me quáles usan en esta tierra; / ca segund es la fabla, quien pregunta non yerra" (955abc; Let me pass, friend, I shall give you mountain jewels: / if you wish, tell me which ones are used in this land; / because, as the saying goes, whoever asks does not err), and to La Chata in the lyric, "Hadeduro, non te espantes, / que bien te daré que yantes, / commo es de la sierra uso" (967efg; Fool, don't be afraid: / I'll provide well so that you dine / as is the custom in the mountains). The Archpriest acknowledges that he is ready to enter into a process of exchange with La Chata, but that he is unfamiliar with mountain customs and values. In this manner, the contrast between the mountains and the urban setting of the other adventures is established, and the Archpriest becomes an alien in unfamiliar territory dependent on women for safe passage, whereas in the other amatory adventures he depends on the mediation of a go-between and the disposition of the object. The exchange also highlights the gender reversal implicit in the Archpriest's reliance on a woman for protection and sustenance.

In the second lyric, custom is linked again to the unfamiliarity of the Archpriest with the mountain environment; however, the erotic potential of finding a young woman in a lonely rural landscape is exploited:

> "Radío ando, serrana,
> en esta grand espessura.
> A las vezes omne gana
> o pierde por aventura.
> Mas quanto esta mañana,
> del camino non he cura,
> pues vos yo tengo, hermana,
> aquí en esta verdura,
> rribera de aqueste rrío."
> Río me como rrespuso
> la serrana tan sañuda;
> desçendió la cuesta ayuso,
> commo era atrevuda;
> dixo: "Non sabes el uso
> comos doma la rres muda"
>                    (989–90f)

( "I wander lost, mountain woman, / in this dense wilderness. / Sometimes one wins / or loses by chance. / But for this morning / I don't care much for the pathway, / since I have you, sister, / here in this green place, / on the banks of this river." // I laugh now at how she replied; / the very angry mountain woman / came down hill; / as she was daring; she said; "You don't know how / dumb animals are tamed")

The Archpriest introduces the idea of risk and play early on in his interaction with Gadea (989cd) before going on to imply that finding her in a lonely place gives him power over her (989ghi). Capellanus's discussion of the love of peasants in which he advises false praise and the use of force in a convenient location forms a clear subtext to the lyric.[75] Ruiz, therefore, engages with the conventions of the pastourelle genre, and the fantasy of male dominion over female physical vulnerability. The mountain woman, however, reverses the power dynamic by assimilating him to the animal, threatening him physically, and striking him with her staff. She makes explicit the impropriety of his mode of approach and lack of familiarity with rural custom by alluding to the domination of livestock. There may be an ironic echo of Andreas Capellanus's view that peasants love "naturally, like a horse or a mule"; Gadea's description of the Archpriest may be recalled by the third lyric, a rural courting song, in which man's dominion over the animal is mentioned. The Archpriest is the butt of an aggressive and slapstick attack, in Burke's analysis a *charivari*, provoked by his inappropriately courtly approach to an unfit object. The clash of courtly and country value systems and modes of address contributes to the humor.

In the urban marital market, where the circulation of women is usually the responsibility of father or husband, access to women is tightly controlled by social convention and by familial action, and women's appetites are constrained. In such a social environment, erotic triangulation becomes a necessary means of control of, and access to, the female constructed as object rather than subject, bringing men into relationship with one another to raise homosocial bonds and kinship links in socially sanctioned inter-sex relationships. Control of women through social codes also brings into existence illicit means of access to them as object. Women of lower social estate, such as Cruz and the mountain women, operate beyond the constrictions imposed on women of higher estate, and are sexually accessible. Nevertheless, the Archpriest either fails to seduce them or becomes the object of sexual predation himself, whether as lover or suitor. Within the fictional framework of the *Libro*, as with a number of fictional genres that deal with illicit sexual desire, such as those dealing with courtly love or that rely on a breech of marital fidelity to create humor, marriage is not at issue. In the *Libro*, the bar on marriage results from the fact that the protagonist is an Archpriest, who, by virtue of his ecclesiastical position, would have been pledged to celibacy and prohibited from marrying. However, as has been well established, despite the proscription of marriage and sexual relations, clerical concubinage was practiced and was even tolerated by secular townspeople. Heath Dillard observes that such were the demands of repopulation of the *meseta* that "secular society took little official interest in the clergyman's concubine except to establish her children's rights to inherit their father's property," and that sons served in town militia.[76] As discussed in the introduction, the church establishment was exercised by the way in which its doctrine could be undermined by the scandal associated with such relationships, and church reformers actively legislated against concubinage in the twelfth to fourteenth centuries.[77] Indeed the "Cántica de los clérigos de Talavera" (st. 1690–709), at the end of the *Libro*, deals explicitly with the issue of clerical resistance to the prohibition of concubinage. Ruiz does not reiterate the Archpriest's clerical standing nor insist on the Archpriest's repeated *concupiscientia oculorum* perhaps because of composing the *Libro* or its constituent elements for episodic performance or possibly because of the widespread secular assumption of the clerical concubinage; however, it should be noted that concubinage and serial adultery are quite different social practices.

The Archpriest adopts the position of an Everyman in his pursuit of women, avowing the prompts of nature, disposition, and habit as explanation in the overarching narrative structure. This is reflected in the protean identity assumed, which is a function of the poetic I, since, at the level of the individual episode, neither the priest's emasculinity and liminal status as a male with access to women nor the scandal particularly associated with priestly desire is foregrounded. However, the scandal and impropriety of a priest relating amorous affairs and tales loaded with tendentious humor to a public audience forms part of the extrinsic context of the *Libro*. The priest, who ought to be concerned with the health of the soul, narrates tales dealing with the failure of his own and his characters' ambition, particularly the urge to achieve coitus. His tales raise the specter of bodily corruption and disintegration and they directly bind the very processes that drive toward life to those of corruption and death. The centrifugal energy that links the compulsion for regeneration with the decay and death is a central facet of the Bakhtinian grotesque realism.[78] In the *Libro*, in my analysis, the potential to abjection is bound in the grotesque representation of the body.

An examination of the Archpriest as an abjected first-person narrator and performer of grotesque and humorous material will help explicate the ways in which Juan Ruiz creates a tension between the poetic I and the empirical I beyond that found in some other first-person medieval narratives. As a read text, the *Libro* is unified through the persistent if not continual presence of the first-person narrator, the Archpriest, whose role is enhanced by the rubrics in MS *S*. Indeed it may have been the case that many of its early readers were themselves clerics.[79] If, however, the majority of the text were being performed, perhaps over several sessions, then the extent of the role of the narrator as character would depend on which episodes actually comprised the total performance, without necessarily including the identity of the narrator as priest. In such a case, Leo Spitzer's pioneering view that "the medieval public saw in the 'poetic I' a representative of mankind," an Everyman, "whose empirical person was immaterial" but that could include the poet's "empirical personality" would be borne out with reference to the Archpriest.[80] Spitzer goes on to argue that Ruiz:[81]

is working within an old literary pattern, a traditional medieval genre (already Andreas Capellanus had written: "quod magis in amore clericus quam laicus est eligendus") which should not be narrowed down to an explicit personal reference.

Nevertheless, I should argue that by labeling the narrator a priest, the dynamics of the poetic I are complicated since the character is no longer a typical Everyman, a man, like every other, subject to sin and whose body is marked by the Fall, even if in particular ways. Rather the priest is a figure from whom his institution and flock expect to see exemplary conduct even should he endure a private struggle with sin. Spitzer himself addresses this point when he argues that with Dante, Ruiz uses the pseudo-autobiographical mode to "preach the *ordo caritatis*." A priest can, of course, be an Everyman since he is as subject to sin as any other man and in such a case heightened expectations of priestly conduct may add to the poignancy of his struggle. However, the ecclesiastical establishment repeatedly warns its own members against the scent of public scandal clinging to priestly cassocks since their sinful behavior is more dangerous than that of the layman because it undermines the church as institution, and threatens the souls of those for whom the cleric ministers.

In performance, whether authorial or minstrel, the conventions of the poetic I position the performer between nature and artifice much like a modern stand-up comedian, as a narrator who purports to speak of personal experience, making public scandal of private indiscretion.[82] Like the figure of the *rribaldo* in the Dispute in Signs, the performer of the *Libro* stands up in a public arena and adopts the personae of a learned and respectable member of a community deemed hierarchically superior—the ecclesiastical establishment—but the face he presents to the unwary public is a mask temporarily concealing his fallen status as narrative protagonist whether he be author or minstrel. Consequently, the issue of clerical virtue and concomitant authority as an embodiment of the values of the church is called into question. In an authorial performance, the narrator—whether posing as a priest or an actual priest—claims the fictional amatory adventures as personal experience, professes the status of poet, adopts aspects of the minstrel's role, and highlights the liminal nature that the roles of priest and minstrel share. The narrator, therefore, lays claim experientially to the cultural repertoire to which he purports in the prologue, and to expertise in secular and sacred domains.

If Vasvári's analysis of the *rribaldo* were accepted and could be applied to the Archpriest, then Ruiz makes his priest a talking phallus. The appearance of phallicism appertains not only to the upright posture of the performer, as was seen in the Dispute in Signs and in stand-up comedy, but to the exposure of the scalp through tonsure, which echoes the baldness of the traditional ribald, as discussed by Vasvári, and which can make of the performer a "kind of personified talking phallus, with his bald head as the *glans penis*."[83] In the traditional treatment of the *rribaldo* this maneuver contributes greatly to the base humor associated with the character. However, to treat a priest as a ribald, a phallus, is to emphasize the aggressive masculinity that the church and society would have him suppress, to render grotesque the gap between his conduct and social and ecclesiastic expectations of his emasculinity, which is consequently satirized. In a non-authorial performance, the narrative persona is a façade erected over the performer's own identity as he ventriloquizes a priapic priest, doomed to failure in sexual love. By focusing on amatory adventures and material that is sexually euphemistic, and presenting a tonsured individual as narrator, the phallic and abjecting nature of performance—in which an individual is picked out as the focus of attention by literally standing up before, or sitting, or standing apart from or surrounded by his audience—is highlighted.

The performer is abjected in that he is marked socially as belonging to a group that, as I discussed in the introduction, was treated as outcast by the ecclesiastical establishment on account of making public scandal out of inappropriate and unedifying material. On account of their ability to transgress barriers and affect the ethical conduct of others, a characteristic shared with priests, minstrels posed the threat of bringing inappropriate material to vulnerable and possibly sinful audiences and this maybe why they were refused absolution. If this analysis were accepted, then those performing pseudo-autobiographical texts with comic content are potentially grotesque and even abject since they occupy an "ontologically obscure" position, which John Limon has described as "the stand-up condition, which is a noncondition between nature and artifice."[84] The performer of the *Libro* realizes the potential to abjection in that he deals with explicitly grotesque and abject subject matter such as snot, sexual failure, lack of bodily integrity, and death.

*Méconnaissance* comes also in the performance of an individual who repeatedly faces the collapse of his ambition, and in the fact that the *Libro*'s narrator does not simply deal with such matters, but more importantly poses as a sick subject, often in proximity to desire and death. The repetition of the confrontation of narrator and characters with their own lack of personal physical integrity, bodily sickness, and the horrifying specter of death, often embodied in the feminine, prefigures Lacanian constructs of the psyche and its relation to desire. Slavoj Žižek is at pains to point out the relationship between the libidinal economy of courtly love played out as masochistic theatre and modern sexual relations in Lacanian analysis, whilst Jacques Lacan himself stated: "I do believe the influence of this [medieval courtly] poetry has been decisive for us," and was adamant that the structure of medieval courtly love bears a direct relation to modern laws of desire in two particulars.[85] First, it is a locus in which the operations of sublimation in relation to raising the Law of the Father against the fear of the maternal are valorized within the symbolic. In courtly love, the Lady becomes, in Žižek's analysis, the traumatic and uncanny Other, the Thing that resists symbolization, and around which desire is organized. Second, courtly love is a mode of erotics that provides a means of engaging in the play of pleasure inherent in an approach—always and necessarily oblique, attempted through detour and repetition—to the Thing, the impossible object, "the beyond of the signified."[86] In this regard, Lacan brings out the uncanniness of the Lady most forcefully in his discussion of the artistic technique of anamorphosis, in reference to the skull in Holbein's *The Ambassadors*, and a syringe-like optical cylinder that reproduces a Rubens crucifixion, concluding "courtly love was created more or less as you see the fantasm emerge from the syringe that was evoked just now."[87] Although Lacan appears to be considering the debate about the historical origins of courtly love at this point, his discussion of the reiteration of indirect and paradoxical Ovidian tenants in courtly love refers to the structure of courtly desire in relation to the organization of the psyche.

Lacan argues that the narcissistic element in courtly love, as in other arenas, functions also as limit indicative of the inaccessibility of the Other, which may be "cet Autre absolu, cet inconscient fermé, cette femme impenetrable, ou bien derrière celle-ci, la figure de la mort" (that absolute Other, the inaccessible unconscious, an inscrutable woman, or even, behind her, the figure of death).[88] Simon Gaunt's account of Lacan's economy of desire in relation to the gaze in courtly lyric summarizes elegantly the crux of the issue:[89]

> Put simply: if I am seen by the Other (or by others who may occupy the position of the Other in my psyche, for instance "an inscrutable women," or "the figure of death," and so on), and if the Other reflects an image of me that is whole, unproblematic, and beyond question, then I must be more than a self-induced illusion, more than a figment of my own imagination.

The gaze of the Other shores up the integrity of the subject by fulfilling the subject's own lack. The integrity of Lacan's Other, however, is also always illusory, already lacking what we desire and seek in it. At the mirror stage, the subject embodies himself physically and psychically through the foundational illusion of his integrity in the eyes of the Other.

The Archpriest experiences the disintegration of self most acutely during his seduction of Doña Endrina through the offices of the go-between, Trotaconventos.[90] Following advice from Don Amor, the Archpriest describes the nature of his plight to Doña Venus in the commonplace

language of the love-lorn, "Só ferido e llagado, de un dardo só perdido: /
en el coraçón lo trayo ençerrado e ascondido" (588ab; I am hurt and
wounded, I am lost on account of a dart, / I carry it in my heart enclosed
and hidden). The love sickness that the Archpriest endures emanates dangers that place him beyond the effects of medicine, "física nin melesina non
me puede pro tener" (589d; neither apothecary nor medicine can have any
benefit for me). In chapters 1 and 2, I argued that descriptions of the body
in the *Libro* are strongly linked to medieval scientific and theological
theories in such a way that the health of the body reveals the spiritual and
ethical status of the individual; for example, the Archpriest's body reflects
his priapic nature but also his lack of sexual success. In the context of the
*Libro* as a whole, the commonplace metaphor of the lover's wounds recalls
the Archpriest's attack on the physically contaminating nature of sexual
love, and problematizes a widely used metaphor.

Doña Venus reiterates Don Amor's advice that the Archpriest take a
reliable bawd. When the go-between suggests that the beloved is inaccessible, the Archpriest responds with a nine-stanza lament (783–91), most of
which describes the psychophysiological effects of frustrated desire. The
disappointed lover first fears the loss of his physical, intellectual, and spiritual
well-being, before turning to apostrophize the organs most complicit in
loving; his heart, eyes, and tongue:

¡Ay que todos mis mienbros comiençan a tremer!
Mi fuerça e mi seso e todo mi saber,
mi salud e mi vida e todo mi entender—
por esperança vana todo se va a perder.
¡Ay coraçón quexoso, cosa desaguisada!
¿Por qué matas el cuerpo do tienes tu morada?
¿Por qué amas la dueña que non te preçia nada?
Coraçón, por tu culpa bivirás vida penada.
Coraçón, que quisiste ser preso e tomado
de dueña que te tiene por de más olvidado,
posiste te en presión e sospiros e cuidado.
¡Penarás, ay coraçón, tan olvidado, penado!
¡Ay ojos, los mis ojos! ¿Por qué vos fustes poner
en dueña que non vos quiere nin catar nin ver?
Ojos, por vuestra vista vos quesistes perder;
penaredes, mis ojos, penar e amortesçer.
¡Ay lengua sin ventura! ¿Por qué queredes dezir?
¿Por qué quieres fablar? ¿Por qué quieres departir
con dueña que te non quiere nin escuchar nin oír?
¡Ay cuerpo tan penado, cómo te vas a morir!

(785–89)

(Alas, all my limbs are beginning to tremble! / My strength and my sense and all my knowledge, / my health and my life and all my understanding—/ for a vain hope everything is going to be lost. // Alas, grieving heart, foolish thing! / Why do you kill the body where you reside? / Why do you love the lady who does not value you? / Heart, it's your fault you live in suffering. // Heart, who wanted to be a seized and captured / by a lady who holds you as more than forgotten, / you put yourself in prison and sighs and cares. / You will suffer, alas heart, so forgotten, in suffering. // Alas eyes, my eyes! Why were you cast / upon a lady who does not wish either to glance at or see you? / Eyes, you wished to be lost on account of what you saw; / you will suffer, my eyes, in suffering and in growing dim. // Alas, tongue without fortune! Why did you wish to speak? / Why do you wish to talk? Why do you wish to converse / with a lady who does not want to listen to or hear you? / Alas much suffering body, how you are going to die!)

Such an apostrophe, in which the rhetorical figure of personification fore-grounds the psychological disintegration and disarray of the lover who then passes into a state of anxious stasis, is a commonplace of medieval love poetry.[91] The suffering and death caused by the organs implicated in sur-render to the beloved are emphasized throughout, using syntactic paral-lelism (785bc, 789abc) with antithesis (786bc), heavy *repetitio* of "¡Ay!" (783a, 784a, 785a, 786a, 787d, 788a, 789ad, 790d), *traductio* of *penar*, particularly at the end of stanzas (786d, 787d, 788d, 789d), reinforced by alliteration on *p-* (787cd, 788cd), with some further alliteration on *v-* (788bc, 790d) and *m-* (790, 791).

Personification of the heart, eyes, and tongue appears to divest the lover of responsibility for the act of loving but in fact attests to the disharmony of his estimative or intellective and sensitive faculties, and his consequent fail-ure to act ethically, and hold to the good. The protagonist's heart loves a lady who does not esteem him and who forgets him; his eyes look upon a lady who denies him sight; his tongue desires to speak to a lady who will neither listen to nor hear him. As a consequence of this action, all three organs will suffer, his eyes will grow dim, and he will die. The Archpriest's experience is predicated upon the visual field and the mind's processing of visual information and its relation to memory and attention. The lover's sensitive and estimative faculties desire the lady by apprehending her image as pleasing, dwelling obsessively upon it, and imprinting it upon the mind. The lady herself denies his image, and consequently the lover, access to her own faculties, withholding opinion, look, and word. The lover fails to hold her attention as a pleasing or desirable object, and she effectively denies his social existence, that is, his existence in the symbolic, thus inhibiting the progression of the affair. More traumatic and mortifying is his failure "to register desire, to leave a trace."[92] Consequently his place in the symbolic and his identity as subject is undermined. Her forgetfulness and failure of attention result in the state of dissolution that the lover experiences since he is constituted as neither subject nor object by another person. The Archpriest's response becomes hilarious as it results not from a genuine rejection by Doña Endrina but as the result of Trotaconventos's manipulating the situation, following *Pamphilus*, to her own advantage.[93]

By representing the lover as forgotten and unseen by an object that he sees and upon whose image he dwells, the lover's complaint predicates the coexistence of the lover and beloved within a single visual field, and in which each has the capacity to participate actively and passively by seeing and being seen. The bar on seeing women of good social standing seems to prevent the exposure of woman in the visual field as objects and subjects, and most likely relates equally to the fear that she may provoke desire in the viewer through a wounding look and that, as seat of a weaker intellectual capacity, she may be unable to put aside *cupiditas* for pleasing objects and thus be moved to sin. Competing medieval theories of vision, based on the extramission of visual rays from subject to object, the intromission of species from the object or a synthesis of both these processes, assume the existence of a visual field within which some objects are the focus of attention and sight, and others are passed over. In her doctoral thesis, Emma Gatland offers an account of the willful turning away from seeing the object in relation to the fourteenth-century female hagiography, drawing on Žižekan analysis and Augustine's treatment of vision in *De Trinitate* (11.2, 11.8). According to her analysis of Augustine's theory, "when appetitive attention is withdrawn from a body, the body ceases to be adhered to, becoming an invisible object over which attention can easily pass." For Lacan, the mutuality of vision is essential in constructing social matrices and locating the self within the symbolic order.[94] He states, "What determines me, at the most profound level, in the visible, is the gaze that is outside."[95] In this analysis, the disembodiment of the lyric protagonist in a moment of stasis is an instance of non-being in which the individual is not constituted through recognition by the collective and ceases to be within the symbolic order; it is an abject moment of the recrudescence of the repressed. However, the context of the lover's complaint exposes the Archpriest's own hypocrisy and forgetfulness since, following Don Amor's advice and as discussed above, he willfully imposed the love object upon his heart (578bc, quoted above).

I have argued that the *Libro* presents a continuum of bodies along a single ontological scale, the chain of being, with the animal and the bestialized human toward the lower end and the human body of divine Christ at the superior end. In the animal fables the beast may stand for the human, and in both animal fables and exemplary fabliaux the wounded body is an indicator of the vices of the fallen individual. I suggested that in the descriptions human characteristics point toward humoral disposition, whilst animal ones tend to be suggestive of particular categories of sin. In the case of the crucified Christ, the wounded body points toward the human aspect of his nature. My argument rests on the supposition that this is not incidental to the material that Ruiz uses in the *Libro*, but has come about as the result of a process of selection and adaptation, perhaps even as a conscious aspect of design but more likely arising from Ruiz's particular ideology as a cleric versed in schoolroom discourses about the nature of the human body and its relationship to the animal and the divine. I hope to have offered enough evidence to sustain this argument as viable.

The lover's complaint foreshadows the lyrics that deal with Christ's crucifixion and wounds (discussed in chapter 2) toward the center of the *Libro* and recalls Ruiz's treatment of wounded animal bodies, such as in the Horse and the Ass or the tales dealing with the wounded or sick lion. Each is couched as direct address and in both the wounded and debilitated body is the object of first-person lyrical utterance; however, the meditative and contemplative tone of the Compassion and Wounds lyrics contrasts with the lovers' apostrophe to his heart, tongue, and eyes. The assimilation of religious and secular discourses on love brings the two wounded bodies into play with one another, particularly through the meditative strategies of affective piety.[96] The contrast increases the affective impact of meditation on Christ's Wounds, borne for charitable love of humankind, and, by representing the lover's passion in a humorous context redolent of the trauma of personal disintegration, augments the bathos of the lover's malady. The only appropriate focus of the desiring gaze is Christ's body, for he is the only object that can be incorporated and incorporates others.

In this chapter, I examined Ruiz's treatment of the amatory affairs, which is the main element that sustains a thread of continuity in the *Libro*. I analyzed the ten affairs with urban ladies from the perspective of Girard's notion of the erotic triangle to demonstrate that the encounters are worked out within a very narrow paradigm. The Archpriest is prompted to seek a beloved by the need to avoid loneliness or to recuperate from the suffering caused by a previous affair, and, in the cases of the Viuda Loçana and the Dueña Ençerrada, his lust is aroused by mimetic desire, which recalls the Archpriest's tale of the drunken hermit. He adopts a position of radical Aristotelianism to naturalize desire but applies it truantly to insist that the object be pleasing. With the exception of Doña Endrina and Cruz, the amatory object is chosen by sight, perhaps reflecting this justification, or on the recommendation of the procurer; but, contrary to Don Amor's advice, there is no evidence that either the Archpriest or the panderer have had privileged visual access to any of the beloveds. The women display a limited number of character traits and general physical characteristics, reflecting contemporary expectations of female behavior and attractiveness but represent a variety of different social and religious groups. The three named beloveds deviate most from the model. Cruz, a baker, appears to have been chosen only for her easy virtue, and Doña Endrina and Doña Garoça each manifest a small number of the physical characteristics that indicate the sensual nature of a seducible beauty. The expectation of audience and lover that the Archpriest will achieve sexual relations with them is defrauded in all three cases: the baker is seduced by the pander; the widow by Don Melón, a dream counterpart of the Archpriest; and, the Archpriest and the nun enjoy *amor purus*. The seven unnamed women are desubjetivized and located as a members of a set of minimally differentiated types.

Following Girard's model, the affairs are marked by the existence of a mediator, and obstacles, such as prevention of access, a rival, or female resistance. Difficulty of access arises on account of the fact that urban society controls access to women through marriage in order to prop up its symbolic system. In all ten of the encounters a go-between acts as mediator to gain access to the object. Although poor selection of the procurer leads to amatory failure, a good choice of pander does not guarantee success even when the beloved possesses indications of meeting Don Amor's criteria. This is particularly borne out by the fact that Urraca Trotaconventos, the bawd par excellence, fails to set up a prolonged and satisfactory sexually consummated affair for the Archpriest, making the address to women in his lament for her passing especially ironic:

> Dueñas, non me rrebtedes, nin me digades moçuelo,
> que si a vós sirviera, vós avríades della duelo;
> llorariades por ella, por su sotil anzuelo,
> que quanta siguía, todas ivan por el suelo.
> Alta muger nin baxa, ençerrada nin ascondida,
> non se le detenía, do fazía debatida
>
> (1573–74b)

(Ladies, don't condemn me, nor call me a little boy / for if she had served you, you'd grieve for her / you would weep for her, for her subtle fishhook, / since however many ladies she pursued, everyone of them was brought to ground. // Low or high estate, cloistered or hidden, / nothing stopped her, when she swooped down)

There is an increasing movement into the sacred sphere from the attempted seduction of the Viuda Loçana and leading up to that of the Mora, with the irony that the Archpriest enjoys the greatest degree of reciprocation with Garoça, a spiritual lover, and with the Dueña Devota, who rejects him on her marriage, and the least with the Viuda Loçana and the Mora thereby reversing received stereotypes of the merry widow and the lascivious Muslim woman. The rival may be another lover, a legitimate suitor, a specter raised by the go-between to increase the beloved's capital, or the lady's spiritual bridegroom. Ironically, in contrast to the Dueña Devota's new husband, Garoça's spiritual marriage to Christ does not prevent the development of her affair with the Archpriest. The lady's resistance is most frequently on account of the fact that her spiritual and social capital is at stake in an unequal exchange.

At the extradiegetic level, the Archpriest's desire is mediated by heterodox Aristotelianism and, in the urban context, Ovidian tenants of sexual pursuit. This is, of course, most evident in the Doña Endrina episode that Ruiz has recast from the pseudo-Ovidian *Pamphilus de amore* and *De vetula*. The pastourelle and Andreas Capellanus's *Ars amatoria* configure the contours of sexual desire in the Archpriest's adventures in the topsy-turvy world of the mountains, where the lack of social constraints on women allow the lower bodily appetites to come to the fore. The retelling of a basic story in which the meeting between itinerant male and a mountain woman in an isolated location leads to talk, food, and wooing foregrounds the poetic function of the mountain episode and exhibits Ruiz's poetic and narrative virtuosity. The norms of the pastourelle are reversed so that the male subject becomes the object of the predatory female, whether she seeks marriage, concubinage, or sexual relations, and the genre is queered as its charge of voyeuristic pleasure becomes focused on the reified male whose masculinity is undermined by the phallic female subject's sexual predation and violent aggression. The dangers emanating from the mountain women are particularly apparent in the reversal in physical strength, gigantism, and the potential for sadistic violence in the first two episodes, and the final narrative in the *sierra* section. The idealistic setting of the pastourelle is also parodied in the *serrana* section, where the real environmental dangers of exposure and hunger are raised as a further threat to undermine the male subject. The proximity of death and the twin appetitive animal drives first raised in the narrator's misapplication of Aristotle becomes a dominant motif in the mountain adventures, linking them very strongly to the carnivalesque. Further, the convergence of the drives toward survival and reproduction reflects the actual wording of *De anima* in which, in Francisco Rico's analysis, they are taken together as single topic of discussion.[97]

The theme of loss as a result of unconsidered action recurs throughout the mountain adventures where it is linked to the need to apply the evaluative faculties in interpretation. The Pauline *auctoritas*, which opens the episode, alludes specifically to the positive evaluative actions of the faculties of the soul whilst it is made clear that, although the Archpriest reevaluates the experience through its narration, the adventures were undertaken out of curiosity and without due engagement of the intellective and evaluative faculties. The theme is expressed in the first narrative, in the second narrative, and final lyric through *traductio* on the verbs *ver/verse* and *provar*, respectively. *Ver/verse* underscores the immediacy and unconsidered nature of the Archpriest's experiences whilst *provar* points to the need to weigh up actions. Just as, through evaluative memory work during the narration of his adventures, the Archpriest can label his experiences as *loca demanda* and *sin seso* so too does the mountain woman, Gadea. In the second and third encounter, *provar* is used to generate hygienic laughter when it is applied to inappropriately secular and banal contexts producing the truant judgments that a blow to the ear hurts, wine provokes lust, and money can buy anything, particularly love.

Unlike the urban women, the mountain women circulate freely in their environment and, like urban men, are prepared to exchange material goods as part of courtship to win favor. The difference in milieu and environmental conditions leads the Archpriest's sexual drive to dominate in the city, where his other physical needs are easily met, and his need for nourishment to come to the fore in the mountains. In each, he depends on others for his appetites to be met, in the city he has recourse to a pander, usually female, to gain access to the beloved, and in the country he depends upon the women he meets for his very survival. Urban and rural amatory practices are contrasted, but, although Ruiz alludes humorously to Capellanus's "On the Love of Peasants," and positions the mountain women low on the ontological scale, he neither naturalizes peasants' amatory practice as being an animal-like surrender to "nature's urging" nor idealizes it as in the later pastoral tradition. Instead both urban and rural practice are presented as cultural products with specific customary practices controlling their structures in keeping with the assertion in the sermon-prologue that the institutions and products that shape post-lapsarian civilization arise on account of the Fall (see chapter 1).[98] Human sexual desire is constructed as a direct product of the Fall that arises from the post-lapsarian loss of control over the reproductive function thus dissolving the split between court and country even if the laws and customs that regulate its practice differ in each of these environments.

Throughout his fourteen amatory adventures, the Archpriest adopts a protean identity, most likely as a function of his adoption of the poetic I, as discussed by Spitzer, and his religious status is neither reiterated nor emphasized, except perhaps in passing.[99] The first-person narrator's shifts in identity are most evident in the Doña Endrina section where he becomes Don Melón, and in the mountain adventures where he adopts different civil and religious statuses, claiming, for example, to be seeking a marital partner, and to be married or betrothed, and where the different women address him in terms that at a literal level reflect different socioeconomic statuses, but which are likely to be politeness markers of different degrees.[100] Other than in the ironic reference to the Archpriest as *pastor* (994a), discussed above, his civil status as priest is not foregrounded in the narrative; however, it does feature as part of the extrinsic context of the *Libro* causing the aroma of scandal to cling to the character. The Archpriest's amatory adventures render him a sick subject marked by post-lapsarian characterological imbalance, and bring him into direct contact with death, through the passing of two of his beloveds, the Apuesta Dueña and Doña Garoça, and of the bawd, Urraca Trotaconventos, thus linking the processes of life and death. As a sick subject in contact with death, ignobly and unsuccessfully making repeated indirect approaches to the amatory object, the Archpriest becomes abjected, and the depiction of his encounters with the mountain women further desubjectivize and demasculinize him rendering him the butt of tendentious humor. The disintegration of the self is directly presented in the lover's lament, which shows the disharmony of the faculties and represents the lover as failing to leave a trace in the words, thoughts, and deeds of the beloved thereby denying his subjectivity and abjecting him. The figurative dismemberment that takes place in the lament prefigures the meditative dismemberment of Christ in the lyrics dedicated to the Virgin toward the middle of the *Libro*, and calls into question the propriety of the overlap between the medical and religious lexicon by ironically contrasting passionate sexual love, in which the lover suffers on account of the disorganization of the post-lapsarian body and soul, and Christ's Passion, borne to deliver the sinner from the effects of the Fall.

As a performance-text the *Libro* has three important similarities to twentieth-century North American stand-up comedy, as discussed by John Limon: the performance of the self, abjection, and the fetishistic substitution of another object for the phallus. As Spitzer argues, medieval audiences are likely to have taken the first-person narrative voice as an Everyman at the level of the individual episode as representing the type of experiences to which everyone is potentially subject. Nevertheless, I hold that in the context of the whole *Libro* the adoption of the identity of priest problematizes the representative status of the poetic I since the church as an institution was exercised by the need for probity and chastity in its priests, and because, if Dillard's evidence is taken into account, parishioners would have been aware of the widespread truancy of clerical conduct, and regardless of tolerance for clerical concubinage, would have been likely to be wary of priests who engaged in serial relationships. Since priests were a group, like panders, with privileged access to women, they posed a potential threat to the chastity of marriageable women and thus to the two institutions that shored up the symbolic order, marriage and religion.

The narrator of the *Libro* is abjected as literally standing up or apart from the group in order to perform a narrative of sexually euphemistic and tendentious material in which the first-person performer continually describes his own amatory failure, and is engaged in an on-going *méconnaissance* in which he constructs himself as predatory lover whilst displaying a body marked by its fallen status, by sin and consequent sickness, and under threat of or in contact with death. In addition, by adopting the identity of tonsured cleric the performer of the *Libro* becomes himself the fetishistic object that replaces the phallus in stand-up comedy just as, according to Vasvári's analysis, the Roman in the Dispute in Signs was a kind of talking *glans*. This maneuver cancels out the priest's emasculinity, and exposes the dangers to a social order dependent on female chastity of his masculinity whilst striping the individual of threat since he desires but cannot achieve his object.

# CONCLUSION

## SEX, SCANDAL, AND SERMON

### Sex, Biology and the Fall

Psychic forms and the fallen human body are bound up in one another in the *Libro*. The individual human subject is "carried in soul but expressed in body," as exemplified in descriptions of the Archpriest and the seducible beauty, which deviate from schoolbook norms in order to express the somatic state through physiognomy, and in the exemplary fabliaux, where sinful acts lead to the disfigurement of body and soul.[1] The effects of the Fall realized on the empirical person of the Archpriest are emblematic of its consequences on Everyman. Despite being a Venerean subject who enjoys some virility, his physiognomy marks him as an individual prone to failure in love. His ontological and ethical status, and that of Everyman, is called in to question when it is shown that the Archpriest's position on the chain of being is, in fact, a feminized one in which he is less than a perfect and complete male, and shares qualities indicative of a sinful nature with Alda, the mountain woman, and the seducible beauty. Sin, particularly but not solely lust, marks the human body, revising its status down the chain of being away from the divine. Spiritual sloth and curiosity permit desire to direct the memory away from the fit usage of objects, and toward the improper to put the subject at risk of losing life and soul. Lust causes a fragmentation of the male subject, who experiences stasis and disintegration through a confrontation with his own *méconnaissance* and being denied a place in the symbolic. His body ceases to be fit for labor, and he loses his ability to assert masculinity as constructed socially through the imperative to aggression, sexual domination, and reproduction. Its imperfect expression is the female body, which in the higher forms depicted in the *Libro* is marked by the inclination to specific sin, and in its lower forms is assimilated to the bestial, and even the demonic. Although the Virgin is presented as an interlocutor in heavenly glory, and as witnessing the Crucifixion, attention centers on her field of vision not her person.

In keeping with medieval medical views, Ruiz uses a bipolar model of human biological sex, with a tendency to position the male higher ethically and ontologically. Overlap in the characteristics of Alda, the Archpriest, and the seducible beauty points to the continuity of physical being in which the female may display masculine or bestial features, and the male feminine ones. Alda's position is the lowest of the human subjects described since she is bestial, and demonic whilst Christ's participation in the hypostatic union positions him at the apex of embodied creatures. The bipolar sex model is embedded within a continuous, linear, and hierarchical chain of being. Alda's bestial nature, humoral dominance in the human and animal, and human characteristics in the anthropomorphized beasts reinforce this view. The continuity from male to female, and from human to animal on the chain of being render the debased and fallen body a site of doubts about the unique status of the human in the economy of salvation, and raises anxieties about damnation and death as located in the feminine and in desire for women, itself feminizing.

In the mountains, where the codes that govern urban social intercourse do not operate, women dominate social and sexual transactions and the venial appetites come to the fore to expose their debased and debasing nature. The need to control women gives rise to male traffic in women through marriage and generates the internal mediation of access to them in triangular desire. In the amorous adventures, licit access is mentioned in the dream vision of Don Melón and Doña Endrina, in the mountain episodes, in the threat of a suitor as a rival for Doña Endrina and the Dueña Devota, and in the absence of such a threat in the case of Doña Garoça. Instead, the focus is on repeated, indirect approaches to the illicit female object through a pander. When an individual pursues women outside of seeking legitimate marriage within a social order that relies on female sexual continence and honor to shore up its symbolic system, he must resort to secrecy. In this way, scandal and exposure become keynotes in sexual relations, and it appears to be this process that leads to triangulation through rivalry, mediation, and obstacles in the *Libro*.

At the extradiegetic level of the *Libro*, the fact that desire is mimetic and structured by cultural models (heterodox Aristotelianism and the pastourelle to cite but two) points to the abuse of the institutions and codes on which human society is founded through the misdirection of fallen human faculties, particularly memory. Although the *Libro* is an exemplary composition, the Archpriest's behavior and the secular amatory codes that govern it are not offered as models that will lead to sexual success even if they may illustrate some of the ways in which love can be wrongly directed. Rather the Archpriest, along with the other lovers and the truant beasts, is a negative *exemplum* whose grotesque but fittingly disfigured and punished body prompts repulsion and scorn, and from whose imitation self-love and fear of God should keep the reader or audience.

## Scandal: The Role of Priest as Autobiographical Narrator of Amorous Adventures and as Tendentious Joker

Although none of the amatory adventures foregrounds the narrator's status as priest, the issue of clerical probity and celibacy is highlighted. The satire on clerical concubinage, "Cántica de los clérigos de Talavera" (st. 1690–709), amongst the end-pieces in MS *S*, with its parody of epic and courtly love lyric convention, points to the vitiated status of the churchmen of Talavera as fallen, rather than attacking church ideology or the institution of celibacy *per se*.[2] The Archpriest, however, does not engage in the more socially—if not ecclesiastically—acceptable practice of keeping a concubine but in a series of fourteen sexual misadventures thereby contravening the expectations of both church and secular society. In theory, since the clergy, like old women hawkers and minstrels, had privileged access to women of all estates, it potentially threatened their chastity to undermine two of the central institutions of contemporary society: marriage and the church. In practice, in the *Libro*, the Archpriest fails to achieve a sustained—or indeed any—sexual relationship, receives very limited reciprocation, and does not enjoy direct access to the urban women, always employing a go-between. Consequently, any reader or audience member following up the suggestion of the sermon-prologue that ways to practice mad or worldly love can be found in the *Libro* will be sorely disappointed.

As subject of desire, the Archpriest experiences a sick self, marked by post-lapsarian characterological imbalance, who is in contact with death, and who makes repeated failed approaches to the object. However, he engages in series of *méconnaissances* that permits him the ambition of success and allows the forgetting or suppression of previous failure. In contrast to the male protagonists of the exemplary fabliaux, the Archpriest does not directly confront the image of the divided and fragmented self but experiences unrequited desire as a disintegration and disorganization of the self and the body. Whilst the Archpriest acts as a predatory male in town, in the mountains the need to attend to bodily survival over the reproductive drive becomes paramount, and he becomes an object of predation himself. The interconnection between the appetitive drives, nourishment, decay, and death is transformed into the carnivalesque register of inversion where the repetitive nature of the Archpriest's pursuit of women is underlined by the reiteration of each adventure in two different meters. As object of desire, the Archpriest's bodily integrity is threatened by violence and exposure leading to his desubjectivization and emasculation.

The combination of the fact that the protagonist's clerical status remains unremarked, and the protean identity adopted presents a poetic I, standing for the fallen nature of Everyman, despite the presence of details about the character's empirical person. However, the Archpriest, as narrator of the *Libro* as performance-text, is abjected through a complex and interrelated series of mechanisms. First, the performer is literally separated from his public. Second, his performance of a pseudo-autobiographical account of amatory failure is an artifice, in which the character whose identity he adopts is engaged in an on-going *méconnaissance* in which his self-presentation as lover is belied by his actual failure, disposition, and complexion. Third, he relates sexually euphemistic and tendentious material in the grotesque register. Fourth, his somatic and bodily experiences as subject and object of desire bring him into proximity with death. Finally, he describes his own humorally imbalanced body, marked by the effects of the Fall, and is embodied as sick, diminished, and emasculated. Despite this, by performing a tonsured cleric, like the Roman in the Debate in Signs, he himself becomes a fetishistic object whose presence disavows the castration anxiety raised by ecclesiastical expectations of the Archpriest's emasculinity; that is, the conventional limits placed on a priest's performance of socially established markers of masculinity, such as male display, aggression, domination, and reproduction. Given the Archpriest's specific role in a single-sex institution, where he would have had the care of the clergy in his arch-presbyterate, the institutional and fictional denial of his drives is necessary in order to diminish the threat that his sexual appetites pose to a symbolic order dependant on obligatory heterosexuality and female chastity.

## Sermon

The Father God exercises an all-seeing gaze over the individual, whose access to knowledge is vitiated by the effects of the Fall, which determines physiological and ontological status and by the inclination of the faculties of the soul toward good or evil: movement toward good, however, is facilitated in the healthy pre-lapsarian or grace-endowed intellective soul only. The combination of specific corporeal weaknesses made manifest in humoral disposition, and the faculties' ill operation contaminates the body. Overall, Ruiz presents a pessimistic view of humankind's ethical status in which determinism plays a strong role but can be overcome. His pessimism about the incapacity of the post-lapsarian human to do and will good is entirely orthodox. Likewise his use of the sermon-prologue and supporting *auctoritates* locate him in a divinely sanctioned chain of authority within official Church ideology. Human cultural institutions and artifacts shore up the slippage produced by the Fall; but their function and meaning can only ever be contingent since they depend on individual fallen human subjects for their right operation and manipulation. Nonetheless, bodies defiled by sin are a function of the grotesque humor of the indecorous in which punishment is appropriately rendered, and their affective function is opposed to the pathos engendered by meditation on the frailty of Christ's pierced body, subjected to a rhetorical dismemberment when each wound becomes the object of lyrical contemplation. As Sarah Beckwith has argued, by stressing the duality of Christ, that is, the human permeability and fragility of His divine body, the meditative and affective treatment of the Wounds renegotiates the relationship between the sacred and the profane(d) to bring into psychic play the embodied self and its place within the symbolic.[3] Christ's body is not so much a body upon which to gaze but rather one with which to become infused. In the *Libro*, however, it is approached indirectly through the mediation of the Virgin's spectral gaze, and through contemplation, and consumption, of its embodiment in the host.

## The Visual

Ruiz's discussion of the role of text and image in supporting post-lapsarian memory suggests that the *Libro*'s visual images are susceptible to the mnemonic practice in which they would be incorporated or imprinted in the faculties of both the intradiegetic interlocutor to whom they are addressed, and the audience. This is the basis for Ruiz's request that the *Libro* circulate, and be used by whomsoever is adequately equipped to do so. Such a maneuver implies that the descriptions are predicated on a scopophilic pleasure residing mainly in treating the other as an object to be appraised, and constituted by a necessarily spatial dialectic. In each case, the interlocutor's directed gaze tames the dangers emanating from that object as unknown, unknowable, and threatening to achieve specular knowledge and possession whilst the audience enjoys a privileged gaze of a visual field that encompasses the two interlocutors and the object described, and which may interiorize the object as other, as site of specific sin. In all three of the exemplary fabliaux, for example, the visual forms part of the mechanics that construct a grotesque moment in which the protagonists are confronted with their own acts of *méconnaissance*, and it grants the interlocutor and the audience a complex yield of pleasure from the coexistence of fantasies of domination and submission. It is, however, manipulated in the two tales related by Don Amor to raise a homosocial bond that lures the

Archpriest into a *méconnaissance* of his own in which he constructs himself as a successful lover and wielder of a powerful phallic gaze.

The Archpriest's love lament depicts a rhetorical dismemberment of the subject, which reverberates with the later meditative dismemberment of Christ in the lyrics dedicated to the Virgin. The fetishization of body parts and the superimposition of ironically contrasting amatory, medical, and religious lexicons show a continuation in the treatment of all bodies in the *Libro*, whether they be human, animal, or divine. Human beings and animals endure physical disfigurement as a sign of the Fall, Christ endured his Passion as part of the economy of salvation to deliver the sinner from its effects. An opportunity for personal and social renegotiation is offered through meditative and affective compassion, in the sense of fellow suffering, prompted by the internalization of Christ's image in the faculties and, through Communion, of His body in the sinner's own. Human and animal bodies are interjected directly into memory through their verbal depiction by another character; in contrast to this, Christ's body, however, is approached indirectly through the Virgin's gaze, and in the host.

The sermon-prologue implies that God's panoptic gaze, however, is located beyond this scheme as all seeing and all knowing: just as the audience exercises its gaze over a visual field extended beyond that of the interlocutors, God's gaze encompasses its looking. Ruiz employs a similar visual and spatial dynamic in his description of Don Amor's ruby-topped tent (st. 1266–301), which occurs when the Archpriest hosts his triumphant visitation. During the *descriptio*, Don Amor and the Archpriest remain silent and inactive, and the ekphrasis—with its personification characters—is thus foregrounded, positioning it as a mental picture subject to the memorative process of *lectio* and *meditatio*. Intellectual *acedia* may be expressed on the narrative level: the Archpriest is incapable of interpreting the extremely commonplace Labors of the Months, and curtails his description of the tent's interior with a brevity topos alluding to tedium, "por non vos detener, / e por que enojoso non vos querría ser" (1301bc; so as not to detain you, / and because I don't want to be irksome), despite the presence in the tent of incredible oddities (1301a). Likewise Don Amor's powers wane as he retires to bed, "con sospiro e como con coidado" (1303d; with a sigh and as if careworn), and is deserted by his retinue.

Ruiz's description of a tent would also call to the memory of audience members of appropriate disposition and cultural competence other such descriptions whose poets, in their turn, actively selected detail to generate meaning, just as Ruiz himself does with physical description. The luminosity and soporific qualities of the ruby atop Don Amor's tent, for example, may have indicated, along with generic markers, that this episode is, in fact, a dream vision.[4] In the majority of analogues, the cycle of interior adornments has a thematic relevance beyond its literal sense. In the *Libro de Alexandre*, for example, it "places Alexander's deeds in historic and moral perspective" to point to "the futility and fleetingness of human achievement and the vanity of human ambition *sub species aeternitatis*."[5] In art historical sources, such as on the portals of cathedrals, in programs of interior wall paintings in churches, and in books of hours the Labours frequently form part of a totalizing narrative of the place of calendar time, controlled by God's cosmological pattern, in relation to liturgical time to form "a story about the sacramentalisation of history."[6]

In the light of this, in much the same way that the decorative program in Alexander's tent suggests his dominion, what the Archpriest reports having seen in Don Amor's tent appears to place *natura*, in the sense of the created world, under Love's power in accordance with heterodox Aristotelianism. Yet, what the Archpriest sees is marked by confusion and contingency. It is a disoriented and slothful visionary's incomplete report from the domain of sleep, which is not fully explained by a diminished guide. The implicit comparison of Alexander and Don Amor, therefore, suggests that Amor and his powers are fragile and transitory, and places him with the providential plan under the Father Creator's panoptic gaze and exposed to the audience's appraising faculties. *Mappamundi*, such as the one illustrating an English Psalter of ca. 1260, depict the Father God positioned in the top register above his creation exercising his panoptic gaze over the whole of nature, just as the illuminations in the manuscript of the *Primera partida* show God as lawgiver above King Alfonso.[7]

## Ideology

Ruiz presents a largely conservative ideology in the *Libro*. He argues that there is a disparity between the faculties of the healthy or grace-endowed soul, and the fallen ones. The effects of the Fall are writ not only on the imbalanced faculties of the post-lapsarian soul but also on the body through iatromathematical influences, which determine physiognomy and humoral character. The vitiated nature of the human soul leads to the production of cultural artifacts and institutions whose purpose is to shore up human weakness. The individual agents who transmit knowledge and comprise the institutions may seem unfit when subjected to human scrutiny but only God's knowledge of intention is complete. Interpretation should therefore take into account the possibility of polyvalent or contradictory meaning, virtuous use, and the existence of divine intention, even in base human action. Individuals may use hygienic laughter, and put whatever material comes to them to appropriate use, if they are blessed with the appropriate cultural competences, and disposition. The foolish or sinful will laugh but not avail themselves of the hygienic application of laughter, the utility of the content for memorization, or appreciate the artistic virtuosity. The wise will use the *Libro* appropriately but miss or lack the hygienic ability to laugh. The blessed will apply multiple cultural competences to put the humor to appropriate hygienic use by employing the *Libro de Buen Amor* as an *auctoritas*, and in expelling despair about the human condition.

The *Libro* presents a negative view of human sexual desire as pollution of body, soul, reputation, and estate; a view shared by the Archpriest and Don Amor. The exemplary fabliaux of the Young Miller and Don Pitas Payas, uttered by each of the two interlocutors in their debate, are linked by the eroticization and debasement of the male body, and its connection with the spheres of labor, food production, and exchange, and coupled with images of contamination and pollution—which also appear in Two Lazy Suitors—to show a shared ideology of the destructive effects of sexual love on the individual and on social order.

In general, the treatment of female characters conveys received medieval misogynism in an unmarked way in the exemplary fabliaux and in the amorous encounters. Don Amor's view that women can be bought forms a subtext to several of the amorous adventures, even when it is adduced by the lady to protest the nature of the exchange in which she is being invited to engage. In the urban context, erotic triangulation increases the symbolic capital of women but gives rise to illicit practices of seduction; a market dominated by, but not exclusive to, female panders. The preeminence of venial appetites in the female-dominated mountains expresses the fear that unrestrained female desire is socially disruptive, but comic deflation, for example, in Alda's grotesque description, and the presence of fetishistic objects to mitigate the menace of symbolic castration contain anxiety. Ruiz explores common social stereotypes about the sexual availability of women of all estates to defraud expectations that his protagonist will enjoy consummation.

Particular dangers emanate from disruption to the social body, represented by bodily boundaries and the polluted hierarchy of animals. Ontological segregation points to a concern with maintaining strict category boundaries, such as of species, social status, geographical location, and ethical conduct. The maintenance of such boundaries and of the physical boundaries of the body shores up the symbolic order by guaranteeing the unicity of the human soul, and its consequent salvation, the dominance of male over female, and the continuity of feudal and ecclesiastical hierarchies. Rightly ordered human community is present in the endeavor to maintain and transmit knowledge, and in religious communion.

Urban and rural society, however, is disordered, and different customary practices relating to desire operate in each. The ten urban women whom the Archpriest desires are presented as members of a set or series, sharing a limited number of traits that conform to social (and literary) norms of appropriate female behavior. The three named women, Cruz, Endrina, and Garoça, deviate most from type whilst the others are minimally differentiated by the possession to an iconic degree of a specific characteristic drawn from the general ones that the beloveds share. The mountain adventures also play out within a limited scenario, in which the Archpriest rather than the peasant girl is presented as the object of amatory attention. The rural is a particular site for the expression of the humor of the indecorous but the split between town and country is false since in both post-lapsarian or natural animalistic appetites dominate, and the institutions that guarantee order, such as law, the church, and marriage, are undermined.

Ruiz explores the tension residing in the double-nature of the priest as a sinner whose public conduct should appear exemplary. As an individual whose conduct is particularly subject to scandal and public scrutiny, the priest should take particular care in maintaining his boundaries and avoiding pollution. Ruiz's pessimism concerning the fallen status of the human leads him to represent the Archpriest as aware of the contaminating effects of desire yet unable to overcome his animal drives, and prepared to engage in a *méconnaissance* to construct himself as a potent, phallic male. Even so, the description of the Archpriest as possessing virile qualities but condemned to disappointment in love, and his repeated, failed approaches to the object hold in check the potential threat from the priest's emasculinity as a male with access to women but barred from openly engaging in social practices of masculinity, such as aggressive display and reproduction. Ruiz may also be concerned with the blurring of the roles of priest and minstrel, both of which involve public performance and access to the female. He positions himself as a schoolman, with a broad grasp of many aspects of the curriculum, as an able poet, displaying linguistic virtuosity across sacred and profane registers, and he aligns his art with that of the poets of the *mester de clerecía*. In contrast, the empirical person of his protagonist fails to exercise his religious duties, takes on the role of lover unsuccessfully, and his poetry is often rejected or fails to seduce the lady to whom it is addressed. Juan Ruiz, therefore, opens a space between the historical author and his protagonist.

# NOTES

## Introduction

1. All translations are my own unless otherwise indicated. "Debit enim quilibet predicator dare bonum exemplum in opere, et bonam doctrinam in uerbo, quia si bene uiuat et nichil predicet, quantum prodest exemplo, tantum nocet silentio [. . .] Debet enim predicator esse quasi liber et speculum subditorum ut in operibus prelati quasi in libro legant, et in speculo uideant quid sibi faciendum est," *Summa de arte praedicandi*, p. 24.

2. St Augustine of Hippo, *Concerning the City of God*, IX.XVII, p. 364: "[opus est quidem mediatore. . .] sed tali qui nobis infimis ex corporis mortalitate coaptatus [. . .] mundandis liberandisque nobis vere divinum praebeat adiutorium," *City of God against the Pagans*, p. 220.

3. Canon 10 of Innocent III's Lateran IV (1215) decrees that bishops appoint "viros idoneos [. . .] potentes in opere et sermone," p. 239, (suitable men, powerful in deed and word, p. 240) to preach. Waters *Angels*, examines how sermon theorists analyze the embodied and performative nature of preaching.

4. Robert of Basevorn, *Form*, p. 123. "Tria enim sunt necessaria actum praedicationis exercenti, scilicet puritas vitae [. . .] Secundum necessarium actu praedicanti est competens scientia [. . .] Tertium necessarium est auctoritas, qua mittatur ab Ecclesia," *Forma praedicandi*, p. 241. Basevorn's manual often forms the basis for discussions of preaching theory since it is viewed as typical, was widely disseminated, and is available in modern editions and translations. It was available in manuscript form in Castile before 1500: Faulhaber, "Retóricas," p. 203.

5. Robert of Basevorn dedicates chapters six to twelve of his *Forma praedicandi* to the preacher's authoritative forebears, particularly Christ, Paul, Saint Augustine, Gregory the Great, and Saint Bernard. Murphy in *Arts* examines the chain of authority outlined in preaching manuals.

6. I accept Waters' arguments in *Angels*, pp. 30–56, concerning the double nature of the preacher's role, and its imitative function in relation to Christ. On the duplex nature of Christ as embodied God see Beckwith, *Christ's Body*, pp. 46–50, 112–17. Consider, for example, Robert of Basevorn's observation: "Et in hoc [the first thing necessary to preaching, cited above] est magna et maxima praesumptio quod ipse in actus hierarchicos se initiat et divinos, protestans se publice quasi divinum et deiformem cum simpliciter sit

deformis," in *Forma praedicandi*, p. 241: "And in this there is a great, even a very great, presumption that he is initiated into hierarchical acts, yes divine acts, and publicly shows himself to be, as it were, divine and godlike, although actually deformed," in *Form*, p. 123.

7. I have capitalized *Buen Amor* since I interpret the title as referring to Good Love's Book, where Good Love is the nickname of the bawd but I note that this strategy underplays onomastic wordplay. I refer to the author as Juan Ruiz, the first-person protagonist as the Archpriest, and the book as *Libro*.

8. Waters, *Angels*, pp. 41–44. Faulhaber, "Retóricas," does not list Thomas's *Summa* as amongst those available in manuscript in Castile; Murphy, *Arts*, pp. 317–18 notes that it was overlooked until 1938, two years after Charland's *Artes* appeared; and it is from Charland that Faulhaber draws his information.

9. Waters, *Angels*, pp. 36, 37. Faulhaber, "Retóricas," does not list Maurice or Humbert as available in Castile pre-1500; Tugwell, "Humbert of Roman's Material for Preachers," pp. 105–17, lists three manuscripts now in Spanish collections.

10. Faulhaber, "Retóricas" provides a hand list of the sixteen preachers' manuals available in MS in Castile before 1500; of these, four or five (if we include Faulhaber's no. 138, the pseudo-Bonaventuran *Ars concionandi*) are pre-1400. Of these, only Alain de Lille's *Summa de arte predicatoria* is present in multiple copies (Faulhaber nos. 124–28); for the remaining three, I give Faulhaber number, and author and title or *incipit*: F120, "Ab habundandum materia predicationis in thematibus"; F133 [Guillelmus de Alvernia], *Rethorica divina*; and F139 [Robertus de Basevorn], *Forma predicandi*. For sermon studies in the peninsula see Sánchez Sánchez, "Vernacular Preaching in Spanish, Portuguese and Catalan"; for valuable work underway, see the series Catálogo de la Predicación Hispánica Medieval (Salamanca: Seminario de Estudios Medievales y Renacentistas).

11. Alfonso X of Castile (1252–84) oversaw the composition of the *Siete partidas* between 1256 and 1265; they were reworked from 1272, and finally promulgated in 1348 by Alfonso XI, who gave earlier local legal codes, *fueros*, priority, with the *Partidas* to be used to fill lacunae: see Kleffens, *Hispanic Law*, p. 217 and Gómez Redondo, *Historia*, pp. 512–16.

12. Alfonso X, *Primera partida*, p. 150. The *Siete partida*'s compilers drew on standard canon law sources: Gómez Redondo, *Historia*, p. 525. For sermon theorists' concern with bodily integrity and gender, see Waters, *Angels*, pp. 2–3, 16, 20–24, 36–38.

13. Alfonso, *Primera partida*, 150.

14. Martín Pérez, *Libro*, pp. 246–48, 204. I give in-text book and chapter references.

15. I have used the phrase, "undue sexual experience," as a single label for a man who remarries, who marries a woman who is not a virgin, and for bigamous and illegitimate marriages. Martín Pérez, *Libro* gives a similar definition, pp. 233–34, and uses the concept of bigamy for sexual impropriety within marriage. Public scrutiny is explicitly mentioned in laws 16, on public penance; 34, on the secret sins of the clergy; 36, on avoiding scandal

in relation to frequenting female religious houses; 37, on integrity of conduct; 38, on women living with priests; and, 44–45, on priests maintaining kept women. On such priests and their women, see Dillard, *Daughters*, pp. 131–32, Linehan, *Ladies of Zamora*.

16. Martín Pérez, *Libro*, p. 206.

17. On the exclusion of women from public preaching and teaching, see Martin, "The Injustice of Not Ordaining Women"; on the basis of their bodily nature as a prohibitive factor, see Minnis, "*De impedimento sexus.*"

18. Swanson, "Angels," pp. 165–66.

19. Small game trapping is permitted (I.VI.lv). On hunting imagery in the *Libro* see Seidenspinner-Núñez, *Allegory*, pp. 45–53, which she associates with the diabolic, and Phillips, *Imagery*, pp. 88–89, 175–76.

20. Alfonso, *Primera partida*, p. 176.

21. Martín Pérez, *Libro*, pp. 334–35.

22. This is implicit in the emphasis on the public nature of minstrelsy; hunting is explicitly stated to distract the laity from devotion, and to cause the clergy to break from dignified conduct in Martín Pérez, *Libro*, p. 335.

23. Translation from Waters, *Angels*, pp. 49–50: "Vnde, manifeste patet quod qui in predicatione tales gestus faciunt, stulti reputantur et magis uidentur esse histriones quam predicatores," Thomas of Chobham, *Summa*, pp. 302–03; Waters, p. 194.

24. Swanson, "Angels," p. 165.

25. Martín Pérez, *Libro*, pp. 444–47. I have translated *pasafríos* in the second category as "itinerants" since I have not been able to find a detailed definition: it is not listed in Kasten and Nitti, *Concordances* nor Corominas with Pascual, *Diccionario crítico etimológico*, II.

26. Martín Pérez, *Libro*, p. 445.

27. Walsh, "Juan Ruiz." For a defense of the term *mester de clerecía* see Uría, *Panorama*, pp. 15–171.

28. For dating see Arizaleta, *Translation d'Alexandre*, pp. 19–26; Uría, *Panorama*, pp. 197–99 provides a good summary of discussion but, probably because of the proximity of publication dates, does not take Arizaleta's persuasive arguments into account, opting for 1217–27. I quote MS *O*, but give significant variants from MS *P*, resolving all abbreviations, and lightly modernizing spelling and accentuation. Due to syntactical ambiguity I have chosen not to add punctuation.

29. *Libro de Alexandre*, p. 3. These stanzas are ambiguous, and have been the subject of considerable debate: see Uría, *Panorama*, pp. 36–51. The syntactic and semantic function of *ca* may vary so I suppress it in both cases in translation to avoid confusion; this is not an entirely satisfactory solution but has the advantage of facing the modern reader with a similar dilemma regarding the relationship between hemistichs as the medieval audience would have faced. Note that *mester* is also ambiguous, and could refer equally to trade or craft, or to ministry, through an etymological link to *menester*, "duty"; the form found in *MS P*. See Deyermond, "Mester es sen pecado," and Gómez Moreno, "Notas."

30. For dating see Uría, *Panorama*, pp. 228–30.
31. *Libro de Apolonio.*
32. Waters, *Angels*, p. 50.
33. Harpham, *On the Grotesque*, pp. 23–27.
34. Camille, *Image*, p. 12.
35. Rudolph, *Things*, shows that Bernard's *Apologia* is not a condemnation of the Benedictine and Cluniac monasteries but a treatment of excess, and lists (pp. 333–36) other medieval discussions in which recurs the notion of a hybridity defying natural order coupled with descriptive terms broadly similar to those used by Bernard: *ridicula monstruositas, deformis formositas, formosa deformitas.*
36. Rudolph, *Things*, pp. 11–12. "Ceterum in claustris, coram legentibus fratribus, quid facit illa ridicula monstruositas, mira quaedam deformis formositas ac formosa deformitas? Quid ibi immundiae simiae? Quid feri leones? Quid monstruosi centauri? Quid semihomines? [. . .] Quid milites pugnantes? Quid venatores tubicinantes? Videas sub uno capite multa corpora, et rursus in uno corpore capita multa. Cernitur hinc in quadrupede cauda serpentis, illinc in pisce caput quadrupedis [. . .] Tam multa denique, tamque mira diversarum formarum apparet ubique varietas, ut magis legere libeat in marmoribus, quam in codicibus, totumque diem occupare singula ista mirando, quam in lege Dei meditando. Proh Deo! si non pudet ineptiarum, cur vel non piget expensarum?" p. 282.
37. Douglas, *Purity*, p. 33.
38. *On the Grotesque*, p. 74.
39. Bakhtin, *Rabelais*, p. 4.
40. Bakhtin, *Rabelais*, p. 5.
41. Bakhtin, *Rabelais*, pp. 11–12; Stallybass and White, *Politics*, p. 7.
42. Bakhtin, *Rabelais*, p. 21.
43. Bakhtin, *Rabelais*, pp. 24, 27. Bakhtin's formulation has been reoriented to take account of the fact that carnival is socially and politically licensed. The utility of Bakhtin's approach is not lessened by three further caveats concerning his overall thesis; (i) his idealist notion of popular community as "heterogeneous and boundless"; (ii) the way in which his engagement with Rabelais permits him space to engage in a culturally specific critique of his own milieu; and (iii) the gendered nature of his depiction of the carnivalesque body. Stallybass and White, *Politics*, pp. 12–16.
44. Harpham, *On the Grotesque*, pp. 11, 16.
45. For a superb account of medieval optics see Crombie, *Science*, and for its relation to knowledge, love, and redemption, see Biernoff, *Sight*. Medieval visual theory has also been studied in relation to voyeurism in Middle English poetry (Spearing, *Medieval Poet as Voyeur*), to Chaucer (Klassen, *Chaucer on Love*), and to Rojas's *Celestina* (Burke, *Vision*). Since the visual is their primary field of investigation, these critics are able to give a fuller account of the development of medieval ocular theory than I can here.
46. Carruthers, *Memory*, and *The Craft of Thought*.
47. Carruthers, *Memory*, p. 137.

48. I cite here and throughout Arcipreste de Hita, *Libro de buen amor*, giving page numbers for prose and stanza numbers for verse; all translations are my own. Editions whose notes rather than text are cited are listed under the editor's name. The memorative practice of *divisio* need not be relegated only to long texts but might also serve as a method for memorizing a learned sermon.

49. Zahareas, "Parody of the Canonical Hours," Bueno, *Sotana*.

50. On Ruiz's milieu see Haywood, "Juan Ruiz and the *Libro de Buen Amor*."

51. Juan Ruiz is a forename, and, although it is unsatisfactory to refer to him as Ruiz, I shall do so to save space.

52. Excellent summaries of research trends can be found in Nepaulsingh, *History*, and Brownlee, *Status*, pp. 11–22. Burke, *Desire*, gives some space to the discussion of the visual.

53. Dagenais, *Ethics*, pp. 153–213, and Lawrance, "*Libro*," pp. 58–60.

54. Lawrance, "*Libro*," p. 46. Gybbon-Monypenny, "Two Versions," Kinkade and Capuano, "Los folios finales del MS *S*."

55. Blecua, *Libro*, pp. liv–lvi, lxxxi–lxxxvi. Haywood, "Contexts," p. 22 and Lawrance, "*Libro*," p. 46. Note the use of the preterit tense in the prologue, implying the substance of the book was composed first: Lawrance, "*Libro*," p. 45.

56. For further discussion see Haywood, "Pasiones," pp. 943–44 and Morreale, "Lectura," p. 348.

57. Pérez López, "Fecha," and Lawrance, "Audience," and "*Libro*," pp. 48–58, 61–62.

58. On the role of Archpriest of Hita see Kelly, *Law*, and Gonzálvez Ruiz, "La persona de Juan Ruiz," pp. 37–67.

59. Haywood and Vasvári, "Reading the *Libro de Buen Amor* Thirty Years On."

60. However, see Seidenspinner-Núñez, *Allegory* for parody and allegory, and Zahareas, *Art*, on Ruiz's artistic virtuosity, and humor.

61. Sedgwick, *Men*.

62. Lacan, "The Mirror Stage," p. 4; also "Split." For an excellent account of Lacan's reading of the mirror stage, with a feminist critique see Rose, *Sexuality*.

63. Lacan, *Écrits*, p. xi, for Sheridan's discussion of *méconnaissance*, and the difficulty of its translation.

64. Girard, *Deceit*, and "Mimetic Desire."

## 1   Humor and the Humors

1. Klibansky, Panofsky, and Saxl, *Saturn*, pp. 97–112, Cadden, *Sex Difference*, pp. 75–78. In the light of Spitzer's "Note," on the interchangeability of the poetic and the empirical I, I use Everyman throughout when referring to something experienced by the first-person narrator but which has application to the medieval subject in general.

2. Rist, "Augustine of Hippo," p. 17.

3. I use Barry Taylor's tale numbers ("*Exempla*," pp. 101–04 ); my stanza numbers may differ from his since I occasionally include more of the application.

4. The case for a single version of the *Libro* has achieved considerable acceptance: see the introduction.

5. Charland, *Artes*, p. 127.

6. Ullman, "Prologue," pp. 155–56. *Presión* could refer to a literal jail or it could be it being used in its common metaphorical sense: *Libro*, 1dn. I take it metaphorically since it appears in the prayer's closest analogue (*Poema de Fernán González*, 107d) where it rhymes with *Babilon*, as in the *Libro*, and because there is little evidence to support its literal interpretation.

7. It seems prudent to assume Ruiz is drawing on a tradition of prayers using this formula; references to the *Ordo* should therefore be taken to refer to prayers in the tradition in general, and not specifically to the *Ordo* itself.

8. Ricard, "L'invocation initiale"; Sola, "Súplica inicial"; Russell, "Oración," pp. 138–41, 147–48; Gimeno Casalduero, "Oración narrativa," pp. 15–29; Gerli, "*Ordo commendationis*," pp. 436–37 and Baños Vallejo, "Plegarias de héroes y de santos."

9. I list here only those sources prior to the composition of the *Libro*; the *Milagros* prayers address the salvific power of the Virgin, and not God the Father. Ricard, "L'invocation initiale," points out that Ruiz's version includes only three figures, or four if the *Ordo*'s Moses is equivalent to the *Libro*'s Jews, drawn from the *Ordo* (p. 465). Of the *Poema de Fernán González* eleven personages, Ruiz lists seven, and adds two of his own. There are also some verbal correspondences; for example, see note 6, above.

10. I cite the *Ordo* from Gimeno Casalduero, "Oración narrativa," p. 19; Russell gives another version, "Oración," pp. 143–44.

11. Direct knowledge is possible (Walsh, "Juan Ruiz") but I do not judge the similarities to be sufficient to conclude definitively that it was Ruiz's direct source.

12. None of the French antecedents, discussed by Gimeno Casalduero, "Oración narrativa," p. 15, and Russell, "Oración," pp. 119–22, 144–47, and 148–50, open poems.

13. Prof. Duque (University of California at Chapel Hill) kindly sent me a copy of his article, which was first read as "Religious Imagery in the *Poema de Fernán González*" at the 40th International Congress on Medieval Studies, Kalamazoo, University of Michigan, on May 7, 2005, prior to publication in *La corónica*.

14. Direct reference is made to Omnipotent God at 105c, 106a, 107a, 108d, and 111c, with further pronominal or verbal references at 105c, 106bcd, 107bcd, 108abc, 109ad, and 111ad, and to Christ at 112acd and 113.

15. Kupfer, *Romanesque Wall Painting*; and Mateo Gómez, *Temas profanos*.

16. Beltrán, *Razones*, pp. 13–22. "Madre de Dios gloriosa" (1635–41) also has seven stanzas. Compare the structure and the use of a single stanza to conclude with "O María" (20–32; final Joy described in st. 31), and "Mis ojos non verán luz" (115–20; adventures with Cruz and Ferrand Garçía conclude in 119, the messenger is cursed in 120). The following lyrics have similar endings: "Omillo me, Reína" (1046–58), "Madre de Dios gloriosa" (1635–41), "Todos bendigamos" (1642–49), and "Santa Virgen escogida"

(1673–77). The wild women lyrics (959–71, 987–92, 997–1005, 1022–42), and "Los que la ley avemos" (1059–66) do not have concluding stanzas as such. I have excluded lyrics after 1709 from my list.

17. Ullman, "Prologue," pp. 149–51, is correct to rule out the possibility that the prologue is a *sermon joyeux*, a verse vernacular genre that flourished in France from the late fifteenth century. The *sermon joyeux* typically dealt with alimentary or phallic hagiographies, everyday life, drinking, fools, and the business of trades guilds: for edited texts and studies see Koopmans, *Quatre sermons joyeux* and *Recueil*, and Koopmans and Verhuyck, *Sermon joyeux et truanderie*. Ullman, "Prologue," pp. 154, 167, and Jenaro-MacLennan, "Presupuestos intelectuales," pp. 152, 174–75, consider that the prologue is an added justification of content.

18. Jenaro-MacLennan, "Presupuestos intelectuales," p. 152, and Gerli, "Greeks," p. 411, insist on its being read as a prologue and not as a sermon. On the chain of authority through David, see Paiewonsky Conde, "Polarización," pp. 333–34.

19. Beltrán, *Razones*, pp. 30–35, 40–41, 50–53.

20. Zink, *Prédication en langue romane*, pp. 221–23.

21. Many discussions of the scholastic sermon are available: Wenzel, *Preachers*, pp. 61–100 is accessible and appropriately detailed.

22. Bataillon, *Prédication au xiii^e siècle*, pp. 22, 29; Rico, *Predicación y literatura*, pp. 10–11. Ullman, "Prologue," argues for a link by word (Castilian *dar* to Latin *dare*, to give, at 2ac, 4d, 9c, and 10a to *dabo*) and concept between the opening prayer's supplication for succor and God's gift of the faculties; whilst the argument holds, the link is by word between the content of the prayer rather than between the *antithema* and the *thema*, and in his development of the *thema*, Ruiz makes very little of the God-given nature of the faculties.

23. Charland, *Artes*; Wenzel, *Preachers*, pp. 70–72 and *Latin Sermon Collections*, especially pp. 11–16; and Murphy, *Arts*, pp. 293–94. For the peninsula, see Sánchez Sánchez, "Vernacular Preaching in Spanish, Portuguese and Catalan," pp. 781–802, especially 785–88.

24. Biblical quotations come from the Authorized Saint James version; I give references to Psalms numbers in that version in square brackets.

25. See Nepaulsingh, "Rhetorical Structure," for the argument that the whole prologue is a sermon. Burke, "*Libro de buen amor*," argues that the similarities with the scholastic sermon are forced and, instead, it should be seen as a meditative sermon.

26. Dagenais, "Further Source."

27. Beltrán, *Razones*, pp. 49–51, and Amasuno, "Saber médico," p. 251 discuss the introduction of the first person as a movement into the authorial voice from that of the preacher.

28. Paiewonsky Conde, "Polarización," p. 334, argues that Ruiz's interpretation of the text is a misreading since only one of the soul's faculties, understanding, is mentioned in the *thema*; however, Ruiz reads the whole text as dealing with the operations of learning, and consequently, all of the

# 160      NOTES

intellective faculties would be called into action. Kinkade, "'Intellectum,'" p. 304, overlooks the Augustinian trinity and, in the absence of clear allusions to the Thomist model of the soul, interprets understanding as "revelation of the spiritual world to which the soul belongs," will or desire as "an expression of the individual mind," and memory as "the physical world."

29. Ullman, "Prologue," p. 160, argues that, although the sermon structure stops at this point, Ruiz continues to use sermon technique. Nepaulsingh contests this interpretation. In my view his argument has three unaddressed weaknesses: a misconstrual of Charland's discussion of figure of the building; the opposition of the faculty's positive and negative qualities seems inappropriate (human nature's weakness is opposite to good understanding; lack of understanding to goodwill; and poor memory to good deeds, "Rhetorical Structure," pp. 329–30); and he does not take into account the movement into an implied authorial first-person voice.

30. Paiewonsky Conde, "Polarización" pp. 342–43.

31. Green, *Spain*, I: 51, Jenaro-MacLennan, "Presupuestos intelectuales," pp. 168–71.

32. Cuartero Sancho, "Paremiología" shows that Ruiz certainly used Montagnone's *Compendium*, including in the prologue. The use of encyclopedia should not be taken to mean that Ruiz was unfamiliar with the sources from which citations were drawn: Cuartero Sancho, "Paremiología," p. 224, Carruthers, *Memory*, pp. 83–84, 175–76.

33. See Beattie, "Lawyers," pp. 259–82, for an assessment of these sermons, held in the Cathedral Library, Valencia, MS 215.

34. Kinkade, "'Intellectum,'" holds that Ruiz was unlikely to be familiar with philosophy and theology and more probably used vernacular sources; his evidence points toward the wide permeation of literary discourse by medieval theological and philosophical ideas.

35. Jenaro-MacLennan, "Presupuestos intelectuales," p. 156.

36. Klibansky, Panofsky, and Saxl, *Saturn*, pp. 67–112, Harvey, *Inner Wits*, Jenaro-MacLennan, "Presupuestos intelectuales," pp. 180–81.

37. Jenaro-MacLennan, "Presupuestos intelectuales," pp. 162–63. Amasuno, "Saber," discusses the psycho-medical view of memory and love in relation to the *Libro*. I do not agree with Amasuno's conclusions that Ruiz presents a *regimen sanitatis* showing that love of God can be reached through physical love.

38. On voluntarism see Ullman, "Prologue," pp. 151–61.

39. Also see Jenaro-MacLennan, "Presupuestos intelectuales," pp. 159–60.

40. Paiewonsky Conde, "Polarización," p. 338.

41. See, for example, Colish, *Peter Lombard*, II.303–98, especially pp. 336–43. Also Klibansky, *Saturn*, p. 29. Jenaro-MacLennan, "Presupuestos intelectuales," pp. 162–63, observes the *Libro*'s pessimism.

42. Colish, *Peter Lombard*, I.384.

43. Klibansky, Panofsky, and Saxl, *Saturn*, pp. 90–94, discuss the diseased faculties, including an emphasis on the role of memory.

44. Wack, *Lovesickness*, pp. 39–40, 56–59. Despite its difficulties, I use the term 'Averroist' to refer to the medieval reception of Aristotle's teachings

through the commentaries of Averroes, Ibn Rushd (1126–98) of Córdoba, particularly as attacked in Bishop Tempier's Condemnation of 1277, discussed in chapter 3.

45. Klibansky, Panofsky, and Saxl, *Saturn*, pp. 102–05, Wenzel, *Sin of Sloth*.

46. Klibansky, Panofsky, and Saxl, *Saturn*, pp. 97–104.

47. Walker, "Interpretation," and "Con miedo," Haywood, "Contexts," p. 32, and Nepaulsingh, *History*, pp. 126–27, discuss the presence of death throughout the *Libro*.

48. I use *auctoritas* as defined by Minnis, *Medieval Theory*, pp. 10–12: a writer who enjoyed wide acceptance as a source of authoritativeness, and whose work was endowed with truth and wisdom.

49. "Presupuestos intelectuales," p. 151.

50. Nepaulsingh, "Rhetorical Structure," pp. 327–28.

51. I do not take this to be related to the Averroist monopsychistic position, which regarded human intellect to be one and eternal but conditioned in the mortal individual by his or her sensory perceptions since Ruiz makes no allusion to the unicity of memory.

52. Nepaulsingh, "Rhetorical Structure," pp. 327–28.

53. I see little indication here that Ruiz is invoking Augustine's theories on the presence of Christ in the interior person as expounded, for example, by Ullman, "Prologue," p. 165.

54. On the background to this view, see Klibansky, Panofsky, and Saxl, *Saturn*, pp. 90–94.

55. For an excellent summary of this position see Colish, "Peter Lombard," pp. 175–76.

56. Colish, "Peter Lombard," p. 175.

57. I find little evidence in this development of the prologue for the Augustinian insistence on the dependence of grace and the existence of goodwill for revelation to inner man through Christ as the interior teacher. In his seminal "Recta voluntas," Gerli sees this view as a significant ideological underpinning to the Debate in Signs.

58. Walker, "Juan Ruiz's Defence," observes a similar warning in the *Libro del caballero Zifar* and in *Castigos y documentos*, and claims that Ruiz perverts the arguments put forward there.

59. Smalley, "Peter Comestor," pp. 87–88, 97 and Robson, "St Bonaventure," p. 194.

60. Jenaro-MacLennan, "Presupuestos intelectuales," p. 154, Colish, *Peter Lombard*, I.242–45.

61. Ullman, "Prologue," pp. 164–65, Brownlee, *Status*, pp. 47–48, Davies, "Medieval Mystics," pp. 223–24, at p. 224; also Colish, *Peter Lombard*, I.242–43.

62. "Prologue," p. 161; Gerli, "Recta voluntas," and "Greeks."

63. Kienzel, "Typology," pp. 87–88, Wenzel, "Sermon," pp. 252–54.

64. Smalley, "Peter Comestor," pp. 109–15, Wenzel, "Sermon."

65. Gilman, *Parodic Sermon*, pp. 11–30, Wenzel, "Sermon." Gilman, pp. 14–15, 20, discusses the *Libro*'s prologue.

66. Smalley, "Peter Comestor," pp. 110–17, Minnis, *Medieval Theory*, pp. 63–72.

67. Smalley, "Peter Comestor," pp. 110–11.

68. "Peter Comestor," p. 110.

69. Minnis, *Medieval Theory*, pp. 15–33.

70. Minnis, *Medieval Theory*, pp. 63–72.

71. Dagenais, "Further Source," pp. 39–40.

72. Dagenais, "Further Source," pp. 46–47.

73. Deyermond, "Aspects of Parody," p. 59.

74. Dagenais, "Further Source," pp. 38–41.

75. "Prologue," pp. 161, 169.

76. Brownlee, *Status*, pp. 29–30, Carruthers, *Memory*, pp. 192–94.

77. Brownlee, "Autobiography," pp. 71–82 and *Status*, pp. 30–31. In my view, Brownlee is overdependant on a specifically Augustinian hermeneutics, and misunderstands Ruiz's treatment of the soul and its good or healthy faculties as being more proper to the divine than to the fallen individual, and his attribution of his own actions to the same forces of nature under God that affect other sinners' characters (pp. 71–76, 123–27, and 152–53).

78. Nepaulsingh, "Structure," pp. 67–68.

79. Deyermond and Walker, "Further Vernacular Source," p. 196, Gómez Moreno, "Forma,", Dagenais, *Ethics*, pp. 24–26.

80. Gómez Moreno, "Prológos," p. 74.

81. Lawrance, "*Libro*," p. 43.

82. I owe the observation of the commonplace nature of the image to Professor Lawrance himself, to whom I am grateful, and who brought my attention to a number of illuminations showing women at ball play.

83. For a link between promiscuous circulation and concupiscent love see 66, 68a, and 1630, and Vasvári, "Novelness," pp. 174–77.

84. Ekman, "Leçión."

85. Carruthers, *Memory*, pp. 93–94, Dagenais, *Ethics*, pp. 121–220. Dagenais focuses on the scribal division of text in the manuscript tradition; his discussion of memory does not make explicit the connection between the two practices (pp. 89–90).

86. Dagenais, *Ethics*, pp. 153–70, 172–212.

87. See Vasvári "De todos instrumentos," and "Novelness," pp. 174–77 for an obscene level. Brownlee's view that Ruiz refuses to proscribe meaning arises from her insistence on the use of Augustine's *Confessions*.

88. I have translated *puntar* and *punto* as 'notate' and 'note' to convey Ruiz's punning on *puntar* as meaning 'to punctuate' and 'to set to musical notation.' Also see Gerli, "Greeks," p. 420, Vasvári, "Novelness," pp. 154, 174, Burke, *Desire*, pp. 174–76, 269–70.

89. Brown, *Contrary Things*, pp. 132–33, treats the different manuscript readings: see my discussion below.

90. Sturm, "Greeks," pp. 406–07.

91. Klibansky, Panofsky, and Saxl, *Saturn*, pp. 75–78, 90–94, Wenzel, *Sin of Sloth*, pp. 39–41.

92. Zahareas and Pereira, *Itinerario*, p. 36.

93. Sturm, "Greeks," p. 410.

94. For a commentary on variant interpretations of st. 65 depending on manuscript tradition and editorial punctuation see Dagenais, *Ethics*, pp. 91–103, 231n16; he reads 65c as a reference to praise and blame. Hook, "More Melons," p. 193, documents Garrida as a woman's name in 1484.

95. Reckert "'. . .avrás dueña garrida'." When the Archpriest seeks a *garrida*, in the form of the Viuda Loçana, the affair does not progress.

96. Dagenais, "Further Source," p. 42.

97. Ruiz's prose is elliptical since the use of *a* suggests that the types of people listed are the object of a verb, and that the book is the subject; however, the latter would necessitate the introduction of *a* before "cada uno" or suggest that a verb is missing. As it stands, "puede cada uno dezir," seems to mean "as each one [of the types of people listed] can well say. . ." since this presupposes a lesser amendment. Also see Ullman, "Prologue," pp. 164–65.

98. "Semiotics," p. 138.

99. Vasvári's phrase: "Semiotics," p. 138.

100. Zahareas, *Art*, pp. 57–58, discusses narrative control; however, I do not agree with his reading of this episode since he fails to take into account fourteenth-century attitudes to interpretation.

101. Parker, "Parable," pp. 143–44, suggests that the Greeks' pride leads to their purpose being deflated.

102. "En torno al arte del Arcipreste de Hita," p. 105.

103. Carruthers, *Memory*, pp. 51–68.

104. Zahareas, *Art*, p. 57.

105. For the classic analysis of the panopticon, see Foucault, *Discipline and Punish*; also Camille, *Image*, pp. 14–16, Burke, *Vision*, p. 10. Bryson, *Vision and Painting*, argues that in sacred space the spectator becomes "the disembodied presence he will later become," moving under the gaze of God, "not yet of the introjected gaze of the Other" (pp. 96–98). In my analysis, God is the absolute Other; I shall return to this point in chapter 3.

106. Freud, *Jokes*.

107. Deyermond, "Aspects of Parody," p. 59.

108. On Ruiz's vision of the inadequacy of language see Read, "Man against Language."

109. Zahareas, *Art*, p. 56, also sees the analogy as false but draws different conclusions.

110. Brownlee, *Status*, p. 74–75, sees the episode as indicating voluntaristic interpretation.

111. For Sturm, the Dispute shows that the *Libro*'s aim is "to teach man to laugh despite his cares," and she defines "el de buena ventura" as "the reader who, having needed his author's warning against the mistake of the *doctor de grecia*, chooses to lighten his cares with the various *burlas* offered by the Archpriest" ("Greeks," p. 412). She does not connect the *Libro* to the medical tradition, nor observe that Ruiz describes three interpretative positions. Morros, "*Libro de buen amor*," p. 26, notes the three interperative stances but draws different conclusions.

112. Deyermond, "Greeks," p. 91, notes the contradiction.
113. See, for the deterministic impact, Zahareas, "Stars," pp. 85–86, and Blecua, *Libro*, 123dn; Michael, "Function," pp. 188–90, provides a critique of Zahareas's conclusions about this *exemplum*. For my reading of *sentençia*, see Carruthers, *Memory*, pp. 164–65; also Corominas with Pascual, *Diccionario crítico etimológico*, v.209a, who note its derivation from Latin *sentĕntĭa*, "opinión," "consejo," "sentencioso" (opinion, advice or counsel, sententiousness). Brown, *Contrary Things*, pp. 129, 132, notes its use in medieval hermeneutics.
114. Klibansky, Panofsky, and Saxl, *Saturn*, pp. 178–87.
115. Klibansky, Panofsky, and Saxl, *Saturn*, pp. 94–97.
116. On this concept see Kantorowicz, *The King's Two Bodies*, pp. 138–92.
117. Kinkade, "'Intellectum,'" pp. 311–12, draws a similar conclusion, emphasizing the orthodoxy of Ruiz's treatment of free will.
118. López-Baralt, *Islam*.
119. Gerli, "Greeks," Brown, *Contrary Things*, pp. 139–40.
120. See Matthew of Vendôme, *Ars versificatoria*, I.38; I use Matthew's *Ars* to illustrate the view that portraits should be apt rather than to suggest that his, or any other, rhetorical manual was known to Ruiz, who may have observed the technique in practice. Goldberg, "Personal Descriptions," discusses the rhetorical use of descriptions to convey meaning.
121. Morros, "Fuentes," pp. 75–81.
122. Morros, "Fuentes," p. 76n, knows of no other bipartite descriptions.
123. Spearing, *Medieval Poet as Voyeur*, p. 46.
124. Beltrán, *Razones*, pp. 187–89, Morros, "Fuentes," pp. 78–79 (reading it as 'fine eyebrows' and 'tightly bound hair,' respectively), Alarcos Llorach, "*Libro de buen amor*," Blecua, *Libro*, 115n.
125. Joset, *Libro*, I: 166, Morros, "Fuentes," pp. 79–80. On Arabic analogues, see Alonso, "La bella de Juan Ruiz."
126. Zahareas and Pereira, *Itinerario*, pp. 139–40.
127. "Figuras."
128. I draw in part on Michalski, "Description"; his concern is the use of descriptive topoi to generate meaning.
129. Mettmann, "Ancheta," Michalski, "Description," p. 70, Curry, "Wife of Bath," p. 44. Curry cites M. Angellus Blondus, "Ac protensa coxendicorum ossa, uirilitatis signum ni mollis caro contingit" and Rudolphus Goclenius, "Coxarum ossa duriter eminentia, & exterius apparentia, virilitatem monstrant" 1554 and 1661, respectively (And protuberant hips [are] a mark of fecundity and pliant flesh. Strongly prominent and outwardly visible hip bones indicate fecundity).
130. Barbera, "Juan Ruiz."
131. Chaucer, *Wife of Bath's Prologue*, ll. 603–16. On *quoniam* for female genitalia in Chaucer see Davis et al., *Chaucer Glossary*, p. 116, and in the *Libro*, Vasvári, "*Parodia sacra*."

132. Curry, "Wife of Bath," pp. 41–43. Most recent editors accept that "gat-tothed" refers to spaced teeth rather than their similarity to a goat as Skeat proposed: Curry, "Wife of Bath," pp. 45–46, Davis, *Chaucer*, p. 65, Chaucer, *Wife of Bath*, p. 113n.

133. Karras, *Common Women*, p. 111.

134. Klibansky, Panofsky, and Saxl, *Saturn*, pp. 85–86, Wack, *Lovesickness*, p. 44, Cadden, *Sex Difference*, pp. 183, 274.

135. Michalski, "Description," p. 71.

136. The wild woman is named only in the lyric and not in the preceding narrative *cuaderna vía*. Kirby, "*Serranas*," p. 159 observes that distortion is a central feature of the grotesque description of Alda, whilst Zahareas sees this as part of Ruiz's comic technique (*Art*, pp. 149–51).

137. López-Baralt, *Islam*, pp. 66–67.

138. Richardson, *Etymological Vocabulary*, p. 224.

139. Curry, "Wife of Bath," p. 34. *Doncella Teodor*, p. 65. Based on the protagonist of *One Thousand and One Nights*, nights 436–62, Teodor shows encyclopedic knowledge in a dispute. Although extant manuscripts date from the fifteenth century, the translation of the tale has been dated to the second half of the thirteenth century: see Parker, *Story*, and Gómez Redondo, *Historia*, pp. 484–502. I have ruled out Libra, which is also governed by Venus, since, although promiscuous and deceptive in amatory matters, the Libran is ruddy-complexioned (Martínez de Toledo, *Arcipreste de Talavera*, pp. 186–91; dated 1438), sanguine rather than melancholic, and "hombre de buena criança y gran trabajador, y terná muchos amigos" (*Doncella Teodor*, p. 67: "a man of good upbringing, a great worker, and he will have many friends").

140. "Figuras," p. 89. There are parallels with the description of the lover in *De nuntio*, whose lack of experience lessens the sexual threat that he poses (Morros, "Fuentes," pp. 72–73).

141. Martínez de Toledo, *Arcipreste*, p. 184; *cetrino* is first documented from the fifteenth-century (see Corominas with Pascual, *Diccionario crítico etimológico*, II: 58). On *baço*, see *Libro*, st. 417n, Blecua, *Libro*, p. 381, and Dunn, "Figuras," p. 85.

142. Lida de Malkiel, "Notas," pp. 124–26, Dunn, "Figuras," p. 85. Quotation from *Doncella Teodor*, p. 65. Ly, "*Libro de buen amor*," pp. 24–25, 28, notes the presence of sanguine and Saturnine elements in the portrait, and the comparison to the ass in the portraits of the Archpriest and Alda to draw different conclusions.

143. López-Baralt, *Islam*, p. 61.

144. Kane, "Personal Appearance."

145. Goldberg, "Personal Descriptions."

146. On descriptions in *De vetula*, see Morros, "Fuentes."

147. Taylor, "*Exempla*," p. 93.

148. The miniature can be consulted in Alfonso X, *Primera partida*, between pp. XXIV and XXV, and the full folio is reproduced in Herriott, "Thirteenth-Century Manuscript," pp. 286, 287.

## 2 The Gaze and the Grotesque

1. On scopophilia in medieval descriptions see Spearing, *Medieval Poet as Voyeur*, p. 45.
2. Spearing, *Medieval Poet as Voyeur*, p. 22.
3. I refer to these tales as "exemplary fabliaux" because they are broadly analogous to fabliaux, and to differentiate them from Ruiz's *exempla* with animal, Biblical, or historical protagonists and from the amatory adventures.
4. I do not find current psychoanalytical models wholly satisfying in their account of the modern psyche, particularly in their accounts of female and queer identities: more importantly, their application beyond their own domain to literary representation and in relation to the structures of the medieval mind where different models of privacy, family, and relationships to structures of power appertained is problematic. Nonetheless, with these caveats, they currently offer the most potent tool for exposing ideological content by permitting an exploration of latent rather than manifest content. See Rose, *Sexuality*, pp. 1–23, for the shortcomings of psychoanalysis.
5. Vasvári, "Hijo," pp. 462, 468.
6. Freud, *Dreams*, p. 522n.
7. *Casar* can refer to taking a concubine: Corominas, *Libro*, p. 891. Morreale, "Corominas," (1971), p. 286. On the ambiguity of 474d, see Lawrance, "*Libro*," p. 67.
8. Although *cabo* derives etymologically from Latin *caput*, "head," it was used to refer to any extremity, as in the nautical expression, *echar un cabo*, "to throw one end of a piece of rope": Corominas and Pascual, *Diccionario*, I: 714–15; see also Kasten and Nitti, *Concordances*, I: 324–25; definitions 1, "parte extrema o superior de una cosa" and 3, "fin, término, límite," to which Ruiz's phrase may make an allusive reference.
9. Cadden, *Sex Difference*, p. 178.
10. Vasvári, "Hijo," p. 470.
11. Freud, *Sexuality*, p. 67, 68n, 354–55, and *Introductory Lectures*, pp. 393–94.
12. Weir and Jerman, *Images*. At the literal level, the phrase "echó lo por mal cabo," refers to the young man coming to a bad end. The Archpriest returns to make this point about the destructive effects of love in the introduction to the final capital sin discussed: "El que más a ti cree más por mal cabo: / a ellos e a ellas, a todos das mal rramo (MS *S* repeats 'mal cabo')" (398ab; Whoever believes you more (comes to) a worse end: / to men and women, to everyone you give a bad lot (lit. a poor bunch)).
13. *Images*, pp. 10–35.
14. For an excellent analysis of humour in male protagonist slapstick see Lehman, *Running Scared*, pp. 105–29. I should like to thank Dr Santiago Fouz-Hernández (University of Durham) for drawing my attention to Lehman's work, and the strong similarities of its conclusions to my own.
15. Zahareas, *Art*, p. 84.
16. Zahareas, *Art*, 83–84, Vasvári, "Two Lazy Suitors," pp. 194–98.
17. On *entendedor* as lover see 139c, and Impey, "La *fin'amors*."

18. "Widow."
19. Geary, "Pitas Payas," pp. 255–57.
20. Vasvári's phrase: "Pitas Pajas," "Hijo."
21. Cadden, *Sex Difference*, pp. 84, 138, 180, Vivanco, *Death*, p. 48.
22. Russell, *Devil*, pp. 68–73, 245, and Link, *Devil*, pp. 44–45, deal with the negative symbolism of horns, and their association with phallicism.
23. Moffatt, "Pitas Payas," p. 32, considers that there is no *double entendre* on horns.
24. Kuhn, "Lawless Seeing," argues for flexibility in access to a dominant (masculine) subject position in cinema. Mayne, "Paradoxes of Spectatorship," explores the way in which cinema constructs and challenges ideologies through the coexistence of shifting spectator positions, and Clover, "The Eye of Horror," offers a magisterial reading of masochistic scenarios in horror film. I am indebted to their discussions of the modern visual.
25. Pearcy, "Modes," on the obscene language of the fabliaux.
26. Zahareas and Pereira, *Itinerario*, p. 84.
27. Vasvári, "Two Lazy Suitors," identifies the importance of the world upside-down in this tale.
28. Vasvári, "Two Lazy Suitors."
29. Vasvári overemphasizes the courtliness of the milieu.
30. Lehman, *Running Scared*, p. 129.
31. Mulvey, *Visual and Other Pleasures*, p. 31.
32. McGrady, "Story," p. 358.
33. The fabliaux discussed here are edited in the *Nouveau Recueil complet des fabliaux*; full references are given in the Works Cited list.
34. Bloch, *Scandal*, p. 86.
35. Pearcy, "Modes."
36. *Deceit* and "Mimetic Desire."
37. 'Male traffic in women' is Rubin's phrase from her eponymous article. *Between Men*, pp. 7, 10; I would like to thank Prof. Paul Julian Smith, University of Cambridge, for drawing my attention to the pertinence of Sedgwick to my analysis. For an excellent account of the taboo on homo-sexuality in Western culture see Rubin, "Traffic," and Butler, *Gender Trouble*, pp. 81–99. See Blackmore and Hutcheson, *Queer Iberia* for essays on medieval Iberian homosocial desire.
38. Sedgwick, *Men*, p. 25.
39. I follow Grieve, *Death*, pp. 25–54, in representing the erotic triangle diagrammatically.
40. Although the principle of martial monogamy was enshrined in law, only the wife could be formally accused of adultery, and was subject to harsh pun-ishment should her infidelity be discovered. Likewise, female bigamy, a very real possibility in frontier society, was controlled legislatively, with long periods being necessary before the absent husband was declared dead and remarriage permitted. In the Archpriest's adventures, married women do not figure as objects of desire.

41. Zahareas, *Art*, pp. 84–85, discusses the motif only as a contest between two suitors.

42. Mulvey makes a similar point with regard to the narrative conventions of Hollywood film in *Visual and Other Pleasures*, pp. 29–38.

43. I do not wish to deny the possibility of pleasure arising from identification with the female object in these tales but I should argue that their structure places the hero at the center of their drama.

44. Spearing, *Medieval Poet as Voyeur*, p. 125.

45. Deyermond, "Aspects of Parody," p. 69; Chrzanowski, "Estética," pp. 216–17.

46. Vasvári, "Two Lazy Suitors," p. 193.

47. Vasvári, "Two Lazy Suitors," p. 198.

48. For an excellent account of abjection see Grosz, "Body."

49. On interpellation see Butler, *Excitable Speech*, p. 5. The suitors' bodies are given a social existence through naming that emphasizes their fractured and abject nature.

50. On the body as symbolic of social structures see Douglas, *Purity*, pp. 116, 125.

51. Zahareas, *Art*, pp. 60, 114–20 (but see Michael's important caveat, "Function," pp. 216, 217–18), Vasvári, "Digresión," p. 179; but see Taylor, "*Exempla*," pp. 93–95.

52. Zahareas *Art*, p. 120; see also Vasvári, "Digresión," p. 179.

53. Vasvári, "Tale," pp. 16–17. I would like to thank Prof. Vasvári for kindly sending me "Tale." On the desirability of not acting as if the opponent had advanced an unanswerable argument see Murphy, *Medieval Eloquence*, p. 207. The *Libro*'s Arms of the Christian (st. 1579–605) offer protection against the deadly sins.

54. Klibansky, Panofsky, and Saxl, *Saturn*, pp. 29–31, Wack, *Lovesickness*, pp. 6–7.

55. The wild woman is named only in the lyric and not in the preceding narrative *cuaderna vía*. Kirby, "Serranas," p. 159, observes that distortion is a central feature of the grotesque description of Alda, whilst Zahareas sees it as part of Ruiz's comic technique (*Art*, pp. 149–51).

56. Gybbon-Monypenny, "Two Versions," p. 216, Deyermond, "Aspects of Parody," p. 63; for a different view see de Lope, *Traditions*, pp. 127–44.

57. Kane, "Personal Appearance," Lida de Malkiel, "Notas," Zahareas, *Art*, Dunn, "Figuras."

58. Michalski, "Description," pp. 85–86.

59. Zahareas, *Art*, p. 148.

60. De Lope, *Traditions*, discusses the other traditions underlying this episode.

61. For the association of specific animals with sins in the bestiary tradition, and in the *Libro*, see Rowland, *Animals* and Phillips, *Imagery*, respectively. Phillips follows Hart, *Alegoría*, p. 90, to suggest that the *serrana* episode represents man's fight with the devil and the bestial elements in his own nature, concluding that the description of a physically base Alda is a warning to the reader against concupiscent love (*Imagery*, pp. 131–33).

62. Note that the "Enxienplo del ladrón e del mastín" (166–79; The Incorruptible Dog; tale 5) shows the wise dog denying its base, greedy

nature on account not only of loyalty but also of potential loss, "Por poca vianda que esta noche çenaría, / non perderé los manjares, nin el pan de cada día" (176ab; "On account of a little food that I should eat tonight / I shall not lose my daily food or daily bread"); whilst the "Ensienplo del alano que llevava la pieça de carne en la boca" (226–29; Dog and Reflection of Food; tale 8) portrays the dog's natural avarice and gluttony.

63. See, for example, the prone female figure in the bottom center of the Hell's Mouth, Winchester Psalter (1150), in Luca Signorelli's "The Damned" in the Cappella della Madonna di S. Brizio, Orvieto cathedral (ca. 1503), the upright female figure on Satan's left, St Foy, Conquest, Aveyron (ca. 1130); in Link, *Devil*, pp. 77, 140, and 91, respectively. On the association between Alda and hags or fertility goddesses, see Michalski, "Description," pp. 87–89, de Lope, *Traditions*, pp. 127–44.

64. Kane, "Personal Appearance," p. 106.

65. Kane, "Personal Appearance," p. 106.

66. Dunn, "Figuras," pp. 85–86. Seudo-Aristóteles, *Poridat*, p. 65: "de poco entendimiento."

67. Dunn, "Figuras," pp. 85, 87.

68. Goldberg, "Personal Descriptions," p. 5; see Dunn, "Figuras," pp. 89–91, for a different interpretation.

69. De Lope, *Traditions*, pp. 132, 135–36, Spitzer, *Lingüística*, pp. 237–70, and Hart, *Alegoría*, pp. 88–89, also associate Alda with the diabolic.

70. For discussion, see Link, *Devil*, pp. 128, 132, 146–47, and his plates, showing beak-nosed devils in the lower register of the Winchester Psalter's Second and Third Temptation of Christ (1150, p. 127), and of Rafael Destorrents's Last Judgment from the Missal of St Eulalia, fol. 9$^r$ (1402, p. 137).

71. Bakhtin, *Rabelais*, pp. 303–43.

72. De Lope, *Traditions*, p. 132. The comedic and grotesque qualities of the Archpriest's encounter with her are emphasized in the following lyric, in which further disjunctions intervene, such as the shift in use of favorable terms of address to insult, and her response to her interlocutor as a potential marital suitor.

73. Richardson, *Etymological Vocabulary*, p. 224.

74. Haywood, "Pasiones," pp. 943–44, Morreale, "Lectura," p. 348, Kirby, "*Serranas*," p. 159. De Lope, *Traditions*, goes further, and has shown—in my view successfully—the chronological and thematic unity of the adventures in the *sierra*, the *Ditado* section, and the *Pelea que ovo Don Carnal y Doña Quaresma*. I do not fully concur with her conclusions but this portion of her argument is very persuasive.

75. Dagenais, *Ethics*, pp. 105–06, Burke, *Desire*, pp. 133–35, 208 discuss the *Libro*'s affective lyrics; see Beckwith, *Christ's Body*, pp. 50–52, for a discussion of affective piety.

76. In her treatment of the dismemberment of the divine body, Bynum, *Fragmentation*, p. 280, suggests that each of the wounds represents not just physical fragmentation on account of human sin but also a *pars pro toto* in which each fragment of the body, like each fragment of the host, is undivided

God. Douglas, *Purity*, and, later, Kristeva, *Pouvoirs*, pp. 64–132, discuss the strong links between bodily borders, as much those of Christ as those of the sinner, and menaces to Christianity.

77. Silverman, *Male Subjectivity*, p. 197.
78. For a detailed study of dogma related to Christ's body see Rubin, *Corpus Christi* and Beckwith, *Christ's Body*.
79. For a selection of plates see Clifton, *Body of Christ*.
80. Bynum, *Fragmentation*, Vivanco, *Death*, p. 75.
81. The *Oxford English Dictionary* gives the etymology of 'ambiguous' as deriving from the Latin prefix *amb-*, "both ways," and the verb, *ag̃ĕre*, "to drive."
82. Taylor, "*Exempla*," pp. 87–89.
83. Scheidegger, *Roman de Renart*, p. 197.
84. Stone, "Philosophical Beast," p. 25.
85. "Belua fit ex homine dum homo qui naturaliter rationalis et immortalis erat secundum animam nimia delectatione temporalium fit irrationalis et mortalis. Quis anima magis est belua quam cui belue diffinitio convenit? Quis est magis belua quam cui belue inest natura nec aliquid habet hominis preter forma?" Wackers, "Mutorum animalium coloquium," p. 164.
86. Simpson, *Animal Body*, pp. 20–25.
87. Taylor, "*Exempla*," pp. 89–92.
88. Morreale, "Fábula," p. 30.
89. Morreale, "Fábula," pp. 28, 75–77.
90. The Ass and the Lion is the only tale in the *Libro* directed to lady listeners.
91. Douglas, *Purity and Danger*, pp. 116, 125.
92. Adolf, "Ass," pp. 49–57. Mateo Gómez, *Temas profanos*, plate 70, figure 340; such images are common.
93. Mateo Gómez, *Temas profanos*, plate 2, figure 12.
94. Mateo Gómez, *Temas profanos*, p. 44.
95. For *siesta* (893c) as sext, see *Libro*, 893cn.
96. Mateo Gómez, *Temas profanos*, plates 52 and 53, figures 240–42.
97. Vasvári, "Tale," pp. 15–16.
98. Phillips, *Imagery*, pp. 110, 135.
99. Burke, *Vision*, p. 4.
100. Phillips, *Imagery*, p. 127. Despite its unfortunate connotation, Loba appears to have been quite a common name: Hook, "More Melons," p.192.
101. Terry, *Renard the Fox*, p. 9; Bloch, *Medieval French Literature*, p. 114.
102. Vasvári, "Tale."
103. Vasvári, "Tale," p. 20, for *juguete* as having sexual connotations.
104. On its priapism, see Adolf, "Ass."
105. Vasvári, *Heterotextual*, p. 13, and "Erotic Wedding."
106. Michael, "Function," pp. 210–11.
107. See particularly Garoça's opening and closing tales, the Peasant and the Snake (1348–53; tale 23), and the Devil's Vassal (1454–75; tale 32), but equally the Fox that Played Dead (1412–20; tale 28), and the Fox and the Crow (1437–41; tale 30), and Trotaconventos's use of the Greyhound and

the Ungrateful Master (1357–69; tale 24), the Cock and the Sapphire (1387–91; tale 26), and the Lion and the Mouse (1425–33; tale 29).

108. Deyermond, "Women Writers," pp. 46–48, and Vivanco, "Birds," pp. 5–27.

109. Zahareas and Pereira, *Itinerario*, p. 399.

110. "Fabulae sunt quae nec factae sunt nec fieri possunt quia contra naturam." Isidore, *Etymologies*, 1.40; cited and translated in Taylor, "*Exempla*," p. 86.

111. Paxson, *Poetics*.

112. Taylor, "*Exempla*," p. 87.

113. "Sunt autem aut Esopicae aut Libysticae. Aesopice ab Aesopo inventore dictae cum animalia muta vel quae animam non habent inter se sermocinasse finguntur. Libysticae autem cum inter homines et bestias commercium fingitur vocis"; cited and translated in Taylor, "*Exempla*," p. 86.

114. Taylor, "*Exempla*," p. 87.

## 3 The Stand-Up Archpriest

1. Spitzer, "Note," p. 416.

2. Lecoy, *Recherches*, pp. 360–63.

3. Rico, "Mantenencia," pp. 178–79.

4. Gimeno, "Women," pp. 84–96, Arias, "Espacio," Reynal, *Mujeres*, Miaja de la Peña, "*Por amor d'esta dueña*."

5. Rico, "Mantenencia," pp. 173, 180, correctly argues that Aristotle's "primum alimento et generatione" (first nourishment and generation) refers to one subject, *mantenençia*, alluding to survival of the individual and the species as vegetative soul.

6. Rico, "Mantenencia," pp. 169–75. As Joset, "Pensamiento," p. 113, notes, Dagenais, "'Se usa e se faz,'" and *Ethics*, pp. 206–207, remains unconvinced by Rico, whilst, as originally proposed by Zahareas, *Art*, pp. 181–82, Ruiz may also have drawn on *Historia animalium*, VIII, I, 588*b* and V, 542*a*.

7. Wippel, "Condemnations," pp. 187–94, gives a helpful summary of the articles of the condemnation.

8. Rico, "Mantenencia," p. 186, cites item 183 of Tempier's prohibition from Hissette, *Enquête*. Heusch, "Juntamiento," p. 132, glosses "soluti cum soluta" as those who are single. Also Cátedra, *Amor*, pp. 42–46, Blecua, *Libro*, pp. XXXIII–VIII, and Joset, "Pensamiento," p. 113. Heusch summarizes the main tenants of the naturalist argument as regards sexual intercourse succinctly: "en tanto que animal, y como todos los irracionales, el hombre debe conservarse a través de la generación y para no desfallezca en semejante tarea, la naturaleza, es decir Dios, le ha dado la noción de placer, una delectación que, por eso, está libre de todo pecado": "Juntamiento," pp. 132–33. The tenants of the Sorbonne group, and subsequent followers, range further than sexual intercourse, and include the view that man and the world are eternal.

9. Rico, "Mantenencia," pp. 187–89, Heusch, "Juntamiento," p. 132, Joset, "Pensamiento," p. 113.

10. Rico, "Mantenencia," pp. 187, 189–90, Deyermond and Walker, "Further Vernacular Source," Walker, "Juan Ruiz's Defence." Rico, "Mantenencia," pp. 186–92, documents other evidence of peninsular familiarity with the Aristotelian heterodoxy, and considers that the narrator's adoption of the naturalist philosophy aligns him with the foolish. Walker, "Juan Ruiz's Defence," suggests that Ruiz burlesques *Zifar*'s censoriousness. For the date of the *Zifar*, see *Libro del caballero Zifar*, pp. 12–22, and on date and authorship, Walker, *Tradition*, pp. 12–19, and Hernández, "Ferrán Martínez."

11. Girard, *Deceit* and "Mimetic," coins the term "mimetic desire" to refer to the way in which a protagonist is inspired to love by a fictional paradigm on which he bases his own amatory behavior: thus Don Quixote mimics the amatory practice of Amadís de Gaula.

12. "To be nude is to be seen by others and yet not recognised for oneself," usually with a male spectator as principal protagonist: Berger, *Ways of Seeing*.

13. Reynal, *Mujeres*, pp. 184–87, provides a list of the qualities of each of the women, including the seducible beauty, and the wild women mountain.

14. On the lady's wounding eyes see, for example, Spearing, *Medieval Poet as Voyeur*, p. 10.

15. I give the description of the Dueña Ençerrada as the main text, and note alterations in that of Endrina in parenthesis.

16. Although I have elsewhere translated *loçana* as 'elegant,' I give 'lovely' here to convey the overlapping semantic fields.

17. David Hook has rightly advised caution in attributing meaning to the names and bynames of the *Libro*'s characters until their historical context is recovered. He has located medieval uses of them: Hook, "Further Onomastic Footnotes," pp. 156–64, and "More Melons." Hook argues that such names may have been selected because of a specific individual or individuals who bore the name, and who may be the target of personal satire.

18. Lacan, "Courtly Love," p. 149.

19. On the changing identity of the bawd see Márquez Villanueva, *Orígenes*. He considers Trotaconventos a nickname of the bawd Urraca, p. 50. Also Willis, "Two Trotaconventos," with the caveat that his discussion is based on the two-version theory.

20. Walsh, "Names," pp. 160, 162 includes *maçada* in his list of "apt though unsavory and forbidden slang-words" in the *Libro*; Vasvári clarifies the aggressive phallic connotations of terms related to the hammer in her discussion of the proper name "Mazote" from the ballad "Yo me era mora Moraima": Vasvári, *Heterotextual Body*, p. 13.

21. Márquez Villanueva, *Orígenes*, pp. 57–58.

22. Corominas with Pascual, *Diccionario*, I. 443.

23. Vasvári, "Semiología." See, for example, st. 451: "De tus joyas fermosas, cada que dar podieres. . .; / quando dar non quisieres, o quando non tovieres, / promete e manda mucho, maguer non ge lo dieres; / luego estará afusiada, fará lo que quisieres" (Of your beautiful jewels, give whatever you are able. . .; / should you not wish to give, or when you don't have

anything, / promise and command a great deal, in spite of the fact that you don't give it, / then she will be reassured, and she will do whatever you want).

24. For a brief discussion of the centrality of *domus* in women's lives, see Lacarra, "Notes."

25. Walsh, "Names," p. 159.

26. Zahareas and Pereira, *Itinerario*, p. 216.

27. Deyermond, "Vision"; see Dagenais, Review, p. 1206.

28. Note that Vasvári points out that "el clavo echar" plays on the sacrilegious parody of the lyric to manifest a level of sexual euphemism, translating it as "he knew how to drive in the nail / he really screwed me good," where "screw" has the Modern English sense of deceit and sexual intercourse, "Semiotics," p. 140; also see her "Semiología," pp. 306, 310, 317–18. Also Burke, "Again Cruz," Gerli, "*Mal de la cruzada*," Morros, "Liturgía."

29. On widow's in frontier society, see Dillard, *Daughters*, pp. 99, 105–06, 120–25.

30. Joset, *Libro*, 1328–29n. Gybbon-Monypenny, in *Libro*, 1328–29n, follows the suggestion (Blecua, *Libro*, 1328n) that there may be a lacuna in the sole witness, MS *S*.

31. On frontier practice, see Dillard, *Daughters*, pp. 99–100.

32. Vasvári, "Widow."

33. On the lascivious Mora, see Vasvári, *Heterotextual*, pp. 51–57 and "Erotic Wedding," p. 4.

34. *Partida* VII.XII.x; also Ratcliffe, "Judíos," pp. 424–38.

35. Dillard, *Daughters*, p. 131.

36. Vasvári, "Erotic Wedding," pp. 6–7.

37. She uses the tales of the Gardener and the Snake, the Town Mouse and the Country Mouse, the Fox Who Played Dead, the Fox and the Crow, and the Devil and the Thief at the Gallows; tales 25, 27, 30, 32, and 34, respectively.

38. Trotaconventos tells of the Hunter and the Greyhound, the Cockerel and the Sapphire, the Ass and the Lapdog (discussed in chapter 2), the Lion and the Mouse, and Hares Fear the Sound of Waves; tales 26, 28–29, 31, and 33, respectively.

39. See Daichman, *Wayward Nuns* on truant female religious.

40. Gybbon-Monypenny (*Libro*, 1502dn) follows Morreale, "Corominas," (1969), p. 155, and Joset, *Libro*, in rejecting the view that the affair is consummated.

41. Hook, "Further Onomastic Footnotes," p. 158, and "More Melons," p. 188, documents four cases of its use before the composition of the *Libro*.

42. Tate, "Adventures," pp. 219–29.

43. Zahareas and Pereira, *Itinerario*, pp. 268, 278. At p. 279, they observe that rubrics introducing the adventures and their lyrics suggest that the MS *S* copyist, or possibly the author, distinguishes between the Archpriest as protagonist of the prose and as poet of the lyrics.

44. On announced lyrics that are not present in the manuscripts, see Lawrance, "*Libro*," p. 46.

45. Deyermond, "Aspects of Parody," pp. 62–64, Clark, "Ruiz," Marino, *Serranilla*, pp. 42–64, de Lope, *Traditions*, Zink, "*Serrana*," pp. 88–91.

46. De Lope, *Traditions*, p. 150; her discussion of Saint Julian, pp. 148–50, does not focus on the carnivalesque reversal of roles. Rather she points out that both La Chata and Saint Julian are gatekeepers associated with water-crossings: "Acte magique et sacré, dont on trouve la trace aussi bien dans les rites populaires de l'initiation et de la fecondité que dans la devotion aux saints du christianisme" (at p. 150).

47. Morreale, "Corominas," (1971), p. 302 interprets "erizo" as the outershell of a chestnut, which she argues is peeled off by stamping on and hitting it. However, there is no reason to rule out hedgehog since the traditional method of cooking is said to involve caking the unskinned carcass in mud or rolling it in leaves and roasting it under a fire; the spines and skin then easily separate from the cooked flesh.

48. The place name Cornejo may be linked to the appearance of *cornejo*, 'crow,' at 980c ("lieva te dende, cornejo, non busques más contienda" [get up from there, crow, don't keep looking for a fight]) in MS *S*, which has not been adequately explained, and itself may even be a *lapsus scribendi*. MS *G*, the only other witness, has "ca dise la pastrana quien yerra non emienda" (as the saying goes, whoever errs does not make damage good).

49. Zahareas and Pereira, *Itinerario*, pp. 279–80.

50. See Lida de Malkiel, *Masterpieces*, p. 42, on Menga's character.

51. Tate, "Adventures," p. 222.

52. Tate, "Adventures," p. 222, Lida de Malkiel, *Masterpieces*, p. 43.

53. De Lope, *Traditions*, p. 89.

54. See, for example, 285–90.

55. In the light of the predominant taste for pale skin, the reference to her rosy color may not be intended to be complimentary or it may highlight a difference in rural and urban aesthetic.

56. White bread was considered a luxury food in comparison with lower-quality bran or unleavened breads, which were easier to produce.

57. Zahareas, *Art*, pp. 16–20, documents a similar misappropriation of *vanidad*, "vanity."

58. Jauralde Pou, *Libro*, p. 983abn.

59. Jenaro-MacLennan, "Fuentes," pp. 300–14. This view is also seen in Don Amor's admonition in his *ars amatoria* that the Archpriest avoid drunkenness (st. 528–49a), where he cites the *exemplum* about the hermit whom the devil tempts to drink alcohol, and who ends up committing rape and murder after his lust is incited by seeing a cockerel mount hens.

60. Of the serranas, Alda is promised jewelry and a pouch (957d) in the narrative, and clothes and jewelry in the lyric (966bcd), the Archpriest refers to making payment to Gadea (992b), and Alda asks for clothes and jewelry in the final lyric. Of the other women, for example, the Archpriest offers Cruz wheat (119b; see discussion in this chapter), songs to the Dueña Ençerrada (171bcd), the Viuda Loçana (1319b), and, on the Archpriest's behalf, the Vieja gives the Dueña Apuesta songs, a belt, and a ring, the latter two probably as part of a *philocaptio* (918abc).

61. De Lope's *Traditions* extensively documents sexual content.

62. The Archpriest also alludes to an active use of memory at the opening of the first amorous adventure, comprising repentance for, or regret about, that particular affair: "Assí fue que un tienpo una dueña me prisso; / de su amor non fui en ese tienpo rrepiso" (77ab; So it happened that once a lady captured me; / at that time I had not repented of her love).

63. *Verse* does not appear at all in the other adventures nor in the first lyric, where *ver* occurs only once in thirteen seven-line stanzas. In the second narrative, *ver* is used three times in fifteen stanzas and in the fourth, five times in sixteen stanzas, which include the description of Alda.

64. De Lope, *Traditions*, pp. 184–95 and 225–42, discusses intertexts such as the quest and spiritual journey.

65. The weather is described in the first and third narrative, and in both sections of the fourth adventure, and the terrain in the first and second narratives, and second lyric.

66. Bakhtin, *Rabelais*, pp. 17–30, Deyermond, "Aspects of Parody," p. 63.

67. De Lope, *Traditions*, pp. 88–89.

68. See also the discussion in chapter 2, p. 89, on *perdizes*, "partridges."

69. *Luchar* is used in the erotic sense in this episode at 971b.

70. Morreale's suggestion, "Corominas," (1971), p. 313, of "la energía y aplomo de ésta" (her energy and composure) for "con su enhoto" has not been widely accepted.

71. De Lope, *Traditions*, pp. 129–30.

72. Limon, *Stand-Up Comedy*, p. 57.

73. Burke, *Desire*, pp. 194–95.

74. *Desire*, pp. 195–96; also his "Juan Ruiz."

75. Clark, "Ruiz," Marino, *Serranilla*, pp. 57–58, 60.

76. Dillard observes "secular society took little official interest in the clergyman's concubine except to establish her children's rights to inherit their father's property," such were the demands of repopulation of the *meseta* (*Daughters*, p. 132).

77. Dillard, *Daughters*, p. 133; Pérez López, "Fecha."

78. Bakhtin, *Rabelais*, pp. 18–30; discussed in the introduction, pp. 7–8

79. Lawrance, "Audience."

80. "Note," p. 416.

81. "Note," p. 419.

82. On modern performance humour, see Limon, *Stand-Up Comedy*, p. 117.

83. Vasvári, "Semiotics," p. 419. On the phallicism of stand-up comedy see Limon, *Stand-Up Comedy*, pp. 117–19.

84. Limon, *Stand-Up Comedy*, pp. 105, 108–09.

85. Žižek, "Courtly Love," pp. 89–112; Lacan, "Courtly Love," p. 153.

86. Lacan, *Seminar*, p. 54.

87. Lacan, "Courtly Love," p. 153.

88. Lacan, *Séminaire*, p. 431, cited and translated in Gaunt, "Look," p. 82.

89. Gaunt, "Look," p. 82.

90. The transformation of the narrator from the figure of the Archpriest into Don Melón de la Huerta is not made explicit until 727c; for the purposes of

this analysis, I accept Deyermond's proposal that the encounter is to be understood as a dream vision. Deyermond concedes that the fact the dream alter-ego has a different name is odd, "Vision," p. 121.

91. Paxson, *Poetics*, pp. 93–99, 116–17.
92. Gaunt, "Look," p. 86.
93. Zahareas and Pereira, *Itinerario*, p. 212.
94. Lacan, *Écrits*, p. 106.
95. Lacan, *Écrits*, p. 106.
96. On affective piety, see Bynum, *Jesus* and *Fragmentation*, Wack, *Lovesickness*, Beckwith, *Christ's Body*, pp. 50–55.
97. Rico, "Mantenencia," pp. 172–73.
98. *Libro*, pp. 107–08.
99. See, for example, Don Amor's allusion to the need to choose a go-between who is habituated to working for the religious (438, 441), and the emphasis on the participation of nuns and clerics in Don Amor's triumphal procession (1235–41, 1247–52, and 1258).
100. Excluding insults, in the mountains he is addressed as *escudero* (961c; squire), *fidalgo* (965f, 1031b; gentleman), *amigo* (966e; friend or lover), *pariente* (999a, 1027b; friend (lit. relative)), and *huesped* (1032a; guest), is thought to be a *pastor* (994a; shepherd, priest), and he claims to be married or betrothed (1028b).

## Conclusion: Sex, Scandal, and Sermon

1. Bynum, "Why All the Fuss" p. 33.
2. The "Cántica" is based on the *Consultatio sacerdotum*; see Lecoy, *Recherches*, pp. 229–36, Zahareas, *Art*, pp. 105–12 and "Structure," Bueno, *Sotana*, pp. 74–80, and Kelly, *Law*. Gybbon-Monypenny observes that dating formula, "Allá en Talavera, en las calendas de abril" (1690a), with which the episode opens, echoes the synodal constitution promulgated by Archbishop Gil de Albornoz in April 1342, "Datum apud Toletum XVI Kalendas Maii anno Domini millesimo trecentesimo quadragesimo segundo. . .": *Libro*, 1690an. Even if Ruiz deliberately echoes such dating formula, the possibility that the spring opening is a parodic allusion to love lyric cannot be ruled out.
3. Beckwith, *Christ's Body*, pp. 52–63.
4. Haywood, "Imagen," pp. 62–63, 79–80.
5. Michael, "*Treatment*," pp. 266–68.
6. Quotation from Kupfer, *Romanesque Wall Painting*, p. 116; also see pp. 78–80, 121, and Mateo Gómez, *Temas profanos*, p. 226; Mâle, *Religious Art*, pp. 68–69, and Wieck, *Time*, pp. 45–54.
7. For the *mappamundi* see British Library, London, Add. MS 28681, fol 9ʳ; plate 2 in Camille, *Image*, p. 15.

# WORKS CITED

Adolf, Helen, "The Ass and the Harp," *Speculum* 25 (1950): 49–57.

Alarcos Llorach, E., "*Libro de Buen Amor*, 432d: ¿ancheta de caderas?" in *El Arcipreste de Hita: el libro, el autor, la tierra, la época; Actas del I Congreso Internacional sobre el Arcipreste de Hita*, ed. M. Criado de Val (Barcelona: SERESA, 1973), pp. 171–74.

Alfonso X el Sabio, *Primera partida según el manuscrito Add. 20.787 del British Museum*, ed. Juan Antonio Arias Bonet (Valladolid: Universidad, 1975).

Alonso, Dámaso, "La bella de Juan Ruiz, toda problemas," in *De los siglos oscuros al de oro: notas y artículos a través de 700 años de letras españolas*, Biblioteca Románica Hispánica 2.37 (Madrid: Gredos, 1958), pp. 86–99.

Amasuno, Marcelino V., "El saber médico tras el prólogo del *Libro de buen amor*: loco amor y amor hereos," in *Juan Ruiz, Arcipreste de Hita, y el "Libro de Buen Amor": Congreso Internacional del Centro para la Edición de los Clásicos Españoles celebrado en Alcalá la Real del 9 al 11 de mayo de 2002*, ed. Francisco Toro Ceballos and Bienvenido Morros (Alcalá la Real: Ayuntamiento & Centro para la Edición de los Clásicos Españoles, 2004), pp. 247–70.

Arcipreste de Hita, *Libro de buen amor*, ed. G.B. Gybbon-Monypenny, Clásicos Castalia 161 (Madrid: Castalia, 1989).

Arias, Consuelo, "El espacio femenino en tres obras del medioevo español: de la reclusión a la transgresión," *La Torre* 1 (1987): 365–88.

Arizaleta, Amaia, *La translation d'Alexandre: Recherches sur les structures et les significations du "Libro de Alexandre"* (Paris: Klincksieck, 1999).

Augustine of Hippo, *The City of God against the Pagans*, III: *Books, VIII–XI*, ed. and trans. David S. Wiesan, Loeb Classical Library 413 (London: Heinemann; Cambridge, MA: Harvard University Press, 1968).

———, *Concerning the City of God against the Pagans*, trans. Henry Bettenson (Harmondsworth: Penguin, 1972).

Bakhtin, Mikhail, *Rabelais and his World*, trans. Hélène Iswolsky (1968; Bloomington: Indiana University Press, 1984).

Baños Vallejo, Fernando, "Plegarias de héroes y de santos: más datos sobre la 'oración narrativa,'" *Hispanic Review* 62 (1994): 205–15.

Barbera, Raymond E., "Juan Ruiz and 'Los dientes. . .un poco apartadillos,'" *Hispanic Review* 36 (1968): 262–63.

Bataillon, Louis-Jacques, *La Prédication au XIIIe siècle en France et Italie: études et documents*, Variorum CS402 (Aldershot: Variorum/Ashgate, 1993).

Beattie, Blake, "Lawyers, Law and Sanctity in Sermons from Papal Avignon," in *Models of Holiness in Medieval Sermons: Proceedings of the International Symposium (Kalamazoo, 4–7 May 1995)*, Textes et Études du Moyen Âge 5 (Louvain-la-Neuve: Féderation Internationale des Instituts d'Études Médiévales, 1996), pp. 259–82.

Beckwith, Sarah, *Christ's Body: Identity, Culture and Society in Late Medieval Writings* (New York: Routledge, 1993).

Beltrán, Luis, *Razones de buen amor: oposiciones y convergencias en el libro del Arcipreste de Hita* (Madrid: Fundación Juan March and Castalia, 1977).

Berger, John, *Ways of Seeing* (London: BBC, 1972).

Biernoff, Suzannah, *Sight and Embodiment in the Middle Ages* (London: Palgrave Macmillan, 2002).

Blackmore, Josiah, and Gregory S. Hutcheson, ed. *Queer Iberia: Sexualities, Cultures, and Crossings from the Middle Ages to the Renaissance* (Durham, NC: Duke University Press, 1999).

Blecua, Alberto, ed., Juan Ruiz, Arcipreste de Hita, *Libro de buen amor*, Letras Hispánicas 70 (Madrid: Cátedra, 1992).

Bloch, R. Howard, *Medieval French Literature and the Law* (Berkeley: University of California Press, 1977).

———, *The Scandal of the Fabliaux* (Chicago: University of Chicago Press, 1986).

Brown, Catherine, *Contrary Things: Exegesis, Dialectic, and the Poetics of Didacticism* (Stanford: Stanford University Press, 1998).

Brownlee, Marina Scordilis, "Autobiography as Self-(Re)presentation: The Augustinian Paradigm and Juan Ruiz's Theory of Reading," in *Mimesis: From Mirror to Method, Augustine to Descartes*, ed. John D. Lyons and Stephen G. Nichols (Hanover: University Press of New England for Dartmouth College, 1982), pp. 71–82.

———, *The Status of the Reading Subject in the "Libro de buen amor,"* North Carolina Studies in the Romance Languages and Literatures 224 (Chapel Hill: University of North Carolina Press, 1985).

Bryson, Norman, *Vision and Painting: The Logic of the Gaze* (London: Macmillan, 1983).

Bueno, Julián L., *La sotana de Juan Ruiz: elementos eclesiásticos en el "Libro de buen amor"* (York, SC: Spanish Literature Publications, 1983).

Burke, James F., "Again Cruz, the Baker-Girl: *Libro de buen amor*, ss. 115–120," *Revista Canadiense de Estudios Hispánicos* 4 (1980): 253–70.

———, *Desire against the Law: The Juxtaposition of Contraries in Early Medieval Spanish Literature* (Stanford: Stanford University Press, 1998).

———, "Juan Ruiz, the *Serranas*, and the Rites of Spring," *Journal of Medieval and Renaissance Studies* 5 (1975): 13–35.

———, "The *Libro de buen amor* and the Medieval Meditative Sermon Tradition," *La córonica* 9 (1980–81): 122–27.

———, *Vision, the Gaze, and the Function of the Senses in "Celestina"* (University Park: Pennsylvania State University Press, 2000).

Butler, Judith, *Excitable Speech: A Politics of the Performative* (New York: Routledge, 1997).

————, *Gender Trouble: Feminism and the Subversion of Identity* (London: Routledge, 1990).

Bynum, Caroline Walker, *Fragmentation and Redemption: Essays on Gender and the Human Body in Medieval Religion* (New York: Zone, 1991).

————, *Jesus as Mother: Studies in the Spirituality of the High Middle Ages* (Berkeley: University of California Press, 1982).

————, "Why All the Fuss about the Body? A Medievalist's Perspective," *Critical Inquiry* 22 (1995): 3–33.

Cadden, Joan, *Meanings of Sex Difference in the Middle Ages: Medicine, Science, and Art* (Cambridge: Cambridge University Press, 1993).

Camille, Michael, *Image on the Edge: The Margins of Medieval Art* (London: Reaktion, 1992).

Carruthers, Mary J., *The Book of Memory: A Study of Memory in Medieval Culture*, Cambridge Studies in Medieval Literature 10 (Cambridge: Cambridge University Press, 1990).

————, *The Craft of Thought: Meditation, Rhetoric, and the Making of Images 400–1200*, Cambridge Studies in Medieval Literature 34 (Cambridge: Cambridge University Press, 1998).

Cátedra, Pedro M., *Amor y pedagogía en la Edad Media: estudios de doctrina amorosa y práctica literaria*, Acta Salmanticensia: Estudios Filológicos 212 (Salamanca: Universidad, 1989).

Charland, Th.-M., ed., *Artes praedicandi: Contribution a l'histoire de la rhétorique au Moyen Âge*, Publications de l'Institut d'Études Médiévales d'Ottawa 7 (Montreal: Institut d'Études Médiévales, 1936).

Chaucer, Geoffrey, *The Wife of Bath's Prologue*, in *The Riverside Chaucer*, ed. Larry D. Benson et al. (Oxford: Oxford University Press, 1988), pp. 105–16.

Chrzanowski, Joseph A., "La estética grotesca de Juan Ruiz en el *Enxienplo de los dos perezosos*," *Romance Notes* 12 (1970–71): 213–18.

Clark, Dorothy Clotelle, "Juan Ruiz and Andreas Capellanus," *Hispanic Review* 40 (1972): 390–411.

Clifton, James, *The Body of Christ in the Art of Europe and New Spain, 1150–1800* (NeMunich: Prestel, 1997).

Clover, Carol J., "The Eye of Horror," in *Viewing Positions: Ways of Seeing Film*, ed. Linda Williams (New Brunswick, NJ: Rutgers University Press, 1994), pp. 184–230.

Colish, Marcia L., "Peter Lombard," in *The Medieval Theologians*, ed. G.R. Evans (Oxford: Blackwell, 2001), pp. 168–83.

————, *Peter Lombard*, 2 vols. (Leiden: E.J. Brill, 1994).

Corominas, Joan, ed., Juan Ruiz, *Libro de Buen Amor*, Biblioteca Románica Hispánica 4.4 (Madrid: Gredos, 1967).

————, with José A. Pascual, *Diccionario crítico etimológico castellano e hispánico*, Biblioteca Románica Hispánica 5.7, 6 vols (Madrid: Gredos, 1980–83).

Crombie, A.C., *Science, Optics and Music in Medieval and Modern Thought* (London: Hambleton, 1990).

Cuartero Sancho, María Pilar, "La paremiología en el *Libro de buen amor*," in *Juan Ruiz, Arcipreste de Hita, y el "Libro de Buen Amor": Congreso Internacional del*

*Centro para la Edición de los Clásicos Españoles celebrado en Alcalá la Real del 9 al 11 de mayo de 2002*, ed. Francisco Toro Ceballos and Bienvenido Morros (Alcalá la Real: Ayuntamiento & Centro para la Edición de los Clásicos Españoles, 2004), pp. 215–34.

Curry, Walter Clyde, "More about Chaucer's Wife of Bath," *PMLA* 37 (1922): 30–51.

Dagenais, John, *The Ethics of Reading in Manuscript Culture: Glossing the "Libro de buen amor"* (Princeton: Princeton University Press, 1994).

———, "A Further Source for the Literary Ideas in Juan Ruiz's Prologue," *Journal of Hispanic Philology* 11 (1986–87): 23–52.

———, Review of *A Companion to the "Libro de Buen Amor,"* ed. Louise M. Haywood and Louise O. Vasvári, Támesis A206 (Woodbridge: Boydell & Brewer, 2004); *Speculum* 81 (2006): 1205–07.

———, "'Se usa e se faz': Naturalist Truth in a *Pamphilus* Explicit and the *Libro de buen amor,"* *Hispanic Review* 57 (1989): 417–36.

Daichman, Graciela S., *Wayward Nuns in Medieval Literature* (Syracuse: Syracuse University Press, 1986).

"La Dame qui aveine demandoit pour Morel sa provende avoir," *Nouveau Recueil complet des fabliaux*, ed. Willem Noomen (Assen: Van Gorcum, 1996), IX. 183–99.

"La Damoisele qui ne pooit oïr parler de foutre," *Nouveau Recueil complet des fabliaux*, ed. Willem Noomen and Nico van den Boogaart with H.B. Sol (Assen: Van Gorcum, 1988), IV. 57–89.

Davies, Oliver, "Later Medieval Mystics," in *The Medieval Theologians*, ed. G.R. Evans (Oxford: Blackwell, 2001), pp. 221–32.

Davis, Norman, Douglas Gray, Patricia Ingham, and Anne Wallace-Hadrill, *A Chaucer Glossary* (Oxford: Clarendon Press, 1979).

De Lope, Monique, *Traditions populaires et textualité dans le "Libro de Buen Amor"* (Montpellier: Centre d'Études et de Recherches Sociocritiques, Université Paul Valéry, [1984]).

Deyermond, Alan, "The Greeks, the Romans, the Astrologers and the Meaning of the *Libro de Buen Amor,"* *Romance Notes* 5 (1963–64): 88–91.

———, "Mester es sen pecado," *Romanische Forschungen* 77 (1965): 111–16.

———, "Some Aspects of Parody in the *Libro de buen amor,"* in *"Libro de buen amor" Studies*, ed. G.B. Gybbon-Monypenny, Támesis A12 (London: Tamesis, 1970), pp. 53–78.

———, "Spain's First Women Writers," in *Women in Hispanic Literature: Icons and Fallen Idols*, ed. Beth Miller (Berkeley: University of California Press, 1983), pp. 27–52.

———, "'Was It a Vision or a Waking Dream?': The Anomalous Don Amor and Doña Endrina Episodes Reconsidered," *A Companion to the "Libro de Buen Amor,"* ed. Louise M. Haywood and Louise O. Vasvári, Támesis A206 (Woodbridge: Tamesis, 2004), pp. 107–22.

Deyermond, Alan, and Roger M. Walker, "A Further Vernacular Source for the *Libro de buen amor,"* *Bulletin of Hispanic Studies* 46 (1969): 193–200.

Dillard, Heath, *Daughters of the Reconquest: Women in Castilian Town Society, 1100–1300* (Cambridge: Cambridge University Press, 1984).

*Doncella Teodor*, in *Narrativa popular de la Edad Media: 'Doncella Teodor,' 'Flores y Blancaflor,' 'París y Viana,'* ed. Nieves Baranda and Víctor Infantes, Nuestros Clásicos 14 (Madrid: Akal, 1995).

Douglas, Mary, *Purity and Danger: An Analysis of the Concepts of Pollution and Taboo* (1965; London: Ark, 1984).

Dunn, Peter N., "'De las figuras del arcipreste,'" in G.B. Gybbon-Monypenny, *"Libro de buen amor" Studies*, Támesis A12 (London: Tamesis, 1970), pp. 79–93.

Duque, Ariano, "Religious Imagery in the *Poema de Fernán González*," unpublished paper read to the 40th International Congress on Medieval Studies, Kalamazoo, University of Michigan, May 7, 2005; revised version in press, *La corónica* 36 (2007–08).

Ekman, Erik, "'Leçión e muestra de metrificar e rimmar e de troba': *Trobar* in the *Libro de buen amor*," *Hispanic Journal* 24 (2003): 9–12.

"L'Esquiriel," *Nouveau Recueil complet des fabliaux*, ed. Willem Noomen (Assen: Van Gorcum, 1991), VI. 31–49.

Faulhaber, Charles, "Retóricas clásicas y medievales en bibliotecas castellanas," *Ábaco* 4 (1973): 151–300.

Foucault, Michel, *Discipline and Punish: The Birth of Prison*, trans. Alan Sheridan (1975; repr. Harmondsworth: Penguin, 1982).

Freud, Sigmund, *Introductory Lectures on Psychoanalysis*, trans. James Strachey, ed. Strachey and Angela Richards, Penguin Freud Library 1 (1916–17; Harmondsworth: Penguin, 1974).

———, *Jokes and their Relation to the Unconscious*, trans. James Strachey, ed. Angela Richards, Penguin Freud Library 6 (1905; Harmondsworth: Penguin, 1991).

———, *On the Interpretation of Dreams*, ed. and trans. James Strachey, Penguin Freud Library 4 (1900; Harmondsworth: Penguin, 1976).

———, *On Sexuality: Three Essays on the Theory of Sexuality and Other Works*, trans. James Strachey, ed. Angela Richards, Penguin Freud Library 7 (1905, 1910; Harmondsworth: Penguin, 1977).

Gaunt, Simon, "The Look of Love: The Gender of the Gaze in Troubadour Lyric," in *Troubled Vision: Gender, Sexuality, and Sight in Medieval Text and Image*, ed. Emma Campbell and Robert Mills (New York: Palgrave Macmillan, 2004), pp. 79–95.

Geary, John S., "The 'Pitas Payas' Episode of the *Libro de buen amor*: Its Structure and Comic Climax," *Romance Philology* 49 (1995–96): 245–61.

Gerli, Michael E., "The Greeks, the Romans, and the Ambiguity of Signs: *De doctrina christiana*, the Fall, and the Hermeneutics of the *Libro de buen amor*," *Bulletin of Spanish Studies* 79 (2002): 411–28.

———, "*El mal de la cruzada*: Notes on Juan Ruiz's *troba cazurra*," *Revista Canadiense de Estudios Hispánicos* 9 (1985): 220–27.

———, "The *Ordo commendationis animae* and the Cid Poet," *MLN* 95 (1980): 436–41.

———, "'Recta voluntas est bonus amor': St Augustine and the Didactic Structure of the *Libro de buen amor*," *Romance Philology* 35 (1981–82): 500–08.

Gilman, Sander L., *The Parodic Sermon in European Perspective: Aspects of Liturgical Parody from the Middle Ages to the Twentieth Century*, Beiträge zur Literatur des XV. Bis XVIII. Jahrhunderts 6 (Wiesbaden: Steiner, 1974).

Gimeno Casalduero, Joaquín, "Sobre la 'oración narrativa' medieval: estructura, origen y supervivencia," in *Estructura y diseño en la literatura castellana medieval* (Madrid: Porrúa Turanzas, 1975), pp. 11–29.

Gimeno, Rosalie, "Women in the *Book of Good Love*," in *Women in Hispanic Literature: Icons and Fallen Idols*, ed. Beth Miller (Berkeley: University of California Press, 1983), pp. 84–96.

Girard, René, *Deceit, Desire, and the Novel: Self and Other in Literary Structure*, trans. Yvonne Freccero (Baltimore: Johns Hopkins Press, 1965).

———, "The Mimetic Desire of Paolo and Francesca," in *"To Double Business Bound": Essays on Literature, Mimesis, and Anthropology* (Baltimore: Johns Hopkins University Press, 1978), pp. 1–8.

Goldberg, Harriet, "Personal Descriptions in Medieval Texts: Decorative or Functional?" *Hispanófila* 87 (1986): 1–12.

Gómez Moreno, Ángel, "Una forma especial del tópico de modestia," *La corónica* 12 (1983–84): 71–83.

———, "Notas al prólogo del *Libro de Alexandre*," *Revista de Literatura* 46 (1984): 117–27.

Gómez Redondo, Fernando, *Historia de la prosa medieval castellana*, I: *La creación del discurso prosístico; el entramado cortesano* (Madrid: Cátedra, 1998).

Gonzálvez Ruiz, Ramón, "La persona de Juan Ruiz," in *Juan Ruiz, Arcipreste de Hita, y el "Libro de Buen Amor": Congreso Internacional del Centro para la Edición de los Clásicos Españoles celebrado en Alcalá la Real del 9 al 11 de mayo de 2002*, ed. Francisco Toro Ceballos and Bienvenido Morros (Alcalá la Real: Ayuntamiento & Centro para la Edición de los Clásicos Españoles), pp. 37–67.

Green, Otis H., *Spain and the Western Tradition: The Castilian Mind in Literature from "El Cid" to Calderón* (Madison: University of Wisconsin Press, 1963), I.

Grieve, Patricia E., *Desire and Death in the Spanish Sentimental Romance, 1440–1550* (Newark, Del: Juan de la Cuesta, 1987).

Grosz, Elizabeth, "The Body of Signification," in *Abjection, Melancholia, and Love: The Work of Julia Kristeva*, ed. John Fletcher and Andrew Benjamin (London: Routledge, 1990), pp. 80–103.

Gybbon-Monypenny, G.B., "The Two Versions of the *Libro de buen amor*: The Extent and Nature of the Author's Revision," *Bulletin of Hispanic Studies* 39 (1962): 205–21.

Harpham, Geoffrey Galt, *On the Grotesque: Strategies of Contradiction in Art and Literature* (Princeton: Princeton University Press, 1982).

Hart, Thomas R., *La alegoría en el "Libro de buen amor"* (Madrid: Occidente, 1959; repr. in *The Allegory of the "Libro de buen amor," and Other Studies*, Papers of the Medieval Hispanic Research Seminar 58 (London: Dept of Hispanic Studies, Queen Mary, University of London, 2006)).

Harvey, Ruth E., *The Inner Wits: Psychological Theory in the Middle Ages and the Renaissance*, Warburgh Institute Surveys 6 (London: Warburgh Institute, University of London, 1975).

Haywood, Louise M., "Imagen y palabra: algunos aspectos de la alegoría medieval," in *Las metamorfosis de la alegoría: discurso y sociedad en la Península Ibérica desde la Edad Media hasta la Edad contemporánea*, ed. Rebeca Sanmartín Bastida and Rosa Vidal Doval (Madrid: Vervuert Iberoamericana, 2005), pp. 105–25.

————, "Juan Ruiz and the *Libro de Buen Amor*: Contexts and Milieu," in Haywood and Louise O. Vasvári, *A Companion to the "Libro de Buen Amor,"* Támesis A206 (Woodbridge: Tamesis, 2004), pp. 21–38.

————, "Pasiones, Angustias y Dolores en el *Libro de buen amor* de Juan Ruiz," in *Actas del VIII Congreso de la Asociación Hispánica de Literatura Medieval (Santander, 1999)* (Santander: University, 2000), I. 935–44.

Haywood, Louise M., and Louise O. Vasvári, "Reading the *Libro de Buen Amor* Thirty Years On," in *A Companion to the "Libro de Buen Amor,"* ed. Haywood and Vasvári, Támesis A206 (Woodbridge: Tamesis, 2004), pp. 1–17.

Hernández, Francisco J., "Ferrán Martínez, 'escrivano del rey', canónigo de Toledo y autor del *Libro del cavallero Zifar*," *Revista de Archivos, Bibliotecas y Museos*, 81 (1978): 289–325.

Herriott, J. Homer, "A Thirteenth-Century Manuscript of the *Primera partida*," *Speculum* 13 (1938): 278–94.

Heusch, Carlos, "'Por aver juntamiento con fenbra plazentera:' el astuto naturalismo amatorio de Juan Ruiz," in *El "Libro de buen amor" de Juan Ruiz, Archiprêtre de Hita*, ed. Heusch (Paris: Ellipses, 2005), pp. 129–42.

Hissette, Roland, *Enquête sur les 219 articles condamnés à Paris le 7 mars 1277*, Philosophes Médiévaux 22 (Louvain: Publications Universitaires, 1977).

Hook, David, "Further Onomastic Footnotes for the *Libro de buen amor*," *Forum for Modern Language Studies* 29 (1993): 156–64.

————, "More Melons for Doña Endrina: Problems of Onomastic Humour in the *Libro de buen amor*," *Historicist Essays on Hispano-Medieval Narrative in Memory of Roger M. Walker*, Publications of the Modern Humanities Research Association 16 (London: Maney for the MHRA, 2005), pp.185–200.

Impey, Olga Tudorică, "La *fin'amors* y sus términos en la prosa histórica de Alfonso X: un caso de reflexión y refracción," *Revista Canadiense de Estudios Hispánicos* 9 (1985): 369–84.

Jauralde Pou, Pablo, ed. and trans. [Arcipreste de Hita], *Libro de buen amor*, Arbolí 16 (Tarragona: Tarraco, 1981).

Jenaro-MacLennan, L., "Las fuentes de las estrofas 544–545 del *Libro de Buen Amor*," *Vox Romanica* 21 (1962): 300–14.

————, "Los presupuestos intelectuales del prólogo al *Libro de buen amor*," *Anuario de Estudios Medievales* 9 (1974–79): 151–86.

Joset, Jacques, "El pensamiento de Juan Ruiz," in *Juan Ruiz, Arcipreste de Hita, y el "Libro de Buen Amor": Congreso Internacional del Centro para la Edición de los Clásicos Españoles celebrado en Alcalá la Real del 9 al 11 de mayo de 2002*, ed. Francisco Toro Ceballos and Bienvenido Morros (Alcalá la Real: Ayuntamiento & Centro para la Edición de los Clásicos Españoles, 2004), pp. 105–128.

————, ed., Arcipreste de Hita, *Libro de buen amor*, Clásicos Castellanos 14 and 17 (Madrid: Castalia, 1974).

Juan de Mena, *Tratado de amor*, in *Obras completas*, ed. Miguel Ángel Pérez Priego, Clásicos Universales Plantea 175 (Barcelona: Planeta, 1989), pp. 379–91.

Kane, Elisha K., "The Personal Appearance of Juan Ruiz," *MLN* 45 (1930): 103–09.

Kantorowicz, Ernst H., *The King's Two Bodies: A Study in Mediaeval Political Theory* (Princeton: Princeton University Press, 1957; repr. 1997).

Karras, Ruth Mazo, *Common Women: Prostitution and Sexuality in Medieval England* (Oxford: Oxford University Press, 1996).

Kasten, Ll., and J. Nitti, ed. *Concordances and Texts of the Royal Scriptorium Manuscripts of Alfonso X el Sabio* (Madison: Hispanic Seminary of Medieval Studies, 2002).

Kelly, Henry Ansgar, *Canon Law and the Archpriest of Hita*, Medieval & Renaissance Texts & Studies 27 (Binghamton: Center for Medieval & Early Renaissance Studies, 1984).

Kienzel, Beverly Mayne, "The Typology of the Medieval Sermon and its Development in the Middle Ages: Report on Work in Progress," in *De l'homélie au sermon: histoire de la prédication médiévale: Actes du Colloque International de Louvain–la–Neuve, 9–11 juillet 1992*, ed. Jacqueline Hamesse and Xavier Hermand, Textes, Études, Congrès 14 (Louvain-la-Neuve: Institut d'Études Médiévales de l'Université Catholique de Louvain, 1993), pp. 83–101.

Kinkade, Richard P., "'*Intellectum tibi dabo. . .*': The Function of Free Will in the *Libro de buen amor*," *Bulletin of Hispanic Studies* 47 (1970): 296–315.

Kinkade, Richard P., and Thomas M. Capuano, "Los folios finales del MS *S* del *Libro de buen amor*," *La córonica* 34.2 (2006): 229–58.

Kirby, Steven D., "Juan Ruiz's *Serranas*: The Archpriest-Pilgrim and Medieval Wild Women," in *Hispanic Studies in Honor of Alan D. Deyermond: A North American Tribute* (Madison: Hispanic Seminary of Medieval Studies, 1986), pp. 151–69.

Klassen, Norman, *Chaucer on Love, Knowledge, and Sight*, Chaucer Studies 21 (Cambridge: Brewer, 1995).

Kleffens, Eelco Nickolaas van, *Hispanic Law until the End of the Middle Ages* (Edinburgh: Edinburgh University Press, 1968).

Klibansky, Raymond, Erwin Panofsky, and Fritz Saxl, *Saturn and Melancholy: Studies in the History of Natural Philosophy, Religion and Art* (London: Nelson, 1964).

Koopmans, Jelle, ed. *Quatre sermons joyeux*, Textes Littéraires Français 327 (Geneva: Droz, 1984).

———, ed. *Recueil de sermons joyeux*, Textes Littéraires Français 362 (Geneva: Droz, 1988).

Koopmans, Jelle, and Paul Verhuyck, *Sermon joyeux et truanderie: Villon, Nemo, Ulespiègle*, Faux Titre 29 (Amsterdam: Rodopi, 1987).

Kristeva, Julia, *Pouvoirs de l'horreur: essai sur l'abjection* (Paris: Seuil, 1980).

Kuhn, Annette, "Lawless Seeing," in her *The Power of the Image: Essays on Representation and Sexuality* (London: Routledge & Kegan Paul, 1985), pp. 19–47.

Kupfer, Marcia A., *Romanesque Wall Painting in Central France: The Politics of Narrative* (New Haven: Yale University Press, 1993).

Lacan, Jacques, "Courtly Love as Anamorphosis," *The Seminar of Jacques Lacan: VII, The Ethics of Psychoanalysis, 1959–60*, ed. Jacques-Alain Miller, trans. Dennis Porter (London: Routledge, 1992), pp. 139–54.

———, *Écrits: A Selection*, trans. Alan Sheridan (London: Tavistock, 1997).

———, "The Mirror Stage as Formative of the Function of the I as Revealed in Psychoanalytic Experience," in *Écrits: A Selection*, trans. Alan Sheridan (London: Tavistock, 1997), pp. 1–7.

————, *Le séminaire de Jacques Lacan*, IV: *La relation d'objet, 1956–57*, ed. Jacques-Alain Millar (Paris: Seuil, 1994).

————, *The Seminar of Jacques Lacan* VII: *The Ethics of Psychoanalysis, 1959–60*, ed. Jacques-Alain Miller, trans. Dennis Porter (London: Routledge, 1992).

————, "The Split between the Eye and the Gaze," *The Four Fundamental Concepts of Psycho-Analysis*, ed. Jacques-Alain Miller, trans. Alan Sheridan (Harmondsworth: Penguin, 1979), pp. 67–78.

Lacarra, María Eugenia, "Notes on the Feminist Analysis of Medieval Spanish Literature," *La corónica* 17 (1988–89): 14–22.

"Lateran IV, 1215," in *Decrees of the Ecumenical Councils*: I, *Nicaea I to Lateran V*, ed. and trans. Norman P. Tanner (London: Sheed & Ward; Washington: Georgetown University Press, 1990), pp. 227–71.

Lawrance, Jeremy N.H., "The Audience of the *Libro de buen amor*," *Comparative Literature* 36 (1984): 220–37.

————, "*Libro de Buen Amor*: From Script to Print," in *A Companion to the "Libro de Buen Amor,"* ed. Louise M. Haywood and Louise O. Vasvári, Támesis A206 (Woodbridge: Tamesis, 2004), pp. 39–68.

Lecoy, Félix, *Recherches sur le "Libro de buen amor,"* repr. with prologue, bibliography, and index by A.D. Deyermond (1938; Farnborough, Hants: Gregg International, 1974).

Lehman, Peter, *Running Scared: Masculinity and the Representation of the Male Body* (Philadelphia: Temple University Press, 1993).

*Libro de Alexandre: Texts of the Paris and the Madrid Manuscripts*, ed. Raymond S. Willis, Elliott Monographs in the Romance Languages and Literatures 32 (Princeton: Princeton University Press, 1934).

*Libro de Apolonio*, ed. Manuel Alvar, Clásicos Universales 80 (Barcelona: Planeta, 1984).

*Libro del caballero Zifar*, ed. Joaquín González Muela, Clásicos Castalia 115 (Madrid: Castalia, 1982).

Lida de Malkiel, María Rosa, "Notas para la interpretación, influencia, fuentes y texto del *Libro de buen amor*," *Revista de Filología Hispánica* 24 (1940): 105–50.

————, *Two Spanish Masterpieces: The "Book of Good Love" and the "Celestina,"* Illinois Studies in Language and Literature 49 (Urbana: University of Illinois Press, 1961).

Limon, John, *Stand-Up Comedy in Theory, or, Abjection in America* (Durham, NC: Duke University Press, 2000).

Linehan, Peter, *The Ladies of Zamora* (Manchester: Manchester University Press, 1997).

Link, Luther, *The Devil: A Mask without a Face* (London: Reaktion, 1995).

López-Baralt, Luce, *Islam in Spanish Literature from the Middle Ages to the Present*, trans. Andrew Hurly (Leiden: Brill; San Juan: Universidad de Puerto Rico, 1992).

Ly, Nadine, "*Libro de Buen Amor*: L'Autoportrait d'un 'ane' ou les deux portraits et les trois déclinaisons de l'Archiprêtre," in *L'Autoportrait en Espagne: Littérature et peinture; Actes du IVᵉ Colloque International d'Aix-en-Provence (6–8 Décembre 1990)*, ed. Guy Mercadier, Études Hispaniques 19 (Aix-en-Provence: Université de Provence, 1992), pp. 17–36.

Mâle, Émile, *Religious Art in France: The Thirteenth Century. A Study of Medieval Iconography and Its Sources*, trans. Marthiel Mathews, ed. Harry Bober, Bollingen Series 90.2 (repr. Princeton: Princeton University Press, 1984).

Marino, Nancy F., *La serranilla española: notas para su historia e interpretación*, Scripta Humanistica 40 (Potomac: Scripta Humanística, 1987).

Márquez Villanueva, Francisco, *Orígenes y sociología del tema celestinesco*, Hispanistas: Creación, Pensamiento, Sociedad 2 (Barcelona: Anthropos, 1993).

Martín Pérez, *Libro de las confesiones: una radiografía de la sociedad medieval española*, ed. Antonio García y García, Bernardo Alonso Rodríguez, and Francisco Cantelar Rodríguez, BAC maior 69 (Madrid: Biblioteca de Autores Cristianos, 2002).

Martin, John Hilary, "The Injustice of Not Ordaining Women: A Problem for Medieval Theologians," *Theological Studies* 48 (1987): 303–16.

Martínez de Toledo, Alfonso, *Arcipreste de Talavera, o Corbacho*, ed. Joaquín González Muela, Clásicos Castalia 24 (Madrid: Castalia, 1970).

Mateo Gómez, Isabel, *Temas profanos en la escultura gótica española: las sillerías de coro* (Madrid: Consejo Superior de Investigaciones Científicas, Instituto Diego Velázquez, 1979).

Mayne, Judith, "Paradoxes of Spectatorship," in *Viewing Positions: Ways of Seeing Film*, ed. Linda Williams (New Brunswick, NJ: Rutgers University Press, 1994), pp. 155–83.

McGrady, Donald C., "The Story of the Painter and his Little Lamb," *Thesaurus: Boletín del Instituto Caro y Cuervo* 33 (1978): 357–406.

Mettmann, Walter, "'Ancheta de caderas,' *Libro de buen amor* c. 432ss," *Romanische Forschungen* 73 (1961): 141–47.

Miaja de la Peña, María Teresa, *"Por amor d'esta dueña fiz trobas e cantares": los personajes femeninos en el "Libro de buen amor" de Juan Ruiz, Arcipreste de Hita*, Biblioteca Crítica Abierta, Serie Letras 2 (Mexico, DF: Sistema Universidad Abierta; Facultad de Filosofía y Letras, UNAM, 2002).

Michael, Ian, "The Function of the Popular Tale in the *Libro de buen amor*," in *"Libro de buen amor" Studies*, ed. G.B. Gybbon-Monypenny, Támesis A12 (London: Tamesis, 1970), pp. 177–218.

———, *The Treatment of Classical Material in the "Libro de Alexandre,"* Publications of the Faculty of Arts of the University of Manchester 17 (Manchester: Manchester University Press, 1970).

Michalski, André Stanislav, "Description in Medieval Spanish Poetry," unpublished dissertation, University of Princeton, 1964; *Dissertations Abstracts Online* Accession Number AAG6500053.

Minnis, A.J., *"De impedimento sexus*: Women's Bodies and Medieval Impediments to Female Ordination," in *Medieval Theology and the Natural Body*, ed. Peter Biller and A.J. Minnis, York Studies in Medieval Theology 1 (Woodbridge: York Medieval Press, 1997), pp. 109–39.

———, *Medieval Theory of Authorship: Scholastic Literary Attitudes in the Later Middle Ages* (1984; 2nd edn. Aldershot: Wildwood House, 1988).

Moffatt, L.G., "Pitas Payas," *South Atlantic Studies for Sturgis E. Leavitt*, ed. Thomas B. Stroup and Sterling A. Stoudemire (Washington: Scarecrow Press, 1953), pp. 29–38.

Morreale, Margherita, "La fábula del caballo y el asno en el *Libro* del Arcipreste de Hita," *Revista de Filología Española* 71 (1991): 23–78.

———, "Más apuntes para un comentario literal del *Libro de buen amor*, con otras observaciones al margen de la reciente edición de G. Chiarini," *Boletín de la Real Academia Española* 47 (1967): 213–86, 417–97.

———, "Más apuntes para un comentario literal del *Libro de buen amor*, sugeridos por la edición de Joan Corominas," *Hispanic Review* 37 (1969): 131–63.

———, "Más apuntes para un comentario literal del *Libro de buen amor*, sugeridos por la edición de Joan Corominas," *Hispanic Review* 39 (1971): 271–313.

———, "Una lectura de las 'pasiones' de J. Ruiz (*Libro de buen amor*, 1043–1066)," *Boletín de la Real Academia* 55 (1975): 331–81.

Morros, Bienvenido, "Las fuentes del *Libro de buen amor*," in *Juan Ruiz, Arcipreste de Hita, y el "Libro de Buen Amor": Congreso Internacional del Centro para la Edición de los Clásicos Españoles celebrado en Alcalá la Real del 9 al 11 de mayo de 2002*, ed. Francisco Toro Ceballos and Bienvenido Morros (Alcalá la Real: Ayuntamiento & Centro para la Edición de los Clásicos Españoles, 2004), pp. 69–104.

———, "El *Libro de buen amor* como una poética (a la luz de otras obras del mester de clerecía)," *Studi Ispanici* 26 (2002): 13–29.

———, "La liturgía en el *Libro de buen amor*: la 'Cruz Cruzada,'" *Revista de Poética Medieval* 10 (2003): 57–99.

Mulvey, Laura, *Visual and Other Pleasures* (1981; London: Macmillan, 1989).

Murphy, James J., *Medieval Eloquence: Studies in the Theory and Practice of Medieval Rhetoric* (Berkeley: University of California Press, 1978).

———, ed. *Three Medieval Rhetorical Arts*, Medieval and Renaissance Texts and Studies 228.5 (Tempe: Arizona Center for Medieval and Renaissance Studies, 2001).

Nepaulsingh, Colbert, "The Rhetorical Structure of the Prologues to the *Libro de buen amor* and the *Celestina*," *Bulletin of Hispanic Studies* 51 (1974): 325–34.

———, "The Structure of the *Libro de Buen Amor*," *Neophilologus* 61 (1977): 58–73.

———, *Towards a History of Literary Composition in Medieval Spain*, University of Toronto Romance Series 54 (Toronto: University of Toronto Press, 1986).

Paiewonsky Conde, Edgar, "Polarización erótica medieval y estructura del *Libro de buen amor*," *Bulletin Hispanique* 74 (1972): 331–52.

Parker, A.A., "The Parable of the Greeks and the Romans in the *Libro de Buen Amor*," in *Medieval Hispanic Studies Presented to Rita Hamilton*, ed. A.D. Deyermond, Támesis A42 (London: Tamesis, 1976), pp. 139–47.

Parker, Margaret, *The Story of a Story across Cultures: The Case of the "Doncella Teodor,"* Támesis A161 (Woodbridge: Tamesis, 1996).

Paxson, James J., *The Poetics of Personification*, Literature, Culture, Theory 6 (Cambridge: Cambridge University Press, 1994).

Pearcy, Roy J., "Modes of Signification and the Humor of Obscene Diction in the Fabliaux," in *The Humor of the Fabliaux: A Collection of Critical Essays*, ed. Thomas D. Cooke and Benjamin L. Honeycutt (Columbia: University of Missouri Press, 1974), pp. 163–96.

Pérez López, José Luis, "La fecha del *Libro de buen amor*," *Incipit* 22 (2002): 105–42.

Phillips, Gail, *The Imagery of the "Libro de buen amor*," Spanish Series 9 (Madison: Hispanic Seminary of Medieval Studies, 1983).

*Poema de Fernán González*, ed. Juan Victorio, Letras Hispánicas 151 (Madrid: Cátedra, 1981).

"Porcelet," *Nouveau Recueil complet des fabliaux*, ed. Willem Noomen (Assen: Van Gorcum, 1991), VI. 185–91.

Ratcliffe, Marjorie, "Judíos e musulmanes en la jurisprudencia medieval española," *Revista Canadiense de Estudios Hispánicos* 9 (1985): 423–38.

Read, M.K., "Man against Language: A Linguistic Perspective on the Theme of Alienation in the *Libro de buen amor*," *MLN* 96 (1981): 237–60.

Reckert, Stephen, "'. . .avras dueña garrida,'" *Revista de Filología Española* 37 (1953): 227–37.

Reynal, Vicente, *Las mujeres del arcipreste de Hita: arquetipos femeninos medievales*, Biblioteca Universitaria Puvill 2.18 (Barcelona: Puvill, 1991).

Ricard, Robert, "Sur l'invocation initiale du *Libro de buen amor*," *Bulletin Hispanique* 71 (1969): 463–75.

Richardson, Henry B., *An Etymological Vocabulary to the "Libro de Buen Amor" of Juan Ruiz, Archpriest of Hita*, Yale Romanic Studies 2 (New Haven: Yale University Press, 1930).

Rico, Francisco, "'Por aver mantenencia': el aristotelismo heterodoxo en el *Libro de buen amor*," *Anuario de Filología Española* 2 (1985): 169–98.

———, *Predicación y literatura en la España medieval* (Cádiz: Centro Asociado de Cádiz, Universidad Nacional a Distancia, 1977).

Rist, John, "Augustine of Hippo," in *The Medieval Theologians*, ed. G.R. Evans (Oxford: Blackwell, 2001), pp. 3–23.

Robert of Basevorn, *Forma praedicandi*, in *Artes praedicandi: contribution a l'histoire de la rhétorique au Moyen Âge*, ed. Th.-M. Charland, Publications de l'Institut d'Études Médiévales d'Ottawa 7 (Montreal: Institut d'Études Médiévales, 1936), pp. 231–323.

———, *The Form of Teaching (Forma praedicandi)*, trans. Leopold Krul, in James J. Murphy, *Three Medieval Rhetorical Arts*, Medieval and Renaissance Texts and Studies 228.5 (Tempe: Arizona Center for Medieval and Renaissance Studies, 2001), pp. 109–215.

Robson, Michael, "St Bonaventure," in *The Medieval Theologians*, ed. G.R. Evans (Oxford: Blackwell, 2001), pp. 187–200.

Rose, Jacqueline, *Sexuality in the Field of Vision* (London: Verso, 1986).

Rowland, Beryl, *Animals with Human Faces: A Guide to Animal Symbolism* (London: George Allen & Unwin, 1974).

Rubin, Gayle, "The Traffic in Women: Notes on the 'Political Economy' of Sex," in *Toward an Anthropology of Women*, ed. Rayna R. Reiter (New York: Monthly Review Press, 1975), pp. 157–210.

Rubin, Miri, *Corpus Christi: The Eucharist in Late Medieval Culture* (Cambridge: Cambridge University Press, 1991).

Rudolph, Conrad, *The "Things of Greater Importance": Bernard of Clairvaux's "Apologia" and the Medieval Attitude to Art* (Philadelphia: University of Pennsylvania Press, 1990).

Russell, Jeffrey Burton, *The Devil: Perceptions of Evil from Antiquity to Primitive Christianity* (Ithaca: Cornell University Press, 1977).

Russell, Peter E., "La oración de doña Jimena (*Poema de Mio Cid*, vv. 325–67)," in *Temas de "La Celestina" y otros estudios del "Cid" al "Quijote"* (Barcelona: Ariel, 1978), pp. 113–58.

Sánchez Sánchez, Manuel Ambrosio, "Vernacular Preaching in Spanish, Portuguese and Catalan," in *The Sermon*, ed. Beverly Mayne Kienzle, Typologie des Sources du Moyen Âge Occidental 81–83 (Turnhout: Brepols for l'Institut d'Études Médiévales, Université Catholique de Louvain, 2000), pp. 759–858.

Scheidegger, Jean R., *Le "Roman de Renart" ou le texte de la dérision*, Publications Romanes et Françaises 188 (Geneva: Droz, 1989).

Sedgwick, Eve Kosofsky, *Between Men: English Literature and Male Homosocial Desire* (New York: Columbia University Press, 1985).

Seidenspinner-Núñez, Dayle, *The Allegory of Good Love: Parodic Perspectivism in the "Libro de Buen Amor,"* University of California Publications in Modern Philology 112 (Berkeley: University of California Press, 1981).

Seudo-Aristóteles, *Poridat de las poridades*, ed. Lloyd A. Kasten (Madrid: Aguirre, 1957).

Silverman, Kaja, *Male Subjectivity at the Margins* (New York: Routledge, 1992).

Simpson, J.R., *Animal Body, Literary Corpus: The Old French "Roman de Renart,"* Faux Titre 110 (Amsterdam: Rodopi, 1996).

Smalley, B., "Peter Comestor on the Gospels and his Sources," *Recherches de Théologie Ancienne et Médiévale* 46 (1979): 84–129.

Sola, Sabino, "Precisiones a la 'súplica inicial' en el *Libro de Bbuen Amor*," in *El Arcipreste de Hita: el libro, el autor, la tierra, la época; Actas del I Congreso Internacional sobre el Arcipreste de Hita*, ed. M. Criado de Val (Barcelona: SERESA, 1973), pp. 343–49.

Spearing, A.C., *The Medieval Poet as Voyeur: Looking and Listening in Medieval Love-Narratives* (Cambridge: Cambridge University Press, 1993).

Spitzer, Leo, "Note on the Poetic and the Empirical 'I' in Medieval Authors," *Traditio* 4 (1946): 414–22.

———, "En torno al arte del Arcipreste de Hita," in *Lingüística e historia literaria*, Biblioteca Románica Hispánica 2.19 (1955; 2nd edn. Madrid: Gredos, 1961), pp. 87–134.

Stallybass, Peter, and Allon White, *The Politics and Poetics of Transgression* (London: Methuen; Ithaca: Cornell University Press, 1986).

Stone, Gregory B., "The Philosophical Beast: On Boccaccio's Tale of Cimone," in *Animals Acts: Configuring the Human in Western History*, ed. Jennifer Ham and Matthew Senior (London: Routledge, 1997), pp. 23–41.

Sturm, Sara, "The Greeks and the Romans: The Archpriest's Warning to his Reader," *Romance Notes* 10 (1968–69): 404–12.

Swanson, R.N., "Angels Incarnate: Clergy and Masculinity from Gregorian Reform to Reformation," in *Masculinity in Medieval Europe*, ed. D.M. Hadley (London: Longman, 1999), pp. 160–77.

Tate, R.B., "Adventures in the *Sierra*," in *"Libro de buen amor" Studies*, ed. G.B. Gybbon-Monypenny, Támesis A12 (London: Tamesis, 1970), pp. 219–29.

Taylor, Barry, "*Exempla* and Proverbs in the *Libro de Buen Amor*," in *A Companion to the "Libro de Buen Amor,"* ed. Louise M. Haywood and Louise O. Vasvári, Támesis A206 (Woodbridge: Tamesis, 2004), pp. 83–104.

Terry, Patricia, trans. *Renard the Fox* (Berkeley: University of California Press, 1992).

Thomas of Chobham, *Summa de arte praedicandi*, ed. Franco Morenzoni, Corpus Christianiorum, Continuatio Mediaeualis 82 (Turnhout: Brepols, 1988).

Tugwell, Simon, "Humbert of Roman's Material for Preachers," in *De ore Domini: Preacher and Word in the Middle Ages*, ed. Thomas L. Amos, Eugene A. Green, and Beverly Mayne Kienzle, Studies in Medieval Culture 27 (Kalamazoo: Medieval Institute, Western Michigan University, 1989), pp. 105–17.

Ullman, Pierre L., "Juan Ruiz's Prologue," *MLN* 82 (1967): 149–70.

Uría, Isabel, *Panorama crítico del "mester de clerecía*," Literatura y Sociedad 63 (Madrid: Castalia, 2000).

Vasvári, Louise O., "A Comparative Approach to European Poetry and the Erotic Wedding Motif," *CLCWeb: Comparative Literature and Culture* 1 (1999); http://clcwebjournal.lib.purdue.edu/clcweb99–4/vasvari99.html.

———, "La digresión sobre los pecados mortales y la estructura del *Libro de buen amor*," *Nueva Revista Filología Hispánica* 34 (1985–86): 156–80.

———, "An Example of *Parodia Sacra* in the *Libro de buen amor:* 'Quoniam' *Pudenda*," *La corónica* 12 (1983–84): 195–203.

———, *The Heterotextual Body of the "Mora Morilla*," Papers of the Medieval Hispanic Research Seminar 12 (London: Department of Hispanic Studies, Queen Mary and Westfield College, 1999).

———, "El hijo del molinero: para la polisemia popular del *Libro del Arcipreste*," in *Erotismo en las letras hispánicas: aspectos, modos y fronteras*, ed. Luce López-Baralt and Francisco Márquez Villanueva, Publicaciones de la *Nueva Revista de Filología Hispánica* 7 (Mexico City: Centro de Estudios Lingüísticos y Literarios, Colegio de México, 1995), pp. 461–77.

———, "The Novelness of the *Libro de Buen Amor*," in *A Companion to the "Libro de Buen Amor,"* ed. Louise M. Haywood and Louise O. Vasvári, Támesis A206 (Woodbridge: Tamesis, 2004), pp. 165–81.

———, "Pitas Pajas: Popular Phonosymbolism," *Revista de Estudios Hispánicos* 26 (1992): 135–62.

———, "La semiología de la connotación: lectura polisémica de 'Cruz cruzada panadera,'" *Nueva Revista de Filología Hispánica* 32 (1983): 299–324.

———, "The Semiotics of Phallic Aggression and Anal Penetration as Male Agonistic Ritual in the *Libro de Buen Amor*," in *Queer Iberia: Sexualities, Cultures, and Crossings from the Middle Ages to the Renaissance*, ed. Josiah Blackmore and Gregory S. Hutcheson (1994; Durham, NC: Duke University Press, 1999), pp. 130–56.

———, "A Tale of 'Tailling' in the *Libro de Buen Amor*," *Journal of Interdisciplinary Literary Studies/Cuadernos Interdisciplinarios de Estudios Literarios* 2 (1990): 13–41.

———, "'De todos instrumentos, yo, libro, só pariente (*LBA* 70)': el texto liminal como cuerpo sexual," in *Actas del VIII Congreso Internacional de la Asociación Hispánica de Literatura Medieval, 22–26 de septiembre de 1999*, ed. Margarite Freixas and Silvia Iriso (Santander: Consejería de Cultura del Gobierno de Cantabria, Año Jubilar Lebaniego, and AHLM, 2000), II: 1769–79.

———, "The Two Lazy Suitors in the *Libro de Buen Amor:* Popular Tradition and Literary Game of Love," *Anuario Medieval* 1 (1989): 181–205.

————, "Why Is Doña Endrina a Widow? Traditional Culture and Textuality in the *Libro de Buen Amor*," in *Upon My Husband's Death: Widows in the Literature and Histories of Medieval Europe*, ed. Louise Mirrer (Ann Arbor: University of Michigan Press, 1992), pp. 259–87.

Vivanco, Laura, "Birds of a Feather: Predator and Prey in *Celestina*," *Celestinesca* 26 (2002): 5–27.

————, *Death in Fifteenth-Century Castile: Ideologies of the Elites*, Támesis A205 (Woodbridge: Tamesis, 2004).

Wack, Mary Frances, *Lovesickness in the Middle Ages: The "Viaticum" and its Commentaries* (Philadelphia: University of Pennsylvania Press, 1990).

Wackers, Paul, "Mutorum animalium conloquium; or, Why Do Animals Speak?" *Reinardus*, 1 (1988): 163–74.

Walker, Roger, "'Con miedo de la muerte la miel non es sabrosa': Love, Sin and Death in the *Libro de buen amor*," in *"Libro de buen amor" Studies*, ed. G.B. Gybbon-Monypenny, Támesis A12 (London: Tamesis, 1970), pp. 231–52.

————, "Juan Ruiz's Defence of Love," *MLN* 84 (1969): 292–97.

————, "Towards an Interpretation of the *Libro de buen amor*," *Bulletin of Hispanic Studies* 43 (1966): 1–10.

————, *Tradition and Technique in "El Libro del cavallero Zifar,"* Támesis A36 (London: Tamesis, 1974).

Walsh, John K., "Juan Ruiz and the *mester de clerezía*: Lost Context and Lost Parody in the *Libro de buen amor*," *Romance Philology* 33 (1979–80): 62–86.

————, "The Names of the Bawd in the *Libro de buen amor*," in *Florilegium hispanicum: Medieval and Golden Age Studies Presented to Dorothy Clotelle Clarke*, ed. John S. Geary, with Charles B. Faulhaber, and Dwayne E. Carpenter (Madison: Hispanic Seminary of Medieval Studies, 1983), pp. 151–64.

Waters, Claire M., *Angels and Earthly Creatures: Preaching, Performance, and Gender in the Later Middle Ages* (Philadelphia: University of Pennsylvania Press, 2004).

Weir, Anthony, and James Jerman, *Images of Lust: Sexual Carvings on Medieval Churches* (London: B.T. Batsford, 1986).

Wenzel, Siegfried, *Latin Sermon Collections from Later Medieval England: Orthodox Preaching in the Age of Wyclif*, Cambridge Studies in Medieval Literature 53 (Cambridge: Cambridge University Press, 2005).

————, *Preachers, Poets, and the Early English Lyric* (Princeton: Princeton University Press, 1986).

————, "A Sermon of Philosophy," *Traditio* 50 (1995): 249–59.

————, *The Sin of Sloth: Acedia in Medieval Thought and Literature* (Chapel Hill: University of North Carolina Press, 1960).

Wieck, Roger S., *Time Sanctified: The Book of Hours in Medieval Art and Life*, with essays by Lawrence R. Poos, Virginia Reinberg, and John Plummer (New York: George Braziller in association with the Walters Art Gallery, 1988).

Willis, Raymond S., "Two Trotaconventos," *Romance Philology* 17 (1963–64): 353–62.

Wippel, John F., "The Condemnations of 1270 and 1277 at Paris," *The Journal of Medieval and Renaissance Studies* 7 (1977): 169–201.

Zahareas, Anthony N., *The Art of Juan Ruiz, Archpriest of Hita* (Madrid: Estudios de Literatura Española, 1965).

Zahareas, Anthony N., "Parody of the Canonical Hours: Juan Ruiz's Art of Satire," *Modern Philology* 62 (1964–65): 105–09.

———, "The Stars: Worldly Love and Free Will in the *Libro de buen amor*," *Bulletin of Hispanic Studies* 42 (1965): 82–93.

———, "Structure and Ideology in the *Libro de buen amor*," *La córonica* 7 (1978–79): 92–104.

Zahareas, Anthony N., and Oscar Pereira with Thomas McCallum, *Itinerario del "Libro del Arcipreste": Glosas críticas al 'Libro de buen amor'* (Madison: Hispanic Seminary of Medieval Studies, 1990).

Zink, Michel, *La Prédication en langue romane avant 1300*, Nouvelle Bibliothèque du Moyen Âge 4 (Paris: Honoré Champion, 1976).

———, "*Serrana* et femme sauvage," in *La Pastourelle: poésie et folklore au Moyen Âge*, Études 67 (Paris: Bordas, 1972), pp. 86–96.

Žižek, Slavoj, "Courtly Love, or, Woman as Thing," in *The Metastases of Enjoyment: Six Essays on Woman and Causality* (London: Verso, 1994), pp. 89–112; repr. in Elizabeth Wright and Edmond Wright, ed., *The Žižek Reader* (Oxford: Blackwell, 1999), pp. 148–73.

# INDEX OF STANZAS

Note of explanation: The index of stanzas lists those stanzas which are discussed in the text (and not simply cited or quoted). The stanza numbers for episodes treated at length in this book are listed in order in the index of stanzas, and cross-referenced to the episode's title in the subject index, where page references can be found. The subject index notes the pages on which the major topics and those subjects bearing on the major topics discussed are mentioned (i.e. humor, humoral characterology, visual domain, etc) to permit the reader to trace aspects of the argument. Other subjects are only listed if there is discussion in the text, and not simply citation (i.e. not all the pages containing mentions of St Augustine or Leo Spitzer are listed). Episodes are listed by received episode title, and characters by name. The amatory affairs are listed under the beloveds' names.

# SUBJECT INDEX

abjection, 14, 53, 63, 65, 68, 81, 93,
    94, 124, 125, 126, 130, 132, 136,
    141, 142, 146
*accessus*, 20, 26–7, 45, 46
    see also *intentio auctoris*; prologues;
        sermon-prologue; *utilitas*
acedia, 7, 9, 32, 51, 55, 58, 63, 68, 69,
    72, 73, 143, 148, 149
adultery, 2, 73, 130, 141, 167
Aesopic tales, 50, 60, 73, 78–92, 93,
    94, 95–6, 103, 105–6, 111, 136–7
    see also *under individual tale titles*
affective piety, 76–8, 95, 137, 147
Alcaraz, and the Astrologers, King,
    38–40, 41, 46, 47
Alda, 14, 44, 50, 71, 72–5, 78, 95,
    102, 104, 119, 123, 124, 125,
    144, 168, 169
Alfonso X of Castile, 2, 3, 46–7,
    110–11, 154
allegory, 83, 90–1, 95
amatory affairs, 14, 98–113, 137–9,
    140, 141, 144, 150–1
    initial motivation, 99–102, 137
    also see *under individual women's
        names; serrana section*
Amor, Don, 14, 41, 51, 52, 53, 56, 57,
    64, 65, 66, 67, 68–70, 71, 74, 93,
    94, 147, 148, 149, 150
    see also *mesura*
    *Ars amatoria*, 101–3, 104, 105, 108,
        110, 113, 122, 137, 138
    tent, 148–9
*amor purus*, 112, 113, 138
anamorphosis, 133

Andreas Capellanus, 100, 114, 117,
    128, 129, 139, 140, 149
anger, 25, 67–8, 82, 83, 84, 88, 106,
    116, 124, 125
animals, 23, 72, 90–1, 92, 150
    see also *under Aesopic tales;
        chain of being; individual
        animals,*
anthropomorphism, 78–9, 83, 87, 90,
    92, 144
antithema, 16, 19
anxiety, 2, 3, 4, 7, 25, 26, 42, 69, 95,
    123, 146, 150, 151
*Apologia ad Guillelmum*, 6–8, 156
appetites, 14, 60, 87, 126, 127,
    129, 140, 144, 145, 146,
    150, 151
Apuesta Dueña, 99, 102, 108, 109,
    112, 141
Archpriest, 14, 15, 37–9, 40, 43, 44–5,
    47, 49, 50, 53, 56, 57, 66–8, 69,
    71, 72, 73, 74–5, 78, 79, 81, 82,
    83–6, 93, 94, 98, 100, 101, 102,
    105, 108, 109, 110, 113, 114,
    115, 116, 117, 119, 120, 121,
    122, 124, 125, 126, 127, 128,
    129–30, 131, 132, 133–4, 136,
    137, 138, 139–41, 143, 144, 145,
    146, 148, 149, 150, 151, 154,
    166, 175
    amatory success of, 47, 94, 101–2,
        103, 104–5, 109, 110, 112–13,
        124, 129, 138, 145
    description of, 14, 44–5, 49–50, 71,
        72–5, 76, 94, 95, 140

72, 74, 75, 76, 78, 80, 81, 82,
85, 90, 93, 95, 134–5, 136–7,
141, 144, 145, 147, 148, 150
fallen body, 15, 20, 21, 22, 24, 25,
40, 41, 46, 47, 58, 71, 72, 73,
75, 77, 78, 93, 131, 134, 141,
142, 143–4, 146, 149
female, 42–4, 53, 55, 56, 72, 102,
125: *also see under individual
characters; descriptio puellae*
integrity of, 2, 21, 26, 53, 55, 63,
65, 80–1, 93
male, 3, 44, 52, 53–5, 57, 62, 63,
65, 66, 72, 78, 88, 93, 117,
124, 134–6, 143, 148, 150
pollution of, 15–16, 26, 41, 57, 62,
63, 65, 66, 68, 71, 75, 78, 93,
130, 132, 134, 141, 143, 145,
146, 150
/ soul dichotomy, 120
*see also under individual parts*; Christ,
body; grotesque, body;
hypostatic union
Brownlee, Marina Scordilis, 162, 163
Buen Amor, 154
*buen seso*, 31–2, 110
*also see cuerdo*
Burke, James F., 85, 127, 129, 157
butt, 35, 38, 58, 93, 117, 125, 129,
141
buttocks-exposer, 54

*cabo*, 54, 166
*also see echo lo por mal cabo*
Camille, Michael, 6
canonical hours, 9
Cántica de los clérigos de Talavera, 10,
129, 145
*also see* clerical concubinage
*caritas*, 21, 25, 35, 115, 137
*also see* love
carnivalesque laughter, 7, 74, 123
*also see* grotesque
Carruthers, Mary J., 8–9, 30
*casar*, 166

castration, 53, 56, 57, 60, 78, 126, 146,
150
cathedral, 17–18, 46
censure, 82, 86, 88, 90, 92, 93, 96,
106, 127, 145, 147
*also see* charivari; violence
chain of being, 14, 50, 72, 73, 74, 75,
78, 79, 84, 93, 95–6, 125, 136–7,
140, 143, 144, 147
*charivari*, 92, 127, 129; *also see* censure,
violence
Charland, Th-M., 19
Chata, La, 104, 114–15, 116–19, 121,
122, 123, 124–6, 127, 128, 140,
174
Chaucer, Geoffrey, 42, 43–44
cholera, 23
*also see* anger
Christ, 14, 16, 17, 18, 41, 50, 75, 76,
77–8, 147, 148, 161
body, 14, 72, 75, 76, 77–8, 93, 95,
136, 137, 141, 147, 148
Wounds, 75, 76, 77, 78, 95, 137,
147, 169
*also see* affective piety; Corpus
Christi; hypostatic union;
*imitatio Christi*; 'Omillo me,
Reína'; 'Los que la Ley
avemos'
church, 3, 65, 77, 113, 131, 132, 141,
145, 147, 151
*also see* official culture
clergy, 2–3, 4, 6–7, 14, 15, 29, 42, 56,
70, 74, 84, 88, 91, 97, 108, 115,
116, 130, 131, 132, 141, 142,
145, 146, 151
*also see* preacher
clerical concubinage, 129, 130, 141,
145
*also see* Cántica de los clérigos de
Talavera
clerical fornication, 130, 141, 145, 167
*coidar*, 118
comic climax, 54, 56, 58, 94, 96
comic deflation, 57, 58, 64, 150